This book was written on the unceded lands of the melukerdee and palawa people of lutruwita. I acknowledge and pay my respects to the elders, both past and present, and recognise their deep history, culture and continuing connection to Country. Always was, always will be, Aboriginal land.

~~~~~~~~

As author and activist, Kirsten Bradley walks her talk applying the deep and ethical thinking behind permaculture to everyday habits that she and her family have tested and documented through the very successful Milkwood Permaculture Living Course. This book distils the lessons learnt from helping so many others make positive changes in their own lives. In the process it is an accessible introduction to permaculture as powerful thinking tools for regeneration and resilience.

Dr David Holmgren, co-originator of permaculture

In 1975, just as permaculture was emerging, a very wonderful small handbook in black and white called *The First Earth Garden Book* appeared, edited by Keith and Irene Smith. It began generations of articles and books on how to live well, happily and with great consideration for our lovely Planet Earth. Now 48 years later, with experience, wisdom and knowledge of this very changing world, Kirsten Bradley has written this book, based on years of living in different places, listening to people, and looking at renewable and sustainable strategies, techniques and ideas.

The time is right for this volume and it is very welcome.

Rosemary Morrow, permaculture elder and author of
The Earth Restorer's Guide to Permaculture

THE
MILKWOOD
PERMACULTURE
LIVING HANDBOOK

KIRSTEN BRADLEY

THE
MILKWOOD
PERMACULTURE
LIVING HANDBOOK

HABITS FOR HOPE IN A
CHANGING WORLD

murdoch books

Sydney | London

Contents

WELCOME TO MILKWOOD

We both grew up as outdoor kids – Nick under the big skies of Willandra National Park on Wiradjuri/Wangaaypuwan country, and me by the sea in Kiama on Wodi Wodi country. We each moved away to cities, to make art and trouble, and met each other at an illegal dance party where we were both doing live video art (as you do). In 2006 we decided to jump ship from inner-city warehouses to a bare 8 hectare (20 acre) patch on the side of Nick's family farm on Wiradjuri country near Mudgee, New South Wales, in search of a more earthy life.

It was about this time that we discovered permaculture – a design system for creating regenerative farms, communities and landscapes that are interconnected and sustainable – and it turned our lives upside down. We started asking teachers in regenerative agriculture to run courses in our family's woolshed, and people started showing up to learn.

We called this emerging hands-on project Milkwood – for both softness and strength, sustenance and shelter. Over the next eight years we built a small permaculture farm from the ground up, bursting with food, off-grid buildings, water, animals, friends, teachers, family and students. We all learned many things in those years.

The family farm has long since been sold, but our passion for sharing permaculture skills has become the foundation of how we live. Since those years we've learned so much from the ecosystems and communities where we've tended soil and friendships and taught many a workshop, while looking for a place we could call home. Which eventually brought us south to the island of lutruwita/Tasmania, where we now steward half an acre of house and garden in a small green valley by the Southern Ocean on melukerdee country.

From this place, we're raising a kid, growing some veggies, tending bees, chickens and community, and learning to give and receive within our ecosystem. And we continue to share and teach good design tools, ideas and skills with folks near and far, because this kind of knowledge, and the ability to live like it matters, should belong to us all.

The Milkwood Permaculture Living Handbook evolved from an online course called Permaculture Living that we launched five years ago. This course grew out of our weekend workshops that we'd taught for 15 years, as well as the two-week Permaculture Design courses we ran (with amazing teams of teachers from all over) during that time. These workshops (and the online course) have welcomed many thousands of folks – from all walks of life – across Australia and beyond.

Along the way we have met many lovely people who were keen to make life better through learning about and using permaculture as a design

You don't need to design an entire farm or quit your job to move to the country: you can begin right where you are, right now.

system. Many of these folks wanted to 'do it all' as soon as humanly possible (or sooner), inspired by their dreams of self-sustaining gardens, beehives, landscape restoration, energised community initiatives, home-grown everything, a handmade house, and a chicken and a cow and a sheep, as well. Because they had the idea that only in this 'do it all' way could they create a safe future for themselves and their families, and make a difference in this world out of balance.

We were often counselling against this 'everything, all at once' approach, because, simply put, all these types of projects take a *lot* of work – and time, energy, money and headspace. We know from personal experience (and watching others attempt to do this) that it is very easy to have heaps of great ideas about doing all the things at once and then . . . fall in a heap and feel like a total failure.

This is why we teach the way we do, and also why we've created this handbook. We don't want you to fall in a heap trying to do all the things at once to make life better. We want you to thrive and go forward, step by step. And we also know from experience that using permaculture ethics and principles as a framework can be a super-solid way to get started on making changes in your everyday life: changes that edge you towards a day-to-day existence that is more connected to your ecosystem and community. You don't need to design an entire farm or quit your job to move to the country: you can begin right where you are, right now.

This book is intended as an offering to get you started with living like it matters. It's brimful with advice, habits, projects and hands-on ways to make a meaningful difference to your world. We're not trying to map out how to change every single thing that you could possibly do to make a difference. But we see the suggestions in this book as part of an ecosystem of good ideas and small humble habits that can build purpose into your everyday life, while also creating world-shifting change, when done collectively. No-one can do all the things. But we can each do some of the things. And we can each take daily steps towards creating a life where you get to actively participate in building more care and connection, and help create the futures that our ecosystems and communities long for and deserve.

So, at its heart, *The Milkwood Permaculture Living Handbook* is about helping you cultivate habits for living with meaningful connection and purpose. Because this is how we cultivate hope.

Kirsten and Nick
milkwood.net

INTRODUCTION

Habits, hope and connection

Cultivating connection and purpose gives our lives meaning and, importantly, places us in relationship to each other, to land and to other animals and plants. These relationships require reciprocity, attention and care. These relationships also change us.

In this time of ever-escalating and overlapping crises, the health of our ecosystems, our communities and other communities far beyond ours urgently requires us to engage and connect.

We know we have to do *something*, and keep doing it. We know that grassroots movements can change the world. We also know the problems we collectively face are *very big* and it's all incredibly daunting. Despite all of this, you may want to ask, 'How can I become self-sufficient, hole up here and never go out again?'

I'd like to suggest that your ongoing health and resilience – indeed your entire future – lies not in the goal of self-sufficiency, or some bunker mentality where the outside world is no longer connected to you, but rather in *re-establishing and creating more connection* instead.

Connections to your ecosystem and connections to your community. We need the plants, places and people around us to thrive. *Dis*connection – from land, from the people who produce our goods, from our food and from each other – is what got us into this mess to start with.

So, if the urge to establish a mini-fortress (in our backyards or in our hearts) in response to the huge problems we face isn't the best way through this, what can we do, starting from where we are?

I've been asked these questions for decades by permaculture students searching for answers, and the best answer I can give – informed by many thinkers, knowledge-ways, elders and my own experience – is this: the more we can each live in relationship and reciprocity with our ecosystems, and the more we can incorporate connections and meanings into our everyday life through our choices and habits (even if those choices feel tiny against the world's problems), the more connection and purpose we can infuse into our lives.

And the more we can cultivate connection, meaning and purpose in our lives, the more we are able to cultivate hope. A grounding in hope can support us to take action, even when the problems we face seem, at times, overwhelming.

I am not talking about whimsical hope here, pinning our hope on a fancy. I'm talking about tough, robust, active hope. Hope that is cultivated by action.

Hope is a powerful place to be coming from when it comes to endurance and action. In fact, unless you're going to be motivated purely from a place of fear (which I don't recommend, if you can avoid it), hope is *essential* to action.

And, as in the cycles of our ecosystems, there's a feedback loop here, too. Just as hope leads to action, action in turn leads to more hope. It's this momentum that will propel us forward.

But what does hope look like in urgent times, in the face of the scale of our collective challenges and the smallness of our everyday lives? It looks like the things that make up our days: our habits, our choices, our actions, our chores, our work, and our rest and downtime, too.

The power of habits

Day in, day out, our lives are full of actions and habits: some conscious and many unconscious. What if your habits could help create a better world, just a little bit at a time, while you went about your normal day? They can. Your habits can allow you to translate your hopes for the world you want into your everyday life.

Habits are how you eat your eggs, or how you make your coffee, or what you drink, or don't, or how you get to work and back again. But habits can also be a powerful vote for resilience and justice and small-but-significant acts of defiance. Habits are slow, flying in the face of our current culture, and can be used to resist, and revolt, and reimagine more just and lovely worlds. Habits can help us imagine and create the worlds that we need, and the futures that we need. Starting right at your breakfast table, before you've even started your day.

At best, habits can transform your life, and help change the world – on the small scale and on the large.

At worst, habits can be insidious things that damage your body and your mind. And beyond you, they can uphold unjust regimes, reinforce racism, oppress peoples and deplete landscapes and futures.

Simply put, *habits are powerful*. So let's invite better ones into our lives, and create new worlds with more justice and abundance and hope. One little habit and one little step at a time.

But how to get started with habits that are truly world-changing? And how do you ground yourself and create resolve to keep going in the face of so much grief, challenge and change? Happily, there's a design and thinking system called permaculture that can help us chart a course forward to the futures we need.

What is permaculture?

Permaculture is, in many ways, simply a goal: of living in functional, meaningful relation to our ecosystems, with reciprocity at the core of that relationship; a goal of living in a connected, meaningful way that benefits land, waters, life and community, as well as meeting our own needs for a fulfilling life.

By ecosystem, I mean where you are *right now*, not just your nearest forest, river or wild place. Your ecosystem doesn't stop at the forest's edge. It's all around you: right up to your front step, into your kitchen, even inside you. All this is part of your local ecosystem. And it is all part of your duty of care, as a resident of that ecosystem and as a part of nature.

Because you are very much a part of nature. Nature is not 'over there' somewhere. Sure, that bit of nature over there might be greener and prettier than where you're sitting, but you are interacting with and making an impact on multiple living things, both micro and macro, in this exact moment. And how you show up in your ecosystem matters.

Better yet, the animals known as humans – that's you and me – can play an important role in creating abundance within our ecosystem. You are a part of nature just as much as the fruit trees, the forests and the fish swimming upriver. You could be forgiven for thinking that our species is only destructive – there's overwhelming evidence of the harm we can do all around us – but it's also true that you can participate in your ecosystem in a way that tends seeds and people, nourishes plants, pollinators and relationships, and builds soil and community.

So, how can you tend some of these ecosystemic relationships of yours, both known and unknown, by the choices you make and the actions you take on the daily? Is it possible to live in a way that considers your responsibilities to your ecosystem and your community, while building connection and meaning in your own life, all while going about the normal daily stuff in this busy world of ours?

Well, yes. There are many ways and many knowledge systems that have been doing exactly this for as long as there have been people. There are also newer frameworks; though, of course, the new ways are always drawing on and standing on the shoulders of the old ways.

Some of these knowledge-ways are vast, embodied in country, culture and people. Some of the newer, far more simple frameworks have been written down, so that anyone can try them out. Permaculture is just one of the recent frameworks, but we love it because it's simple, flexible and easily incorporated into everyday life, so you can start using it right now.

At Milkwood, we see permaculture as a way of consciously designing, bit by bit, how we meet our responsibilities to our ecosystems and to ourselves. How we eat, the choices we make, how we use energy and how we use our privilege. How we help out, how we advocate, how we garden, how we love. And how we aim to live as meaningfully as we can, both in our personal actions and by getting involved in urgent system change to create communities, societies and governments that prioritise *care over profit* – for the benefit of people, ecosystem and planet.

Like any community-held knowledge base, permaculture is always evolving, especially as it's a design system, a teaching system and a set of thinking tools for daily use. At Milkwood, we have adapted it in our own ways, as others do in their own, and this book builds on our approach.

Where's the word 'permaculture' from? Rewind a bit: the 1970s was a time when climate change was a relatively new topic of conversation, the downsides of industrial agriculture went largely unquestioned, and *Silent Spring*, Rachel Carson's classic book explaining the toxic legacy of pesticides in our ecosystems, had not long been written. The damage that we were doing to our world and its peoples in the name of progress, through capitalism and colonisation, and the realisation that the promise of endless plains and untamed wilderness ripe for the taking was a destructive, catastrophic myth were only beginning to dawn on many, especially in Western countries.

In this context, the term permaculture (permanent agriculture, permanent culture) was coined by Bill Mollison and David Holmgren in lutruwita/Tasmania. At the time, Mollison and Holmgren were both thinking deeply about what a grassroots, principles-based, holistic system for designing agriculture and human habitats could look like; a system that was based on regeneration rather than extraction. Believe it or not, this was quite an unusual concept at a time when much of the developed world was doubling down on the promise of endless growth.

This design system needed to be grassroots enough to be used by just about anyone, with design principles that could hold true across different ecosystems and landscapes, and be used to design both human habitats and *actually regenerative* agricultural systems (as opposed to ones that were simply less destructive). And so, drawing on many diverse influences and their own learning, Mollison and Holmgren defined the design system that they called permaculture.

Permaculture was – and is – a weaving together of ideas inspired and informed by Indigenous knowledge and science and many thinkers, both past and present, working in the realms of landscape design, ecology, ethics, perennial agriculture and architecture.

And . . . guess what? Drawing this knowledge into a grassroots design system that could be used to regenerate landscapes meant that it was one that could regenerate community, too. These principles that focused on designing in partnership with ecosystems, rather than separate from them, could also be used to support the re-emergence of regenerative communities, from the individual to the city level. This should come as no surprise, if you look at Indigenous wisdom and practices, which remind us that Country and people are indivisible: we are not separate from nature. *What's good for Country is good for people.*

But it bears repeating here: like most of modern thought and design, permaculture theory – including its ethics, principles and skills – is all, directly or indirectly, based on the wisdom, knowledge and science of traditional and Indigenous peoples the world over.

Some permaculturists actively acknowledge these legacies, while others are criticised for not adequately recognising such histories. For us, this recognition is central to permaculture.

Concepts like our reliance on the regeneration of and reciprocity within our ecosystems are not 'new' information – quite the opposite. And yet, in our current society, we seem to have forgotten this. These are fundamental truths that we each need back at the centre of our lives, no matter where or how we live now. It is vital that these truths once more become a core part of our decision-making for ourselves, our families, our communities and our ecosystems.

I'm not just talking about other people's ancestors or unbroken lines of traditional knowledge here; your own family histories also form a part of this traditional lineage. While we're well versed in the collective damage previous generations have done to our ecosystems, you are *also* the direct descendant of people who held land-based knowledge well; who cultivated community, knew their local waterways like family, and saved and passed seeds from hand to hand through generations. So some of this is your people's knowledge, too.

The point of permaculture design and thinking, as we see it, is to respectfully draw on these fundamentally excellent concepts and principles to inform our everyday lives. And you can do this in a way that works for you, your household and your ecosystem, to make your life better, while actively practising gratitude for and solidarity with traditional and Indigenous knowledge-keepers to whom we owe pretty much everything.

Since the 1980s, the permaculture movement has decentralised into a worldwide, mycelium-like network of designers, thinkers, makers and doers. Permaculture principles are used all over the world, by all sorts of folks – to design ecovillages in Argentina, accountancy practices in London, schools and entire suburbs, community centres and university courses, to create alternative currencies and community resilience plans, and many a garden, home, homestead and farm, too.

Permaculture has even been used, on occasion, as a principle-based toolbox to help reboot traditional agricultural systems, which, once up and running again, no longer use the word 'permaculture', because the old ways have re-emerged and been reclaimed. It's an incredibly useful framework for thinking about how we relate to place, and *how we can live like it matters*. Because it does.

For many of us wanting to do better by our planet, we need all the help we can get when it comes to principles and frameworks for living well and in relationship to our ecosystems. Permaculture is just one set of ideas – scaffolding you can use – to build an amazing and resilient life, home and community, to build reciprocity with your ecosystem, and to enable a future of possibilities, even in a world out of balance.

So, what could this all look like at your place? To help make these ideas more clear, permaculture is broken down into three ethics and twelve principles that you can use as thinking tools, goals and guides to build a meaningful life.

This is care of the big Earth, our combined home, and care of the small earth, the soil beneath our feet.

Permaculture ethics

At the foundation of permaculture are three ethics: Earth care, people care and fair share.

> *These core ethics, or some form of them, can be found in all traditional cultures. Bill Mollison and I, back in the 70s, saw that this ethical foundation was an essential basis for sustainable design – or what we called permaculture.* **David Holmgren, Permaculture Living course**

We see these ethics as top-level thinking tools, and a good 'first things first' guide for how to live. You can use these ethics as a framework to guide your decision-making and actions while planning for a life worth living. Here's what they mean to us at Milkwood.

Earth care

This is care of the big Earth, our combined home, and care of the small earth, the soil beneath our feet. Earth care can be many things, including but not limited to organising, voting and taking action on things like climate justice; tending the earth that sustains each and every one of us with just and equitable food systems; and understanding that we are part of our ecosystems, not separate from them, and need to step up to the responsibilities that go along with that.

People care

This is living our lives in a way that is kind, safe and healthy – for ourselves, our households and our communities – while doing the least harm possible to others. People care is supporting mutual aid, considering what we consume and its impacts on people far away, and how we vote. It's how we show up in our communities – both in times of plenty and in times of crisis – to ensure the best outcome for everyone, not just ourselves. It's how we work on decolonising our thinking and our actions, along with dismantling our inherited and internal racism; how we seek to be lifelong learners, to co-create a more just world; how we attempt to do the work, and not carry destructive patterns forward – for ourselves, our families and our communities.

Fair share

This is passing on the surplus and, importantly, ensuring our portion is no larger than it needs to be. It's reassessing what 'need' is to us, and making do with less if we can, to ensure there's more for others – people, plants and all the other life, too. Planting more than we need, so that there's enough to share. Voting and taking action in a way that creates equity for those in our community who do not have our privileges. It's sharing seeds, skills and knowledge, so that more folks in more communities can thrive, and so that ecosystems and biodiversity can thrive, too.

Permaculture principles

Combined with the ethics, David Holmgren defined 12 permaculture principles. You can use these to help you think about, plan, design, create things and act with a view to the greater whole. These principles are flexible thinking tools that you can adapt to designs, situations and challenges both big and small.

They're not 'rules' by any means; they are simply tools to inform your thinking and decision-making. These principles can be used to design big projects, but they can also be used to help you make better daily choices, and to form new habits.

> *The strategies and techniques in permaculture are constantly varying . . . and what might be appropriate in one context is not in another. But the design principles are general guides that we can use to help shape what we're doing, or reflect on whether a particular solution is a good one, or not.*
> **David Holmgren, Permaculture Living course**

Observe and interact

This principle reminds us to use all our senses and our powers of observation to truly assess things before taking action, rather than charging in based upon something we've read or been told.

Catch and store energy

This principle helps us remember that energy is flowing through our systems all the time – in sunlight, wind, water, money, the harvest and a million other forms – but that this energy often only comes in pulses; therefore, it's important that we learn to store it so that we can use it when we need it.

Obtain a yield

Along with storing energy, this principle helps drive systems forward. It's essential to obtain a yield in some form to carry on, whether that's veggies, stored power, stored heat or stronger community relationships. Otherwise, it's just not possible to survive long term.

Apply self-regulation and accept feedback

This principle balances the two before it, and is just as important. It's a constraining principle, to ensure ongoing evaluation, and that you take the time to adjust to whatever you discover as a result.

Use and value renewable resources and services

A familiar concept to us all by now, this principle is about designing for and choosing services and resources that are renewable, rather than ones that will deplete and disappear.

Produce no waste

You'll be familiar with this one, as it thankfully creeps back into our society. It's the concept of using every part of something, making choices to only work with, buy or choose things that you can use entirely.

Design from patterns to details

This reminds us to look at the whole, rather than just the parts, when we begin to design something – which we often need to be reminded of in this reductionist world! The whole is more than the sum of the parts.

Integrate rather than segregate

This principle encourages us to integrate elements and functions rather than keep them neatly apart, because separation usually ends up requiring more resources. It's about using one element's output as another's input: to reuse everything we can, reduce pollution, conserve energy and make the most of the resources that we have.

Use small and slow solutions

Think about the ways we can mimic the simple process of planting a small seed and watching it grow slowly into a big, beautiful tree. This principle is about elegance and efficiency of design: considering the simplest solution possible to achieve our goals –

rather than doing something big and fast that inadvertently has negative impacts – while staying within our limits.

Use and value diversity

This is about valuing the biodiversity of life to create stable systems, using and valuing diverse solutions to a problem, and striving to live outside the binary (in *all* the ways!).

Use edges and value the marginal

This reminds us to look to the periphery, because that's often where, frankly, the most interesting stuff is happening! These peripherals may seem small, but they're often significant and can hold great value for all of us.

Creatively use and respond to change

This final principle is particularly powerful. It's about acknowledging biological and other processes, and responding to them in a constructive way, rather than using extra energy to block or work against them. It's going with the flow, and using that flow to your advantage, on both the micro and macro design level.

> *Planting a tree or a seed, these acts are expressions of sacred reciprocity, because these seeds and young trees often need tending to by humans to survive. These are acts that say,* humans belong. *Humans have a role in keeping life abundant, in the same way that a salmon swimming upstream does by delivering nutrients from the sea far into the interior forests.*
> **Sonya and Nina Montenegro, The Far Woods**

Can small changes in big times matter?

We live in unprecedented times – or so we're often told these days.

The negative effects of hundreds of years of industrialisation, colonialism and capitalism on our planet are now completely undeniable: scarred landscapes and hurting soils; cultures, languages, lives and wisdom lost to the violence of colonisation; depleted watertables; species gone forever; civil unrest; even the air we breathe with its rising levels of carbon dioxide. I know it's easy to feel like you're living at the end of the world, right now.

And on top of all *that*, we're fed the message that the environmental devastation and the plastic bags choking our oceans are our fault, as individuals; that the reason these problems exist is that we didn't try hard enough, or turn off our lights when we left the room, or we drove our cars more than we should, or we forgot our reusable cups again.

This individualised blame fits neatly into an individualised culture and has been deliberately cultivated by the fossil-fuel giants to distract us from their climate wrecking.

So, I want to be very clear here at the start of this book: *the responsibility for the environmental and cultural devastation of our Earth and peoples rests primarily with the huge companies and unjust power structures in our societies – from imperialism to multinationals – that have consistently, over hundreds of years, put power and profit before people and ecosystems.*

And *then*, as if that wasn't audaciously evil enough, these same industries have created massive marketing campaigns to place the responsibility to 'do the right thing' entirely on you – the end user – rather than owning their impact as the cause of so much harm, all in the name of power and profit.

There's plenty to get angry about with this global gaslighting. And I believe you should be angry;

exercise your democratic rights and do whatever else you can to hold the systems and powers that created this complete mess to account. Grassroots movements of people joining together can change the world for the better: they have done before and will do again.

However, everything is connected, and what each of us does matters, especially when it's combined with what others are doing. This forms the foundation of connected, collective action: these small actions (or habits, if you're doing them regularly) can create powerful networks and systems. We need collective power, and we need to work together.

Thousands of small acts create positive change. Look at nationwide, citizen-led projects of renewal, fossil-fuel divestment movements, workers' picket lines and the school climate strikes. Look at our previous successes, such as when ordinary workers banded together to push for an eight-hour work day and an end to child labour in the face of huge, profit-focused opposition. It wasn't thought possible, until ordinary people began working together and forced the change. We are all individuals, not corporations, so we can only ever do small individual acts. But when done with others in our local communities, these small acts can shift power bases, make a new future possible and change everything.

Yes, you have responsibilities to your ecosystem and your community – now and always. But that's not the same as being the cause of this enormous mess that we're all in, or bearing the guilt for it. *That is not on you.*

And yet, we must each participate in finding the solutions to these massive challenges. This part *is* on you, as a member of your ecosystem and your community. The power structures that created this damage and injustice are not going to suddenly dismantle themselves, or spontaneously repair the damage they have caused. In reciprocating the gift of being alive and nourished by this incredible Earth, we must all be part of the solutions our planet and ecosystems need, right now.

So being a good ancestor is about understanding the sources of the damage, and using your vote and your body and your words and your head and your heart to stand up alongside others and effect change, as part of whichever movements, petitions, marches, creative interventions, campaigns or class actions you choose, or whatever is within your abilities to participate in and show up for.

Another part of being a good ancestor is figuring out how to live your days in between the protests and the big actions in a way that sustains and nourishes you, while creating as little harm as you can.

And also

You can fight the powers that be *and also* choose to live like it matters – wherever you live. You can take big action *and also* practise accountability in your daily habits. You can resist, defend and help create a new world *and also* practise gratitude for the ecosystem you live in by tending to the reciprocity required of you by your local soils, waters and other living things.

These traumatic times call for *living with intention* and with care, to ensure we can keep going while keeping our heads on straight and our hearts open. It's hard. Fortunately, your ecosystem has a lot of wisdom on this 'how to keep going in unprecedented times' front, and can really help you out if you're willing to learn from it.

There is so much to be thankful for. Our ecosystems are so generous to us, even as they're hurting and changing. They're committed to life, and you get to be a part of that generosity.

You will be part of your ecosystem each day of your life. You owe the simple fact that there's oxygen for you to breathe to the plants and algae around you. Your daily sustenance depends on the soil, plants, insects and animals of both your ecosystem and other ecosystems far beyond.

With this residency of yours comes a life lived in relation to the plants, animals, microbes, water and people in your ecosystem, whether you know their names or not. City or country, it doesn't matter. The life of your ecosystem is all around you and inside you – it *is* you. You're part of it all, and it's helping to sustain your every breath, meal and movement.

So, how will you choose to live – at this time on Earth, with all our collective problems, in this damaged-but-still-generous ecosystem in which you find yourself?

Will you live in a way that cultivates a sense of reciprocity and belonging? Would you like to live your days in a way that creates minimal harm, while contributing purposefully to a more positive future for you, your household, your community and all the life around you? This is big stuff. And it is also the smallest stuff.

In the face of all this bigness, there's a small but enormous question I'd like you to ask yourself.

How do you want to live?

How we live our hours is how we live our days, and how we live our days is how we live our lives. This book is all about ways that you can cultivate new habits and practices to make your life better. And more wild, and more precious. After all, you are stardust accumulated into human form for such a brief period of time, in the greater story of your ecosystem, and the story of life on Earth.

How do you want to live? How can you provide for your needs while enhancing your community and the ecosystem around you? It's easy to get overwhelmed with all the possibilities, so articulating your goals can be a small but powerful pathway to get to the heart of what matters to you.

The power of setting goals

Before you go any further with this book, I suggest that you start with the simple step of articulating a personal goal. This could be a one-month goal or a five-year goal based on your answer to the question: how do you want to live?

When you clearly articulate a goal before beginning a new project or a new permaculture design, you're creating a powerful tool to help you make better decisions about that project or design. Setting a goal can be an anchor that helps you untangle the many options, and helps steer you to where you'd like to get to. But goal-setting is not just for one-off projects or backyard garden designs; you can use goal-setting to help you figure out how to chart a path towards more daily goodness and purpose, too.

Articulating a goal about how you want to live on the daily will help you get the most out of this book. It's *full* of good ideas and habits that might be a great fit for you, but choose too many too quickly and you'll soon feel overwhelmed. To succeed and make those new habits stick, knowing where you want to go will help you to choose wisely.

This personal goal articulation will not evaporate injustice or discrimination. Your current life context is your own, and it may well contain unwanted influences, limitations or oppressions that are not fair or equitable, and are ongoing. Goal-setting is, however, useful in whatever context you find yourself because it allows you to clarify what you want, and where you want to get to.

So, back to the question. Starting from wherever you are right now, with the resources, constraints, context and time that you currently have, ask yourself *how do I want to live?*

Your goals might include:

- Having time to garden and build an amazing backyard ecosystem with enough produce to share.
- Living in a place where community is growing, and people's health is prioritised; a place where everyone has access to fresh food and effective health services.
- Spending more time together as a family, saving money and improving your physical health.
- Helping dismantle the patriarchy, eating delicious home-grown fruit and creating a meaningful livelihood for yourself.
- Having a deeper relationship with your ecosystem – to better know the trees and plants and birds in your area – and living in a community where marginalised voices are raised up and heard.
- Living with less chronic pain, more access to support, fresh herbs at your back door and a community taking strong steps to mitigate climate change by investing in regenerative economies.

Goal-setting prompts

Once you've dreamed up your personal goal, write it down as if it's already happening. Think of it as an inspiring description of your life, from the future.

A love letter from future you, to current you.

If you're feeling a little stuck, you might find it easier to articulate a personal goal simply in terms of the areas of your life that you want to improve, such as:

- health
- diet
- family
- screentime
- exercise
- connection to others
- community participation
- free time
- rest
- hobbies
- adventure
- love

Your goal might be something as simple as:
Each day I take action to improve my physical health, the food that I eat and my relationship with my family and my community.

Or maybe something more specific, such as:
I wake up rested, and walk each day before breakfast. I have enough spare time to see friends and volunteer in my community. My home is filled with plants and I sit in the sunshine on the back step, with a cuppa in my hands and the sun on my face, listening to the birds, at the start of each day.

Or it might be more like:
I eat delicious food that nourishes my body and mind – some of it home-grown – and get lots of exercise from working in the garden I have created. My kids are happy and often engaged in outdoor hobbies, and we eat around our backyard campfire every weekend.

Or maybe it's:
I live in a neighbourhood with lots of friendships and community, and my local food system is gaining momentum all the time. I balance my work with time to preserve and ferment food, using produce from swaps with my neighbours. I know all the plants that grow in the cracks of my street, and which ones are good medicine. I have friends of all ages in my community, and feel that my contributions are worthwhile and help to create more safety for us all.

Write it down!

Once you've identified the areas of your life you want to focus on first, the timeframe you'd like to achieve this in and what you want your life to look like, you're ready to articulate your own personal goal. Write it down!

Use the space below, a favourite journal or wherever makes the most sense for you. An extra copy pinned up in your kitchen, beside your desk or inside your wallet – some personal space that you look at every day – is a great reminder too.

_____

_____

_____

_____

_____

_____

_____

_____

Now, when you encounter a new habit or project that resonates with you, either from the pages of this book or more generally, or you need to make a decision – from making a big purchase to switching jobs to deciding whether to get involved in a new community initiative – take a moment to reflect on that new idea or decision in relation to your personal goal of how you'd like to live.

First, is the thing you're considering actually doable for you, considering where you are, at this moment? This is an exercise in actually getting there, and that means choosing things you can definitely do, given your current context and resources.

Second, ask yourself: will this new habit or decision take me towards my goal, and where I want to be?

If your answer is, 'Yep, I'm pretty sure it will' then give it a go. You may be surprised where this goal-setting takes you. I can't wait to see how you go.

Start practising

Once you have deeply thought about how you want to live and set your goals accordingly, you'll have a clearer idea of how to make the most of this book.

Love five ideas within these pages? Twenty-five? Great! Mark those pages or write those ideas down, and make a plan for tackling your first and second choices. I recommend you take on one new habit or idea at a time: one that suits your life at the moment. Nail that one thing, make it such a habit that it's just 'what you do', then add a second. And a third. And, before you know it, you'll be moving slowly and solidly towards a more connected, meaningful everyday life, with more purpose – and possibly also more pickles.

This is not about doing all the things, or getting everything right, or the idea that unless you succeed at being a power-homesteader with a two-year supply of preserved peaches and home-grown dried beans in your cupboard, you're not doing enough.

This book _is_ about using permaculture thinking to bring small new habits and practices into your daily life that will have meaningful, positive effects – both in ways that you can clearly feel, enjoy and benefit from, and in other ways, with effects that may be beyond your understanding, but no less powerful for that. Because how we live our days – from what we eat to what we advocate for – creates our relationship with our ecosystem as well as our community, and with ourselves.

This book is a small offering to help you cultivate big change by creating more connection and purpose in your daily life, with you as a valued resident of your ecosystem, at its centre. You can work from that grounded place to rise up and be part of the change we all need: with your hands full of goodness, and your heart unbroken.

HABIT ZERO: LEARN WHOSE COUNTRY YOU'RE ON

Let's start with what I see as an utterly essential habit for those of us on the Australian continent, and also everyone else: learn whose land you are on; learn how to show respect for and solidarity with Indigenous peoples and Country where you live, and beyond.

Why is this habit so important? Because showing respect for First Nations peoples and the Country they have had stewardship of for millennia, and which currently nurtures *you*, is fundamental to permaculture ethics, and to being a good human.

This habit also helps to connect you to the Country that you're on, which can only be a good thing.

If you've lived where you are for a while, perhaps you already know this – or maybe it's *your* Country. Or maybe, like us, you've moved around a lot.

Step 1: Do some research and find out who the Indigenous people are of the place you call home, and the language that they speak. For example if you live in inner-city Sydney, you live on the land of the Gadigal people of the Eora nation – and their language is also known as Eora. If you live in New York City, you're on the land of the Lenape nation, people who speak the Lenape languages, Unami and Munsee. Write the names down, and stick them up on your fridge so you see it regularly.

Step 2: Research the original names of the places where you live, and any other landmarks that you can find reference to: mountains, rivers, beaches, plains. Write all those names down on a map of your local area. If these are publicly available and it's appropriate, start using those names.

Step 3: Find the closest Indigenous organisation to you – they may have online or inhouse resources that you can access to help with your research. They may also have events you can attend, to learn more about where you live, from their perspective.

Step 4: Educate yourself on what has happened to First Nations people on the land where you live – from the point of colonisation, if that's the story of your area – until now. Be real about it. Don't look away. Seek to understand what has happened, and what is still happening. This is often a dark story, but it's important to understand what has gone before, to create the place where you live, now. Read books by Indigenous writers and seek out documentaries about history such as SBS television's *The Australian Wars*.

Step 5: Pay the rent. I'll step you through this in Habit 3 (see page 29).

Step 6: Use your knowledge. Share what you've learned with your family and friends. Initiate discussion on these topics. Get involved in reconciliation processes or other campaigns led by Indigenous people nearby.

Place names in addresses

One simple, everyday habit you can do is add your traditional place name to your postal address. In Australia, putting the Country that you're on between your name and the first line of your address is Australia Post's recommended way to do this.

Principle 1

Observe and interact

*

Identify five useful
wild plants

*

Research the life
cycle of something
you use daily

*

Pay the rent

*

Regulate your
household's
temperature

*

Learn about your
local waterways

What does it mean to truly see something?
And how can we best make good decisions, and
take positive action, as a result of that seeing?

For all the other animal species around us, the principle of **Observe and interact** is a constant state of being. Observing with *all* of your senses is a given if you're a small fluffy thing that lives in a forest (pick whatever species works for you; I'm going with bandicoot, but you do you). Without this constant, awakened level of observation and interaction on multiple levels, life in the forest can be short.

For humans, however, there's a certain sense that we've outsourced this decision-making process of 'what to do next'. And while some of this outsourcing has yielded some excellent results, you could be forgiven for thinking that we've lost more of our animal, instinctual, observational selves than is healthy along the way.

We still notice, observe and react to plenty of the 'in your face' happenings of life, of course. But what about the smaller, everyday things that are all around us, and inside us? What can we learn, and what can we reclaim of ourselves, by gathering a deeper understanding of these smaller things?

This chapter is all about reclaiming a little of your inner bandicoot – and giving yourself permission to deeply consider everything: the feelings in your tummy, the ground in front of your feet, the clouds in the sky and everything in between.

What might observing look like in your day-to-day life? How can you cultivate new skills in observing, learning and interacting in a way that empowers you to take actions that make life better?

Don't worry; you don't need to be standing in a pristine ecosystem or a beautiful garden to get started with this. Engaging with your immediate environment can begin at a very practical level, without even going outside; for example, by simply choosing different ways to regulate your own temperature. Can you put on a jumper, instead of turning up the heat? Should you open the blinds this morning to let the warm sun in, or keep them closed so the house stays cool?

Now take a step further out. Do you notice how much water is washed down the gutter, or how much fresh food seems to go to waste in your fridge because you just don't get to it? When was the last time you truly noticed the seasonal changes in your neighbourhood? Have you seen any bees in your yard lately? Simply observing these things is the first step in engaging with them.

The 'interact' part of this chapter is where the fun really starts. What you choose to do with the new-found knowledge you gain from observing, and how you can make changes as a result, is limited only by your imagination . . . which is a good thing. Because I know you have plenty of imagination. And may I let you in on a little secret? Every single small change you decide on, each small habit you form, and each action you take adds up to – your life. So how do you truly want to live? It's the habits and actions of every day that will get you there.

IDENTIFY FIVE USEFUL WILD PLANTS

Learning to identify your local weeds (which we prefer to call 'wild plants') is an excellent way to build your observation skills and your relationship with your ecosystem any time, in any place. Because these are the types of plants that will often grow literally anywhere. You don't need a backyard, or a garden, or a farm to be in relationship to these lifeforms: a willingness to learn and eyes tuned to pattern-recognition mode will get you started, wherever you live.

But why bother learning about, gathering and using weeds? Well, it's a simple way to build your resilience, and connect you to the place where you live. Once you become a proficient forager, you can gather wild plants locally and use them at home to make tasty, nutritious dishes and simple medicines. Minimum food miles, zero packaging and maximum connection to the place you call home. And all for free.

Our local wild plants tell us about where we live and what the landscape is going through: where the wet patches are, where the soil is compacted, what used to be there. They also connect us with histories – our own and those of families who came before us – medicine, food, fibre and stories. By learning to use your local weeds, you can reinvigorate this ancestral knowledge and pass it forward, so others can develop vital and functional connections to the plants and places where they live, too.

Cultivating this habit will change the way you see your street, your local parks and even what pops up out of your pot plant's soil. It's a great honour to meet the wild plants where you live; they have a lot to teach you. So listen well and learn.

An important note

Weed species – which are not indigenous to an area – are what you're looking for here, especially as a beginner. Indigenous plants come with extra considerations and are best left alone until you know a lot more about that species – its cultural status, whether it is endangered and its role in the ecosystem. Learn all you can about these plants, by all means, but don't harvest them for now.

Keeping it clean

If you're concerned the wild plants near you might not be very clean, because they grow in places with lots of herbicides or dog poo or whatever, that's okay. This is firstly an exercise in learning to observe and interact with wild plants around you. Even if you decide not to use the specimens you gather, you will have learned pattern recognition for these plants, and that's the most important bit. Once you can positively ID wild plants, you can look for them in places you know are definitely clean.

Foraging ethically

Know that gathering from the wild – even the wild of your local street – comes with responsibility. This, too, is part of observing and interacting: becoming an active participant in your ecosystem, respectfully! Some plants will be fine to harvest whole, especially if they need removing, while for others you will need to only gather the tips, or the fruit. Look up each species before you dive in. A good foraging rule of thumb is 'Never take the first one that you see'. And only take a little from each patch, no more than what you need.

Cross-check for a positive ID

Think you know what you're looking at? Great! Now, before you go any further, cross check. Some edible wild plants will have not-so-edible lookalikes, and it's worth being *really* clear about what you've found before you eat or use those plants. Find a local weed ID guide for your area, or ask a local expert.

Let's get outside and see what there is to see . . .

Five common and useful wild plants

All around you, wild plants are peeking through the cracks in the suburban landscape, full of goodness. They're often hiding in plain sight – on that bit of land next to the railway line, by your local stream, in the park at the end of your street, even on the footpath in front of your home. So come meet five of our wild favourites: they're among the most common 'weeds' growing worldwide.

Dandelion *Taraxacum officinale*

One of our planet's most widespread weeds. Every part of the dandelion is useful, edible or medicinal. It's fairly easy to identify with its sawtooth leaves, taproot and bright yellow flowers. It dies off over winter in most places and reshoots from the root in spring.

Chickweed *Stellaria media*

This gentle and soft herb usually pops up in springtime and likes to grow in damp places. To ID chickweed, look for a single line of hair on the stems. It's high in iron, has anti-itch properties, and is traditionally used to combat conditions such as anaemia and bronchitis.

Dandelion, top, and chickweed.

Left to right, mallow, dock and plantain.

Mallow *Malva neglecta*

Mallow leaves, flowers, roots and seeds are all edible – and its high mucilage content can help thicken up soups and stews. Mallow is hardy and tough, with a long taproot that keeps this wild plant alive even in very dry seasons. Look for almost circular leaves on a plant growing 30–60 cm (1–2 feet) tall.

Dock *Rumex obtusifolius*

Many types of dock have a tart lemony flavour that is great in salads and cooked meals. But dock does contain oxalic acid, so don't go eating mountains of it at once. Still, a little in moderation is highly nutritious, full of vitamins C and A, iron and B vitamins.

Plantain *Plantago* spp

About 200 plantain species grow worldwide; maybe you have already tried psyllium? The most common 'weed' species is ribwort plantain (*Plantago lanceolata*), with spear-shaped leaves growing in a clump, often in lawns and degraded spaces. Young leaves can be cooked, and herbal medicine can be made from plantain, too.

It's a great honour to meet the wild plants where you live; they have a lot to teach you. So listen well and learn.

Using wild plants as food and medicine

You've successfully found and identified some useful wild plants growing near you – great work! Now you have the 'observe' bit of this new habit sorted, let's have a go at the 'interact' part, which means collecting and using what you've found.

First up, pack a basket or bag, a pair of scissors and your enthusiasm – a local foraging guide or weed identification book can be helpful too – and collect some clean local weeds. Snip samples, ensuring you are 100 per cent certain about what you're collecting, and bring the lot home for a wash in fresh cold water.

Here's where the fun begins: you can research what each plant can be used for and what to do with them. You might discover a new salad green, tea ingredient or medicine right under your feet.

Eating fresh and cooked

The easiest way to start using edible wild plants is fresh in salads. Chickweed and young dandelion leaves are particularly delicious (although older dandelion leaves can be a little bitter). Nibble the leaves and use whatever tastes good to you, creating your own hyper-local salad mix. You can also throw many wild greens into pies, soups, quiches and curries, in much the same way as you'd use spinach or kale. Don't forget to use the flowers too; they're great in fritters and salads.

Drying for later

Drying weeds is a great way to preserve their nutritional and medicinal benefits for later. The dandelion taproot, if you can get it out with a trowel or some wiggling, is delicious when chopped and roasted slowly to make dandelion tea. You can also dry the roots to make a medicine that helps calm digestion and is excellent for treating menopause symptoms. Or dry bits of everything you find and make your own wildwood tea (see the recipe on page 24).

Infused vinegars

We make medicinal herbal vinegars each year that go into the cupboard until winter, then come out to treat colds and flu. It's as simple as this: pour apple cider vinegar over dandelion flowers (or whatever suitable medicinal wild herbs you've found) and set aside for at least a week. A few teaspoons each day when you're feeling yuck works wonders. You can add honey to sweeten it, if you like.

Indigenous edibles

Learn to identify these, but don't harvest them until you understand a bit more about the context (both cultural and environmental) where you find them growing – they're doing important work in your ecosystem! You can also grow these in your garden.

- Warrigal greens (*Tetragonia* spp)
  A fleshy-leaved, spinach-like groundcover often found in sandy soil or along waterways.

- Pigface (*Carpobrotus* spp)
  There are both invasive *and* native varieties of this plant, and they look pretty similar. Pigface fruits can be delicious when ripe – the taste is between strawberry and kiwifruit, with a dash of salt.

- Lilly pilly (*Syzygium* spp)
  Often planted as garden screens and street trees, their fruit may be white, blue or electric pink, and are about the size of a fingernail. Great popped into your mouth straight off the tree, pickled, or made into jam.

Make your own wildwood tea

Wildwood tea is as individual and unique as each household that makes it. Whatever grows in the nooks, trees, dunes or parks around where you live, that's your tea. That's *your* wildwood.

So, when it comes to ingredients, use what's growing wild near you, and good to eat and drink. We like a mixture of briar rosehips, turkey tail mushrooms, hawthorn, aniseed myrtle and dried citrus peel. But let your tea become an expression of *your* place, in a teapot. A warm hug, from where you live, and from all of your seasons, too.

What you'll need

Forage and collect ingredients in season: things like briar rosehips, mushrooms, hawthorn, aniseed myrtle, dried citrus peel, dandelion root, tea tree, small plums, wild fennel seeds, nettle, cleavers, lemon balm and hibiscus.

1. Dry each ingredient in the sunshine, in an oven on its lowest setting or in a dehydrator until all the water content has evaporated. This could take between 6 hours and 2 days.
2. Combine all dried ingredients together in a big jar with an airtight lid. Keep it in your pantry.
3. When you feel like tea, put a few tablespoons of wildwood mix into a teapot and pour boiling water over it. Steep for anywhere from 5 minutes to many hours. (We leave ours to brew slow and long on our wood stove.)
4. Strain the infusion into a mug and drink to calm the soul and quiet the mind.

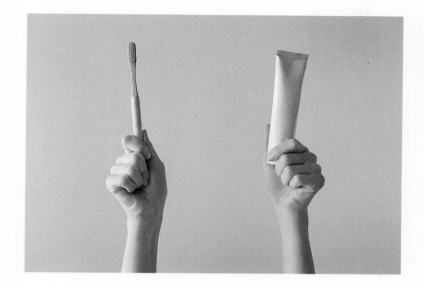

An item you use every day, such as toothpaste, can have a long and varied life cycle.

RESEARCH THE LIFE CYCLE OF SOMETHING YOU USE DAILY

When was the last time you thought about where your toothpaste comes from, or what it was before it was turned into toothpaste? Let me guess: never? That's the thing about everyday household products; they're all around us, yet we rarely pause to actually 'see' them. We're too busy brushing our teeth with them, washing up with them or cleaning the bench with them.

Yet each product we purchase comes with an impact, especially the items we buy regularly and don't really think about. Taking time to dig into one (yes, start with just one!) of these products can be eye-opening. You might observe how your toothpaste, say, connects you with faraway supply lines, raw materials, manufacturers and communities of people and their landscapes, all of which are implicated each time you brush your teeth.

This deep knowledge can inform all sorts of choices or changes. It's possible you will discover previously unseen impacts that don't quite sit right with you, now that you know. Perhaps the ingredients in that 'nature scented' cleaner you use each week are actually not very good for you or your family. Or a faraway ecosystem is being damaged by your go-to dental floss. Or landfill is the only disposal option for a certain item, once you've finished with it.

Where to start

To get a true picture of the impact of a product, you need to step back and observe that item's life cycle from cradle to grave (this is called life-cycle mapping). It sounds like a big job (and it can be!) so starting with just one thing is the way to go here: maybe your dishwashing liquid, your favourite kind of biscuit or your moisturiser.

Keep in mind that the fewer ingredients the item contains, the more straightforward this process will be. If you're up for a challenge, and are ready to have your mind blown, consider choosing something more complex: life cycle of a smartphone, anyone?

Life cycle research checklist

Choose a product you use every day and answer the following questions:

What are the raw materials? These might include minerals, chemical compounds, plastics, alcohol, water and a billion other options.

Where does it all come from? Think about the origin of all these ingredients. Mineral compounds are often mined, chemical compounds are often made in a lab, then there are plant-based ingredients and all the other possibilities.

How is the product made? Is it a multi-stage manufacturing process? Or a 'mix it all in a (very big) bowl' situation? Which country was the product manufactured in?

How is the product packaged? How many layers of coverings are there? Where did they come from, and what are these layers made of?

Who made this product? What are the labour laws in the country of origin? How much were the workers paid to make the product? What were their working conditions like?

What are the distribution channels? What was the likely method of transport? Was there any special packing required during this process?

What happens once the product is all used up? What parts of the product (and packaging) can be recycled, composted or reused? How easy is it to do this? How much of the packaging will end up in landfill?

Once you've answered all these questions – by a combination of research and 'best guess' – have a look at what you've learned.

How do you feel about what you discovered? If you're not okay with it, what can you do about it? Sometimes the action you might take at this point is finding a less-awful alternative that doesn't have a particular dodgy ingredient in it, or is made somewhere with better labour laws.

This habit is about building awareness, first and foremost. The more we understand about our choices and the impacts of the products available to us, the more empowered we are to make better choices, advocate for better alternatives, or reconsider our use of that product. But without awareness, you can't begin this process. This is one-step-at-a-time stuff. And beginning is a good start.

This habit is about building awareness, first and foremost.

Awareness doesn't need to be a guilt trip

This habit is an exercise in observation and interaction, not a guilt trip. You may find that a product that you use every day is not great for the environment, but you may not have an alternative at this point. Committing to this habit is a way to build awareness, which will lead to choices that better align with your own personal ethics – maybe right now, or maybe later. Whatever you decide, life-cycle mapping of an everyday item will help you understand the value and impact of what you're bringing into your home.

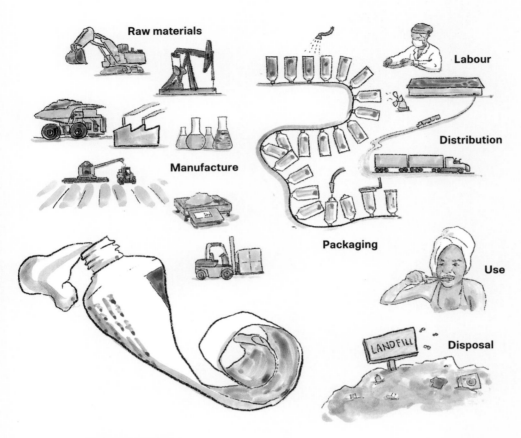

Raw materials

Labour

Distribution

Manufacture

Packaging

Use

Disposal

LANDFILL

For example: toothpaste

Raw materials – Flavours, sweeteners, binders, sudsers, fluorides, whiteners, humectants, preservatives and water.

Where it comes from – Mineral compounds make up many of the ingredients, and some are chemical compounds. Minerals are mined from the earth, but chemical compounds are often made in a lab.

Manufacturing – Measurements need to be exact for toothpaste, so often each ingredient is weighed both manually and mechanically, before being mixed together.

Packaging – Most toothpaste tubes are plastic. The plastic caps are put on and the tubes are filled from the other end before being crimped and sealed.

Labour – This will depend on which brand you buy. Check out the country of manufacture and research the labour laws in that place.

Distribution – Most toothpaste tubes are boxed individually and then placed in a bigger box that's sent to warehouses, and then on to stores. How far did your toothpaste travel from the factory to the store? What forms of transport (and fuel) might have been used?

Disposal – Tubes can be recycled, but it requires a bit of effort: you need to cut the tube open, wash out any toothpaste and remove the cap before putting it in the recycling bin, otherwise it will end up in landfill.

You now have the ability to change your relationship with that item or what it does for you, for the better.

What to do with this new-found knowledge

So now what? You've observed this everyday product, and you have a better understanding of what it is and the responsibilities that come with it. You have also become empowered! Because you now have the ability to change your relationship with that item or what it does for you, for the better, if you choose.

That doesn't necessarily mean rushing out to buy some pricey eco-brand alternative. You might simply decide to find a toothpaste that doesn't have an especially questionable ingredient in it. Or, if you researched cooking oils, next time you might choose chips fried in a type of oil that isn't as destructive when produced.

A good first question to ask is, 'Do I really need it?' Perhaps that item is not as crucial as you thought. Or check if you can make something similar at home, from basic ingredients. For example, some folks use a very easy DIY toothpaste alternative – dunking a wet toothbrush in baking soda. Or could you occasionally swap plastic-packaged chips and snacks for dried fruit, which you bought fresh when in season and dried at home?

For things you do need to buy – or maybe you just don't have the time and resources to make your own – research better options via online ethical shopping guides. Even better, investigate local alternatives for your product, reducing transport miles and supporting your local community. Or perhaps get really clear on what your local recycling services can handle, and commit to diverting as much of your product's packaging from landfill as you can.

Keep going!

Once you're happy with whatever alternative you settled upon, perhaps it's time to dive into the life cycle of another product you use frequently? By observing more closely, and building this habit little by little, you can gradually increase your awareness and create a household that is better for your health, your community and your planet.

PAY THE RENT

Australia is founded on land that was stolen from Indigenous people. The wealth that has been generated by that theft is disproportionately distributed. All people who live here today, or who have lived here in the past, have not benefited equally from the continuing dispossession of Indigenous people. Indeed, many are deliberately and profoundly marginalised from power and the spoils of colonialism.

Paying the rent is a step towards acknowledging these facts. It is part of a process that all non-Indigenous people – individually and collectively – need to enter into if we are to move towards justice, truth, equality and liberation for First Nations people. **Pay The Rent Grassroots Collective**

This fundamental habit is very simple, and you can start doing it today. Pay the rent to the people upon whose traditional lands you live and work and benefit from, each and every day. Nearly everywhere (in Australia, at least), the Country beneath your feet was never ceded – it was colonised. Taken. And whether you're a homeowner, renter or otherwise, you now directly benefit from this Country, as well as its traditional owners' knowledge and stewardship. So, pay the rent.

Hopefully, in the future, we will all work together to achieve reparations for traditional owners. But we're still a fair way from achieving this kind of large-scale, coordinated response. What you CAN do though, right now – without waiting for further permission or structural reform – is pay the rent yourself.

This is not about white guilt, or colonial settler guilt – it's about simply checking your privilege. And doing the right thing.

Paying the rent relates to climate justice: by supporting positive action you are contributing to making things that tiny bit better for First Nations communities, and to how well-resourced they are to respond and adapt to the climate crisis.

Paying the rent also relates directly to climate mitigation and creating resilient futures for all of us. Throughout the world, lands managed by Indigenous peoples have the highest biodiversity, and this may be overwhelmingly responsible for maintaining ecological stability into the future. By paying the rent, you'll be helping to support and strengthen extensive Indigenous knowledge bases, which are essential to repairing and adapting our ecosystems (and our communities) moving forward.

Not living on stolen land, but part of a nation or state that is or was a force of colonisation, and thereby deeply associated with the extraction of resources and historical injustice to Indigenous peoples that goes along with that? This action is for you, too.

Suggestions for how to pay the rent

The most important thing about paying the rent is that your money needs to end up in the hands of First Nations people, and how it is used needs to be determined by them. You pay, they decide what to do with it. This is not conditional funding. This is the simple act of paying the rent.

Not living on stolen land, but part of a nation or state that is or was a force of colonisation? This action is for you, too.

Step 1: Decide on your rental budget.

This is up to you, but activist and Gunnai elder Robbie Thorpe, one of the founders of the Pay the Rent movement in Australia, suggests one per cent of your annual income. Your rental payment might end up being $5 a week. Or it might be $50. Be honest with yourself, and also consider how many years you've lived on Country, without paying the rent, while benefiting from this place and the far-reaching stewardship of its First Peoples, in all kinds of ways.

Step 2: Figure out (if you're not already clear) whose Country you're on.

If you're in Australia, there are online maps to help you identify where you live. If you live further afield, check out online maps such as LandMark and Native Land.

Step 3: Find your closest Indigenous council or community, and ask them who you could pay the rent to.

They should be able to point you in the right direction. Sometimes, this may take a little work to figure out. Stick with it! This matters. Once you figure out how to pay the rent, let your local mates know how they can do it, too. If you can't locate your local Indigenous body or community (many communities have been intentionally fragmented by colonial interests), see what Indigenous-led organisations you can find in your region. In Australia, there are also organisations like the Pay The Rent Collective to check out.

This is important work and we encourage you to commit to doing your bit. Because reparations and justice go hand-in-hand with regeneration. We're co-creating a better world, and the only way forward is together.

We pay our respects to those who have developed and promoted the Pay the Rent concept, including, in Australia, Bruce McGuinness, Bejam Kunmunara Jarlow Nunukel Kabool, the National Aboriginal and Islander Health Organisation (NAIHO) and Robbie Thorpe, and many others in Pay the Rent movements across the world.

REGULATE YOUR HOUSEHOLD'S TEMPERATURE

We all like to keep warm in winter and cool in summer. But all that gas or electricity for heating and cooling can be your household's single biggest contributor to carbon emissions, a driver of climate change. Plus these systems are often expensive to run. The good news is you will see a *huge* difference by making simple, small behavioural changes or adjustments to your home and environment that will have positive effects on your health, household budget and carbon footprint, too.

Actively managing the temperature of your home when possible – and turning off the air conditioning and heating whenever you can – is actually quite easy. And it is possible no matter where you live: in every country and city, in rentals and farmhouses, and everywhere in between. Because this is as much about your own behaviour, and rethinking that, as anything else.

Can you put on a jumper before you turn the heater on? Or move your body to warm up? Great – you've just changed your behaviour to better fit the climate. Can you learn to cook outside on hot days, rather than heating up your kitchen? Or grow some beans on a trellis in front of a window that cops afternoon summer sun? Hooray – you've helped keep your household cool without switching on air conditioning.

So actually, this habit isn't just about heating and cooling – it's about living a little more, getting active and trying new things, plus observing and interacting with where you live. All the good things, really, disguised as an energy-saving exercise!

Let's look at how to actively manage the temperature of your house in small but significant ways.

Adding a glasshouse to the equator-facing side of your home, like this one at Melliodora in central Victoria, is another way to capture extra heat in winter.

Getting started

Like so many habits we can adopt to reduce our impact on our climate – often boosting our health and happiness in the process – this one is as much about *you* and your own actions as any external factors. So ask yourself some questions, do a little research, and then you can start to act on your answers.

Good questions to ask yourself

How can I change my behaviour so that it better fits the climate? Can I use natural sources of heating and cooling: the sun for winter warmth, breezes and shading for summer coolness? Here are some things to try:

- Use rooms when they are the most comfortable: what might be great as an office in winter, when it's warm and bright, could become a spare bedroom in summer when the afternoon sun makes it unbearably hot.
- Close windows, curtains and external shutters early on a hot day.
- Open windows in the evening to let cooler air in.
- Use fans, which are much more energy-efficient than air conditioners.
- Cook outside in summer: see Habit 52 (page 243) for ideas.
- Work in the garden in the morning to warm yourself up on cold days.
- Shuffle your summer day around, doing more indoor jobs during the heat of the day, and completing outdoor tasks in the cooler hours.
- To keep warm when sitting inside, layer your clothing, have a thermos of tea at the ready and a hot-water bottle on your lap or under your feet. Get up every half hour or so to bust some moves to a Prince song!

How can I adapt my environment to manage temperature?

- Seal gaps that let in drafts to prevent winter heat loss. Get a door snake and consider floor-to-ceiling curtains with pelmets.
- Find out what insulation you have (if any) and research options. Cellulose insulation is one of the lower-impact options.
- Check out electric heat pumps as a super power-efficient (and climate-friendly) way of heating and cooling, when extra input is needed.
- Consider double glazing for your windows.
- Grow deciduous vines, shrubs or trees directly outside west-facing windows to screen them in summer.

This habit is about living a little more, plus observing and interacting with where you live.

LEARN ABOUT YOUR LOCAL WATERWAYS

This habit is subtle but powerful: how much do you know about the water that flows around where you live? Where does it come from and where does it go? These waterways were once intrinsic to your community's health on a practical, day-to-day basis. Water is life, after all.

These days, many of us are disconnected from our local waterways. No matter how urban our local 'hood, we can deepen our sense of connection to place. This is an exercise in observation, interaction and discovery, which can reveal all sorts of things about your place – in a similar way to learning about the wild plants where you live.

Discovering your local waterways can involve looking at maps, doing some research, possibly using your feet and committing some time. While investigating, you might pause to reflect on what the state of your local waterway says about your community. What does the health of your waterway mean for ecosystems and communities downstream too?

While pondering all that, you might also find yourself thinking, 'Hey, wait a minute – where does the water from *my* sink and shower go?' Well, it goes to a variety of places, depending on where you live, but it will always wind up in your local water table, waterway or ocean. So, how you interact with the water in your house has a flow-on effect to larger water bodies near and far. Yes, those same water bodies you're about to get more acquainted with! Knowing more about the health – or lack thereof – of these waterways might spark questions, such as: 'What biosphere-safe soaps and detergents can I use or make, to minimise my impact?'

Even if you opt only for discussing what you've learned about your local waterways, this observing and interacting will add richness to your daily routine, and depth to your understanding of your place.

Getting to know your local water catchment

Your water catchment (also called a watershed) is the area of land – suburbs, forests, hills, all of it – bounded by ridge lines that cause all the rainwater that falls within them to drain inward. This water passes through soil, across hard surfaces and through your local ecosystem in all kinds of ways, eventually feeding the creeks and rivers of the catchment. Some catchments are big, and some are quite small – but no matter where you are on Earth, you are standing in, and contributing to the health of, a local water catchment.

First of all, figure out where the boundaries of your local water catchment are. Searching the name of your nearest city and the word 'catchment' online will often return local government websites with information on your area. Get an aerial map, or look one up online.

- Where are the ridge lines, the highest points in the landscape?
- What creeks flow down from them?
- What about the rivers, lakes and dams?

Identify elements that you are familiar with; the bridge you cross on your way to work, or the gully where you harvest blackberries in autumn. Link what you see on the map with what you know on the ground.

See if you can find out the original names of the waterways – names used by the people who have been the waterkeepers of your area in the past and into the future. In some places, the names of the waterways will have changed over time, and will reveal all sorts of things about the ecosystems and people who have lived alongside them over the years.

Then get out there and say hello to your local waterway. Go for a walk or bike ride along your local river or creek, in each direction. If you can, walk your entire waterway, from its source to your kitchen sink – a fascinating and revealing way to better understand the place where you live. Even if your local creek has been paved over, walk the waterway regardless. This is your place, so get to know it. Some cities have historic walks that follow submerged waterways, so poke around and see what you come up with.

Once you've discovered your local waterways, continue to observe and interact with them over time, taking note of how they change with the seasons, and after heavy rain or a dry spell. Chat to friends and family about what you notice: sharing what you've experienced is valuable for others, too. And if you feel inspired to do more, you can join a community group working to clean up your waterway. Or investigate the *many* ways you can help ensure stormwater leaving your property is as clean as possible, before it enters and joins your local stream. Do whatever you can that is within your scope – this is all part of caring for your watershed.

Principle 2

Catch and store energy

Store the season by preserving food

Harvest rainwater

Build a mini greenhouse

Create a budget and start saving

Grow a storage crop

Energy is all around us: in the sunlight that falls on our faces and the sugars that plants produce via photosynthesis. It's the force that drives all living things . . . and beyond-living things.

We often think of energy in terms of electricity, or glucose, or the force of waves and wind, but energy can also be found in the form of compassion and care – how we show up for each other.

> *Energy is flowing through systems in nature all the time, but it comes in big pulses, in waves, and then it's gone. We all need energy. And, because of that pulsing nature, we need to catch it and store it in ways that are useful for later.* **David Holmgren, Permaculture Living course**

This principle is about thinking ahead and planning how you can capture abundances when they occur. Everything from catching and storing rainwater, to saving money, to preserving seasonal gluts of food, to capturing the heat and light of the sun so that you can use it, at your place, when you need it.

This principle – *Catch and store energy* – reminds us how crucial it is that we collectively divest from fossil fuels as a source of energy and turn towards renewable power and energy sources: sun, wind, waves and more. There are huge challenges in developing ways to effectively and ethically 'store'

these types of energies, but we can do this. Your personal choices, and our collective advocacy, can help us all get there.

The importance and value of this principle is also highlighted as we become more attuned to the seasons of the places where we live, and understand the waves of energy that flow through those places, in the form of seasonal foods, rainwater, building materials and even money; or the goodwill of community that comes with sunny summer days and can be harnessed to raise a barn or hold a fundraising concert. Energy can be caught and stored for use in so many ways to get a big project done.

This principle is about rolling with the seasons, making the most of different times of year, and understanding the fundamental concept of pulses of energy, rather than on-demand everything. This is really important to get your head around when it comes to creating resilience at home and in your community.

habit 6

STORE THE SEASON BY PRESERVING FOOD

The act of preserving is hopeful. It's a gesture of goodwill to future meals, incorporating a past season's bounty.

Getting your preserve on, and making the act of 'storing the season' something you do regularly, is a delicious way to catch and store energy. When you bottle up the red summer goodness of tomatoes for cold winter days, or preserve fruit to keep in the cupboard for months to come, you're making the most of produce when it's abundant, in the knowledge that you'll need it later, when there's less to eat. It's like capturing sunshine in a jar! And you don't need to be growing your own food to get started with preserving. You can just as easily buy produce in bulk when it's in season and therefore cheap and plentiful in shops.

The act of preserving, like gardening, is hopeful. It was once essential to survival, to ensure that foods were available year-round. Now it's a gesture of goodwill to future meals, incorporating a past season's bounty. We do it so our kids' winter lunch boxes will have slivers of last summer in them – not just any summer, but *our* summer; the one we lived and worked and sliced and laughed in.

Preserving is a great habit to bring into your life for a bunch of reasons. It saves you money, because you can buy or pick seasonal food when it's cheap to make batches of your favourite foods for later. It reduces waste, because you can preserve your bounty in reusable containers and don't have to buy, use and throw away yet another packet every time you cook. It's a great opportunity to explore food cultures from around the world, too. Many preserved foods have become proud signifiers of specific regional flavours and cultural food traditions. There's a whole world of tangy, delicious ferments out there, just waiting for you to discover them.

Learning this skill is also highly empowering. You get to control exactly what is in your bottled fruit or tomato sauce or those dried apple snacks that you're making. This means no toxic nasties or hidden ingredients and no reliance on multinational corporations to tell you what they put inside each packet. With real ingredients and just a bit of your time, you'll have a shelf full of good food whenever you need it. What's not to love?

Five basic ways to preserve food

Freezing

If you're pressed for time and have freezer space, preserving food can be as simple as freezing it. Make a big batch of basil pesto and freeze some in small jars, for example, or buy a big load of sweet corn while it's cheap and put the cobs in the freezer for future meals. Note that freezing does rely on your power being on (obviously) and for this reason it's not as high up the resilience scale as shelf-stable options that don't need energy inputs. That said, freezing is a great first step towards storing your season.

Drying

Drying is a great low-energy preservation method: once dried, your food is shelf stable, meaning it doesn't require any further energy (such as freezing) to stop it from going bad. Surplus apples, pears, peaches and other fruit can be simply sliced and dried in a dehydrator, or on a tray in the sun for a day or two, set atop the trampoline or even on your car dashboard. When dry, store in airtight containers: big glass jars are good.

Fermenting

Ah, fermenting – possibly the tastiest way to catch and store energy. Lacto-fermentation is the easiest way to get started, requiring simply salt, clean water, veggies and some waiting time. While you wait, the *Lactobacillus* bacteria that are present on all plants get to work, converting natural sugars to lactic acid and thus preserving all the flavour, texture and nutrients in a form that is additionally beneficial for your digestive system. We've included our favourite lacto-fermented kraut recipe on page 44. Once you get more confident, you can extend your repertoire to spicy kimchi, dill pickles and even pickled mushrooms.

Bottling

Another way to preserve the harvest is bottling, either by water bath or pressure canning. The basic method for bottling is this: put your fruit or veggies in a clean jar and add some water plus either sugar or salt. Then put those jars into a big heated vessel and hold them at a simmering heat for as long as is needed, according to the recipe you follow. When you're done, the jar of food will be shelf stable for months, if not years. There are many good recipes out there for this technique!

Cooking

Then there are all the delicious cooking options, including making jams, sauces and pickles, that rely on high heat to preserve the food. The fruit or vegetables are cooked with sugar or vinegar, then ladled into piping hot jars with lids that are immediately screwed on tight. The food contracts as it cools, pulling the lid inwards and sealing the jar shut. Some folks cook their sealed jars in a water bath as a final stage of preservation.

Beans and cucumbers ready to have brine poured over them for pickling. Experiment with cuts and shapes to fit more pickles in your jars.

A simple lacto-fermented sauerkraut recipe

Sauerkraut is a primary cog in the engine of our kitchen. We eat it hot, we eat it cold, on eggs, in soups and on the side. While traditional sauerkraut is made from just cabbage and salt – and it is deee-licious – this recipe can be applied to other vegetables, too; in particular, most of the root veggies and brassicas.
In the interests of keeping things as local, seasonal and fresh as possible, we now 'kraut' whatever we can. Diversity in all things!

What you'll need

Mixed veggies, such as cabbage, carrots, radishes

Your favourite herbs and spices for flavouring (garlic and seaweed are also good flavour options)

Salt, ground or flaked (straight up, no additives: sea salt or rock salt is fine)

A fermentation crock or bucket or a big jar with a lid

1. Wash the veggies. Save the outer leaves of cabbage, then core and chop your veggies. Choose and chop your flavourings.
2. Put it all in a bowl and weigh it. Add 1 tablespoon of salt per kilogram (2 lb 4 oz) of veggies.
3. Get squishing: squeeze with your hands, or bash with a rolling pin. The aim here is to bruise and break down the cell walls of the veg, which releases the moisture and mixes everything with the salt. It's ready when the veg is very soft and loads of liquid has been released.
4. Firmly pack the kraut in a jar, squishing the veg down under its own liquid. Push in a folded cabbage leaf as a lid to cover the top of the kraut. Make a carrot stopper: trim a whole carrot into a length that will press down on the mixture when the jar lid is closed. It's important to keep all your kraut below the liquid.
5. Put the lid on gently and place the jar on a plate to catch any juices. Leave it on the bench for

1–2 weeks, depending on the ingredients and your room temperature.
6. Open the lid once or twice a day so you can 'burp' your kraut to release any built-up fermentation gasses.
7. When it's tasting delicious – salty, sour, yum – secure the lid properly and store in the fridge to slow the fermentation to a minimum.

Tips

Trust your nose! If it smells great, eat it. If it smells bad, some other bacteria got in (it happens), so throw it in the compost and start again.

Kraut can be made any size, from finely shredded to using whole cabbages, but we recommend keeping your slices thin, or grated.

White smudges on the cabbage leaves are actually the good bacteria that helps ferment the kraut into delish probiotic food.

Some kraut combos we love:

Chinese cabbage (wombok), fennel, carrot, basil, collard (or kale) and cumin seed.

Carrot, fennel and orange.

Red cabbage and caraway.

Green cabbage, mustard greens and chilli.

How to bottle peaches in syrup

Preserved peaches are a grand, go-to classic in our household. They're plentiful in summer from the fruit growers of our area, store really well and taste amazing. This recipe uses a light sugar or honey syrup; it's also perfect for other sweet fruits such as nectarines, apples, cherries, berries and grapes.

For fruit varieties that are more tart or sour, add more sugar to make a heavier syrup: up to 50 per cent sugar to water. You'll need a thermometer to monitor the water temperature during the cooking process.

1. Prep peaches by washing, trimming and cutting off any brown/mushy bits. Cut in half and remove the stones. Place peaches in large jars, layering stone-side down, and leaving 1–2 cm (½ inch) of space at the top.
2. Combine the sugar or honey with 4 cups (1 litre) of water in a saucepan and bring to a boil.
3. Pour the syrup evenly into the jars, covering the peaches and leaving 1–2 cm (½ inch) of space at the top, and clip or screw the lids on tightly.
4. Place the jars on a metal rack in the bottom of a large stockpot and fill the pot with water. Make sure the jars are not touching each other. Heat the pot until the water reaches a temperature of 92°C (198°F) then maintain the water at that temperature for 45 minutes.
5. Use bottle tongs or a similar tool to carefully remove the jars from the hot water and set them aside to cool completely.
6. Once cooled, label the jars and store in a cool, dark spot – they should be good for at least 12 months.

What you'll need

A couple of kilograms (4–5 lb) fresh peaches

Glass jars with metal lids

2 cups (440 g) sugar OR 1½ cups (525 g) honey

Tip

You can use this method for preserving veggies, using salt as the preservative instead of sugar. Some veggies will need more or less salt, depending on the water content (and therefore the final percentage of salt in the jar), so check a good preserving guide for the right amount.

habit 7

HARVEST RAINWATER

Every living thing needs water to survive: you, your garden, animals, insects, soil microbes and the ecosystem in between. Rain is a crucial part of the water cycle; however, like all forms of energy, rain mostly comes to us in pulses. We get waves of high availability, which may then be followed by long, dry periods of no rainfall.

Planning for these times of plenty and times of need by capturing rainfall where and when it falls and storing it for later use is an excellent strategy to increase your household's resilience. It's a habit available to almost everyone. Got a sky that rains sometimes? You very likely can begin collecting rainwater at your place.

Your goal with this habit is to capture, slow down and store rainwater as it passes through your local system. You don't need huge tanks or an expensive plumbed-in system; rainwater harvesting can be done on a small budget with easily accessible DIY materials and the biology of your garden, in ways that work even if you're renting.

Why is this important, when water flows freely from the taps in your house? It's all about resilience: having a little (or a lot) of stored water enables you to use that water, no matter what is happening with the town water where you live. Collecting rainwater also benefits your community, and your local watershed, because it reduces the pulse loads of stormwater. That water you catch and store WILL still make its way downstream, eventually, but you can slow it down and use it productively before releasing it onward. This means your local stormwater system will be less overloaded in big rains, and your slow release of that water, over time, also helps reduce soil erosion and therefore the amount of sediment making its way to our rivers and oceans.

All in all, catching and storing rainwater is a benefit to your family and your community. It makes life more abundant, in all sorts of ways.

Got a sky that rains sometimes?
You very likely can begin collecting
rainwater at your place.

CATCH AND STORE ENERGY

How to harvest rainwater at your place

Rainwater can be collected in many different ways, from simple systems to seriously sophisticated methods. The best solution for you really depends on your situation and budget. The most basic option is just to leave a bucket or other container out in the open so it fills during rainfall: this might be enough water to keep plants on your balcony happy for a week, for example. It's a start!

To work out what might be best as a more permanent system for your place, get outside during your next rainstorm and observe the patterns. Ask yourself, 'Where does the water pool? Where does it run? How much water falls? What's my largest catchment? How many uses could I get out of this water before I let it flow out of my yard?'

Many properties are on some sort of slope, so start harvesting rainwater at the top if you can, to slow it down as it runs through your yard. You can catch and store rainwater in your soil by using mulch or planting living groundcovers to help keep the soil porous and able to soak up the rains when they come. You might also be able to divert overflows off hard surfaces and away from stormwater drains into a bucket, pond, an earth berm or soil. Perhaps you can even make a rain garden to soak up excess water (see page 52).

Another great way of increasing the amount of water you have at your disposal is to create a small rainwater barrel to capture water from your roof and store it for use in your garden (see the diagram on the next page). This is a great DIY approach to get you started. If you want to become more self-reliant with rainwater, you will need to install medium to large rainwater tanks – a larger project with associated costs and expert help. Which is great if that's within your scope, but if it's not, start with catching just a bit of your rainwater, and take it from there.

Potable water

In most places, rainwater is good for drinking, but do first check that your roof and collection container are made from food-safe materials. Also, consider what's around you: is there a risk of contamination because you're close to heavy industry or an industrial agriculture system? If you're not sure, you might choose to catch and store rainwater just for using in your garden.

Making a simple rainwater barrel

Harvesting rainwater for your garden in a small-scale barrel is a good DIY step you can sort yourself – no expensive large tanks or plumber required. While it won't supply all your household water needs – a rainwater barrel is about 250 litres (65 gallons), compared to tanks that may hold thousands of litres – it will give you some really useful quantities of water for your garden.

Tip

Check with your local council: some have outdated restrictions about capturing and using rainwater and, sadly, it may not actually be allowed in your area (so hide it! Hehe).

1. Choose a location: for example, a downpipe from a smallish roof catchment (garden sheds or verandahs are great) near to your garden and with space to place a barrel next to it.
2. Choose a container: ideally food-safe polypropylene, such as a 200 litre (50 gallon) olive drum, with a tight-fitting lid to prevent mosquitos from getting in.
3. Lift it up: raise the barrel off the ground using concrete breeze blocks or something sturdy. You need to use gravity to get water out, so, at the very least, make it high enough to get a watering can underneath.
4. You will need to make two holes in the barrel, so you can attach a tank flange or bulkhead fitting (allowing you to add threaded fittings like taps). Make one hole as close to the base as possible, and attach a tap.
5. Make the second hole near the top, and attach a diverter. The diverter allows water from the downpipe to be diverted to the barrel. Choose a diverter that allows the overflow from the barrel to go back to the downpipe, joining the original storm-water system. They are cheap and easy to find at hardware stores. Connect the diverter to the downpipe.
6. Use the water! Don't forget, *a full rain barrel can't catch anything*, so use that water while it's available to you, then catch and store some more.

Deep-rooted plants that don't mind wet feet

Mulch your rain garden with pebbles

Overflow to second rain garden

Rock-lined French drain from downpipe to garden bed

Gravel in base of rain garden

How to make a rain garden

A rain garden is a garden bed that collects rain run-off from hard surfaces – your roof, pavers, driveway, shed roof – and filters the water to remove nutrients and toxins. The cleaner water either sinks into the soil or can be redirected to other thirsty parts of your garden. It's a simple way to help protect both your house foundations and local waterways at the same time.

1. Choose the best location for your rain garden; ideally downhill from your house, about 3 metres (10 feet) from foundations and 15 metres (50 feet) from any septic systems.
2. Choose a water catchment area to work with, such as your driveway, your shed roof, or part of your house.
3. Connect your rain garden to the output of that catchment by building a French drain (a ditch filled with rocks) to direct the run-off to the garden.

4. Dig out a garden bed that sits lower than the surrounding soil level, and quarter fill it with gravel. The aim is to have this hole drain within 24 hours of filling.
5. Build up the ground level around the rain garden hole, to prevent water washing out.
6. Plan for overflow: consider another French drain to another rain garden, or a pathway to your stormwater system, or some other solution to manage the overflow from a larger rain event.

7. Plant the bed with useful and beautiful plants that are deep-rooted (to carry the water down) and require average-to-moist conditions – they need to be happy with a flood, but the aim is to sink that water quickly, so they won't always be in wet soil.
8. Mulch the garden bed with pebbles or shredded hardwood (pine or woodchips will float away).
9. For the first year, care for the plants with regular watering and weeding. After that, the rain garden should look after itself.

CATCH AND STORE ENERGY

BUILD A MINI GREENHOUSE

You want to grow tomatoes, but it's still too cold. Or you'd like to grow some ginger in a pot, but you live in a cool climate. What can you do? One option is to build a time-warp machine: that is, a mini greenhouse!

Greenhouses allow you to extend your growing season by catching the energy and warmth of the sun and storing it in happily growing seedlings. Greenhouses can give you an extra month or two in spring to get plants started (come on, tomatoes) and extra time in autumn to ripen things.

Mini greenhouses are suitable for anywhere from a balcony to acreage, and work for both renters and homeowners. Crucially, small ones are often moveable, so you can shift them around with the seasons to get just the right spot depending on where the sunlight is, and also take them with you if you move house. Even a windowsill, or an old window propped up against a wall, can have a 'greenhouse' effect for your plants.

Designing a mini greenhouse (or heck, a full greenhouse, if you have enough room) into your growing space is an excellent way to ensure strong spring seedlings, as well as reducing the impacts of weather shocks in your garden.

If you're feeling brave and creative, build yourself a DIY greenhouse, perhaps made from recycled glass doors and windows.

And if you get really keen, a greenhouse can even be positioned beside your house, to warm your living space. Combining function with lower heating costs while you raise the next crop? Yes, please.

Some mini greenhouse ideas

While greenhouses come in many shapes and sizes, the good ones all follow this basic premise: sunlight comes into an enclosed space, through either glass or clear plastic, and this solar energy is captured to heat the space and trap moisture inside.

But a word of caution: airflow is key. Without it, your greenhouse quickly becomes an oven. (Yes, we did fry many a seedling in our early greenhouse experiments.) So no matter what kind of greenhouse you end up making, remember to balance heat, light and airflow.

A windowsill

An old window propped against a wall

A wooden box with a hinged glass lid

A small prefab portable greenhouse

CREATE A BUDGET AND START SAVING

Money can be seen as a kind of energy, ebbing and flowing, coming into our pockets and out again. And because most of us live in a world driven by and dependent on money, it's helpful to learn how to catch and store this energy, so that when money comes in, you have the skills to accumulate some for future use via savings.

It's important to acknowledge that the habit of setting a personal budget is not feasible for everyone: those who are struggling to access a living wage will have other priorities. However, if you earn more than you need to cover the basics of life, this habit is worth cultivating.

Saving money empowers you to plan and implement big life goals and invest ethically, perhaps by converting your house to solar energy, bringing goats into your life, choosing to work fewer hours, or some other big, beautiful thing.

That nest egg – or a specially set aside emergency fund – can also be essential for reducing financial stress in unexpected lean times, while helping you plan for times when you know less money will be coming in, such as taking extended parental leave, or pausing a job to study or care for a loved one, or just to regroup yourself.

Which all sounds great, but how do you 'catch' that money for storing? The simplest way is to create a personal budget and get clear on the flow of monetary energy in your life: how much you require, how much is coming and going. This can be daunting when you first do it: it's quite hard to face up to our spending sometimes! But be kind to yourself and keep going. The point here is to empower yourself by getting real about where this energy flow leaks out of your life, and making choices about that.

Knowing how much cash you need to cover the basics helps you get smart with spending. You might realise the only way to accumulate savings right now is to spend less from day to day, which may lead you to investigate more frugal approaches. Can you buy second-hand clothes for that party? Could you build that garden bed using free materials found in your neighbourhood? Would investing in LED lights lower your energy bill? And – very importantly – how can you make sure you still have fun while you do all this?

Creating and sticking to a budget can be a bit like having a small superpower in your pocket, which just might blow up the way you think about your spending habits, and put it all back together in a more meaningful way.

How to start a personal budget

A simple way to get started with budgeting is to keep track of your spending over one month. Track to see where your money really goes! Jot down everything you spend money on, using a notebook or an app. This will give you powerful data and you might be surprised at where your money is going. At the end of the month, take a look at your spending, then ask yourself: 'Am I happy to expend XX hours of my energy to earn the money to have these things?'

The next step is to prioritise your spending by collating two lists: needs and desires. Number them in the order of priority, thinking about creating the life you really want to live. Map rough weekly or monthly costs against each item, perhaps placing an asterisk next to items that you have to spend money on at the moment, even if they aren't high priority (for example: a university debt or utilities bill). Analyse these priorities against your budget: you might realise that an expensive course, for example, is a high priority as it will teach you crucial skills for the future you want, while buying your lunch every day is a low priority that can be scrapped to free up funds. Shuffle money and priorities around until you are spending less than you earn, if you can.

At this point, it might be helpful to set goals for bigger-picture investments. If you're saving for a home, planning to finally sort out that dental work, fix the roof, or upgrade your garden, or you're keen to learn a new skill, work out how much money you will need for that. And thinking about when you'd like to get started, how much money will you need – and can you afford – to set aside each week or month to reach your goal?

Now, have a go at implementing your budget over a month or two. You can try a few different approaches to making it work, one at a time, to see what works best for you. Keep the ones that suit you, ditch the ones that don't. Everyone is different!

And as you're working with your budget, don't forget to track your spending and regularly review it all. Keep note of how much things cost and determine if your budget was correct. Perhaps it was over- or underestimated? Once this rhythm of maintenance is established and you're being honest with yourself, assess the feedback loop. What's working, and what isn't? What changes would make it more efficient? Keep tweaking, keep assessing, and keep showing up for yourself.

Creating and sticking to a budget can be a bit like having a small superpower in your pocket.

Top: beans growing. Above: 'Cherokee Wax' pods, in basket, seeds in top bowl; scarlet runner beans, centre; red kidney beans, right; and blue lake bean seeds.

habit 10

GROW A STORAGE CROP

The idea of growing a storage crop in your garden is a great idea for a few reasons. Firstly, you might get lots of food for later! Beyond that, you'll develop a very real appreciation for what's involved in growing, harvesting, processing and storing enough of something to see you through other seasons – and the reality of this task will give you a newfound respect for your food (and your food system) in a way that you may not have considered before.

If you have the space, an easy crop to start with might be potatoes or pumpkins: these can be stored for six months after harvest. But you know what stores for years, once they're dried? Beans. Collecting and keeping dried bean seeds for cooking is an excellent, simple way to catch and store energy at your place.

Beans are a deeply useful and nutritious crop that take comparatively little time and effort to grow. Actually they are just about the easiest storage crop you can grow. They don't take up much garden space and there are varieties that can be grown year-round in most climates.

Then you get to eat them, which is really good for you! Beans are packed with protein and antioxidants, and are a nutrient-dense source of fibre. And because you've grown these beans and dried them for storage yourself, you know they're just beans – with no extra salt or preservatives or who-knows-what added. Plus, they taste great in everything from soups and pies to dips and salads.

Beans come in two types – bush and climbing – so choose according to the space you have in your garden. Climbing beans will need a trellis and take up more vertical space. Bush beans will take up more horizontal space. You'll also need to choose beans suitable for your particular climate. Broad (or fava) beans are a tall-bush type – a great crop for a cool temperate climate. Snake beans and winged beans are happy growing in a tropical environment. And for folks in the subtropics, pole beans, runner beans and scarlet runners are good choices.

There are other benefits for your garden here, too. Beans are part of the legume family, which means they have a special skill: they can catch nitrogen from the air and store it in the soil via nodules on their roots, where it then becomes available for other plants to use.

This is rather handy, as nitrogen is one of the main nutrients all plants need to thrive, and some plants we love to eat – such as tomatoes, cucumbers and corn – need a lot of nitrogen. So you can plan for your next nitrogen-hungry planting by growing beans first. After your bean harvest, snip the plants off at ground level to ensure the next planting gets all that goodness that is attached to the bean plant's roots.

The life cycle of a bean storage crop

We usually sow three successions of each bean variety we want to store for eating, planting the last round as close to the longest day of the year as we can. Within about three months, we'll be harvesting bushels of delicious beans, which we can dry and keep for months or even years in airtight containers.

Part 1: Grow beans
- Get yourself some bean seeds that are suitable for drying.
- Prepare your garden bed, then plant the bean seeds directly into the soil. Watch them emerge in a week!
- Beans generally need very little attention as they grow, other than weeding the garden bed to ensure the bean plants aren't competing with anything else for sunlight and space.

Part 2: Harvest dry pods
- Most dwarf beans take about 110 days, seed to seed. You want to harvest the pods when they're as dry as possible.
- It's best to harvest in the heat of the afternoon when there is no dew.
- Remove the whole plant by cutting the stem above the ground and laying it on a sheet.
- Leave the beans on their sheet somewhere dry and warm for 5 days.
- Pop some beans out of a pod, and check the beans' readiness with the Bite Test: bite a seed, and if there's no indent from your teeth, it's dry and ready.

Step 3: Get those seeds out!
- Place all pods between two big sheets on hard ground. Then put on boots and stomp on them!
- The bean seeds should shell out and settle in the bottom of the sheet. Remove the dry pods and pour the beans into a bucket.
- Winnow the beans from bucket to bucket over a sheet, in a mild breeze, to remove the last of the plant material (chaff).
- Store your beans away from light or temperature fluctuations in airtight buckets or jars.

Step 4: Cook and eat
- Soak the beans overnight and cook them in boiling water for about 20 minutes (depending on variety) and then use them in *all* the ways.

Step 5: Sow again
- Ensure you save enough of your best bean seeds for planting next season! And around the cycle goes, with your locally adapted, tasty beans: energy caught, stored and enjoyed.

Principle 3

Obtain a yield

＊

Grow sprouts and
microgreens

＊

Use what
you have

＊

Start a
herb garden

＊

Do a life/work
time audit

＊

Pest-proof
your garden

At first, the most obvious and, perhaps, aspirational example of obtaining a yield that you may think of is growing food that you can harvest and eat. And most of us put this principle into practice in our normal lives every week: working, to make money.

This principle, along with *Catch and store energy* (Principle 2), is so much more fundamental to life than that: these are the power principles that drive systems forward. Natural systems, economic systems and ecosystems, too. And while these principles can cause harm in the wrong hands – by concentration of power and wealth or exploitation of workers, for example – these principles can also be used to regenerate ecosystems and communities alike.

This principle of **Obtain a yield** is important because it reminds us that in order to keep going – and to build abundance, health and community – we have to set up systems that will bring us a return. We need sustenance, clean water, beauty, rest, safety, stable housing, love and companionship in order to survive – not just money and vegetables. And so it's crucial to plan for, design and build systems that allow these things to flow our way, and into the arms, lives and hearts of others, too. We need to behave in a way that brings this goodness into our lives.

So this principle reminds us that it is essential that we get real, direct rewards from what we do in order to sustain motivation: this is true for establishing a veggie patch *and* for establishing a social movement.

Design your system to create yields, wins and happy results – even if they're small ones – to keep you and everyone else motivated to keep going, and nourished while you do so.

So when you're considering a new habit or undertaking a new project, make sure you consider how to obtain a yield as part of your plan. Yields nourish us, and others – and ensure that new possibilities can emerge as a result of this nourishment.

These represent important psychological yields that maybe in the past were just a by-product of people going about their everyday lives. People in the modern world have been so disconnected from their sources of sustenance, they are often not aware of how important it is to obtain a yield – or they're very focused on a very narrow form of it: 'How do I earn money?' In capitalism, this is the one essential truth. In permaculture, we take that one truth and reduce its scale to being just one of 12 principles.
David Holmgren, Permaculture Living course

If you have spare garden-bed space for a few weeks, a carpet of lettuce and rocket can work well, to be harvested as microgreens.

GROW SPROUTS AND MICROGREENS

Growing even just a little bit of your own food is a powerfully positive habit to cultivate, because every chunk of resilience we can cram into our household and community counts – including knowing how to grow your own food at home, if and when you need it.

Growing food helps build a connection with our ecosystem: it connects us with our soil, plants, other animals, insects and water. It allows us to eat more locally, avoid buying from giant multinational companies just a little bit more often, and it gives us access to food grown without plastics and chemicals. It's good for you, and everything around you.

If you don't have the time or space to launch full steam into a veggie patch just yet, no worries at all. You can grow your own nutritious sprouts and microgreens on your kitchen bench or windowsill – no garden required. All you need is a few jars, a few seeds and a bit of basic know-how. The results you'll get are fast, cheap and delicious: nutritious fresh food, grown right in your kitchen where you need it most.

Sprouts and microgreens are essentially baby plants – vegetable and herb seedlings – that you eat when they're just a few days or weeks old. At this point, they're still in the 'leafy greens' stage, which is excellent, because leafy greens are just about the most expensive vegetable you can buy. Plus, greens spoil rapidly after being picked. So fresh is definitely best, and microgreens are incredibly quick to grow in small spaces, without needing a heap of sunlight. You can do this year-round in your kitchen, regardless of where you live or what's happening outside.

You will need

Sprouting seeds, organic if possible (you might find these in the drygoods section of your local store); 2 tablespoons small seeds, such as mustard or alfalfa OR ½ cup big seeds, such as adzuki beans, chickpeas or whole lentils

A clean jar, around 1 litre (4 cups) capacity, but use whatever you have

Netting or tulle fabric, or even an old handkerchief will do

Elastic band or hair tie

A small bowl

1. Put the seeds in the jar and fill with cool, clean water.
2. Cover the jar with netting and secure it with the elastic band.
3. Let the seeds soak for 4–8 hours or overnight. (This ensures you get good germination.)
4. Drain the water off the seeds then give them a rinse in cool water. To fully drain the seeds, upend the jar at an angle in a bowl so all the water drains out.
5. Place the jar, still upside-down in its bowl, on a windowsill or on the kitchen bench, out of direct sunlight.
6. Every 12 hours or so (at least once a day), fill the jar with cool, clean water, then rinse, drain, and put the jar back in the bowl on its tilt.
7. In 3 or 4 days (or sooner) enjoy your fresh young sprouts! Delicious.

How to grow sprouts in a jar

Sprouts are plant seeds that have germinated successfully; they have literally sprouted for you, entirely within a jar. No soil required! You can sprout almost any seed that produces edible adult plants. The result is crunchy homegrown veg that's packed full of nutrients, all grown in a space that's not much bigger than your hand.

How to grow microgreens

Microgreens are seeds sown in trays with growing medium and grown for a week or two until their 'true' leaves appear. (A seedling's first set of leaves are 'cotyledons', or seed leaves, which look similar in many plants. You're waiting for what appears next: the first set of 'true' leaves.) Cut the shoots close to the base with scissors and eat!

The real trick to growing great microgreens is to make a habit of it. If you plant a tray every week, you will constantly have new greens coming on. So find a windowsill, and let's get growing.

You will need

Seed-raising medium, such as coir fibre

Seed-raising trays (clean)

Suitable seeds (organic if possible)

Water spray bottle or hose

Hessian or other coarse cloth

1. Spread seed-raising medium in the tray to a depth of 2.5 cm (1 inch) and level it out gently. Scatter seeds over the surface. For larger seeds, place them 1 cm (½ inch) apart.
2. Gently mist with water until soaked through (when the shiny wet look takes longer than 10 seconds to fade away).
3. Cover the tray with hessian or cloth, or stack trays on top of each other: this keeps the moisture in and improves germination.
4. Each day, uncover the trays, water and check for germination. If nothing's popped up, cover them over again.
5. When leaves first form, move the trays into a spot that gets indirect sunlight, and continue to water daily.
6. Your microgreens will likely be ready for harvest in 1 to 3 weeks. Harvest only what you need to eat right now, by cutting close to the base. Keep watering what's left and harvest as needed.
7. Once all is eaten, you can restart the tray by loosening the growing medium, topping up with a little fresh medium and scattering with new seeds.

Lettuce microgreens grown from seed.

Our favourite seeds to grow for microgreens

- Lettuce and rocket
- Herbs such as coriander and basil
- Buckwheat
- Amaranth
- Beetroot
- Broccoli
- Spinach
- Sunflower
- Daikon radish
- Mustard greens

You might already have some of these seeds in your pantry – why not give them a try?

Using sprouts and microgreens

Microgreens and sprouts are supremely versatile and can be added to almost anything. We put them in salads, sandwiches, soups, stir-fries and pasta sauces, and we can often get several meals from one small tray. Happily, their mild flavour goes down well with the whole family, picky eaters included. Here are some ways we use them:

- Sprouts on top of peanut-butter toast
- Sprouts sprinkled into carrot and cumin soup
- Sprouts in a halloumi burger
- Microgreens as a salad with tomato and mozzarella, or roast pumpkin and quinoa
- Microgreens on pizzas
- Microgreens in omelettes
- Sprouts or microgreens stirred through a stir-fry just before serving.

habit 12

USE WHAT YOU HAVE

Stick with us here, because this one might seem a bit counterintuitive at first: you're going to learn how to obtain a yield by first giving something away, because we all have an abundance of something, and some of us have an abundance of many things.

Swapping and sharing your abundances can form the beginnings of a rich, connected, informal economy, sometimes called the non-monetary economy, gift economy, 'freeconomy' or barter network. It's a way of practising your own sense of 'enough-ness', helping others and cultivating community, while often obtaining a yield for yourself in the process – which is excellent for everyone!

The trick is taking time to consciously identify what your abundance is. Look around: what do you have plenty of and how could you share that? We're not just talking about physical things here – it could also be time, skills or knowledge. Once you've identified what you have in abundance, you can figure out how to pass it along to others who might need it. You might be able to swap or share or trade. And this, in turn, is likely to bring yields of something new back around to you.

So, for example, you might have some spare time on a Thursday afternoon. Or a tree with far too many lemons on it. Perhaps you know how to speak French or Italian, unlike most folks around you. Or you've got what seems like a thousand cardboard boxes or clean jars. This is abundance, and others are likely to be grateful for the opportunity to share in your surplus.

This kind of thinking is at the heart of permaculture, and also at the heart of many natural systems. It's the beginning of reciprocity, a fundamental trait of all functional ecosystems. Surpluses become yields which beget other yields which create new surpluses. And around it all goes. In the process, the fabric of your community interweaves, everyone gets to know each other a little more, and life gets a little better each time you engage.

And all because you had too many lemons or a free Thursday afternoon.

It's a way of practising your own sense of 'enough-ness', helping others and cultivating community.

OBTAIN A YIELD

How to join the non-monetary economy

The next step is deciding whether you want to swap or trade for something specific, or if you're happy to just help and see where this sharing of your surplus takes you.

The gift economy

This is all about giving forward, without a specific yield expected: what you receive in return can be as simple as the satisfaction of helping with something you care about.

We've observed that this kind of economy functions best when there are commonalities between the gifters. This might be friendships, values, access to land or another combination of factors. When everyone feels somewhat 'on the level' with each other, gift economies work beautifully.

You might choose to give your spare time to a good cause: your local food bank, a new community project or an online climate crisis campaign, for example. You can find volunteer programs for everything from fixing lawn mowers to breastfeeding support.

The swap economy

In some contexts a barter or swap approach sits more comfortably, and helps move towards equity for everyone. A straight-up barter – my 'this' for your 'that', rather than gifting – enables people to not feel indebted, which can be so very important when fostering community where there might be disparity, such as wage inequality, privilege, racism or other structural inequity or imbalances. So go carefully – but DO keep going. Your participation in creating these structures mindfully, and learning as you go, will help the greater whole.

And sometimes a straight-up swap creates more sharing, because everyone feels comfortable with the equal give-and-take of the outcome. This in turn can encourage more swapping, and then more swapping, and onwards to other awesome outcomes.

So you might swap your lemons for your neighbour's eggs; car parts for a load of firewood; or your seedlings for a casserole delivered to your door. Some places have crop swaps where everyone brings their surplus garden produce and swaps for things they don't have. And some communities have 'time banking' schemes, where you can exchange skills via direct time swaps, such as an hour of your time making a spreadsheet in return for an hour of someone's cleaning time.

Really, you can choose to engage in whatever way works best for you and your community. Get started, and give it a go.

Some ideas for sharing: if you've got spare time, make dinner and deliver it to a neighbour; volunteer your skills as a handyperson to make others happy.

Ideas to get you started

Stuck for what your specific surplus might be? Here's a non-exhaustive list of ideas that might help spark some clarity for your situation. You might be able to share or swap:

- A language
- Your computer skills
- Skills in mending and repairing clothes, electronics or machines
- Woodchopping skills
- Your gardening knowledge
- Enormous amounts of citrus, when the season hits. Or really, any kind of fruit – don't let the glut fall to the ground and rot; share it instead!
- Cardboard boxes, jars and other containers
- Your food scraps: that gardener down the road may be searching for compost ingredients
- Homegrown seedlings or veggie seeds saved from your organic patch
- Home-brewed beer, kombucha and tibicos (water kefir)
- Soups, casseroles, lasagnes and other delicious homemade meals
- A few hours of cleaning help
- An hour of the thing you do as a day job: marketing, massage, fundraising, trade services, building, hairdressing, etc
- Your baking services for someone's big birthday celebration
- Some of those spare computer cables you have lying around
- Schoolkid pick-up help – especially if you're already heading that way to collect your own small person.

What else do you have in abundance?

Teach your language skills to someone who'll make you your favourite cake; swap lemons from your tree for eggs from the neighbour's chooks; reprogram a computer in exchange for dinner.

START A HERB GARDEN

If we're talking about the value of positive feedback – of seeing and using the results of our efforts – growing your own herbs is a yield that rates pretty high for satisfaction. Most herbs are easy to grow, even if you're a beginner. They don't require much space – even just a windowsill will do — and they taste delicious, always.

Once you get into the habit, a herb garden can be something you tend, and use, most days. Homegrown herbs add a delicious fresh flavour punch to your meals, and picking your lunch or next tea brew fresh from that planter box by your back door is much more nourishing (and sustainable) than having to buy herbs wrapped in plastic from the supermarket.

You can choose to grow medicinal herbs too. Pick them fresh and add them to your favourite herbal tea blend, for extra goodness. Or you might like to get more adventurous and experiment with making your own herbal creams, salves or lip balms from your herby harvest.

Probably the most important step is considering what herbs *you* actually like to use or eat. Write down your favourites, and then cross-check what's possible to grow in your climate. No matter where you live, there will definitely be herbs that you can grow, starting now.

You'll also need to consider the space you have. If you're a complete beginner, we recommend you start small. Choose a small windowsill planter box and a few seedlings and see how you go, adding to your herb garden as your confidence grows.

A lot of herbs are at their best over spring and summer, and may die back during the cooler months. So if you're growing in a bigger space than a window box, you could try your hand at storing the season, too, by picking your herbs when they're flourishing and hanging them upside down in small bunches – in a shady, warm place with good airflow – until they are dry. After about a week, you can put them in labelled jars and store them somewhere away from light, ready for adding to teas and cooking come winter. Herbs all year round? Yes, please.

Once you get into the habit, a herb garden can be something you tend, and use, most days.

Easy herbs to start with

Good choices for small herb gardens with some sunlight

- For delicious flavour and aromatics: parsley, tarragon, basil, kitchen mint and thyme.
- For herbal tea and medicine: chamomile, calendula, peppermint and lemon balm.
- For attracting beneficial insects: borage, comfrey and fennel.
- For a drought-tolerant, low-care garden: rosemary, sage and oregano.

Considerations for windowsill herb gardens

Unless you have a perfectly placed, equator-facing window (you do? Great! See the list above), your windowsill herb garden will be getting only a few hours of sun per day. Choose a windowsill that gets some direct sunlight though, if you can. And choose herbs that go well in a few hours of sunlight per day, such as:

- mints of all kinds: spearmint, peppermint
- sorrel
- coriander (cilantro)
- chives
- thyme
- lemon balm.

Pick herbs when they are in abundance and tie them in bunches to share or dry and store them for the cooler months.

DO A LIFE/WORK TIME AUDIT

Time is a funny thing. So many of us wish for more of it – for more hours to lie in the sun with a good book, or to grow great food, or hang with our family, or make friends with that interesting person we met, or whatever makes your heart expand. Yet often we spend this finite resource without really thinking about how or why, racing from one commitment to the next, and the days fly by.

So have you considered that, maybe, gathering some precious time could be an amazing 'yield' in your life? As boring (and time-consuming!) as it sounds, auditing your time can be a way to obtain more of this yield. Because to audit is to become aware of how we might be spending time that actually doesn't do us much good, while discovering that the things we love are getting pushed aside due to a perceived lack of time.

All this pondering and realignment might gradually lead you to big decisions: to downsize, downshift, radically simplify, and perhaps even say goodbye to that nine-to-five office job and its questionable impact on your health and happiness.

Or perhaps your work/life balance audit could lead to small life tweaks that have unimaginably big consequences. Maybe you commit to adjusting your sleeping patterns to follow the seasons, and suddenly you discover a beautiful annual cycle of winter rest that leaves you pumped with energy and ready for more action in the warmer months. Or you decide to set firmer boundaries with your workplace and quit all that overtime, giving you a much healthier balance between work for other people and time for yourself.

For this habit, let's assume we each spend about nine hours each day sleeping and on basic wake-up and wind-down routines. That leaves 15 hours per day, or 100 hours a week, to do everything else. What do you do with your 100 hours each week? Where are you currently, and where would you like to be? What steps can you take to get there?

This is about ways to find more time – within your finite resource of 24 hours a day – to live a good and happy life filled with more community, more great food, less carbon, less waste and more spine-tinglingly good possibilities.

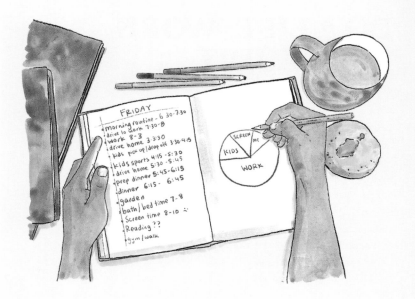

How to audit your time

The easiest way to reclaim some balance in your life is to figure out where you're spending your time in the first place. Once you have a clear picture of it all, decide what's truly important to you – this will look different for everyone! – and see if you can gently realign and reassign a little of your time towards more of what you really want.

1. For a week, keep a daily activity log, where you roughly track how you spend your time, both at work and elsewhere. Be as honest as you can with yourself. This gives you full visibility, and you might uncover a few surprises about where your time is going. Add up those hours, and write them down.

2. Look at your list: are you surprised by anything you see? Is the number next to 'work' eye-wateringly large? Do you actually not spend nearly as long cooking, or exercising, or reading each week as you thought you did? And where is your average weekly screen time in that list?

3. Next, get out your goal statement (see page 12). Have a look at that, next to your time audit. How does it make you feel?

4. If there's not enough of what you really want to be doing in your time audit, that's okay. You can start to change that as soon as you like, tiny bit by tiny bit.

What can you tweak? Can you add 30 minutes of reading when you're on the train? Can you add a short walk in the park each lunchtime? Tiny changes add up, and affect everything. And sometimes, when that's all the wriggle-room you've got, it's in this tiny, piece-by-piece way that you can slowly change things, and cultivate new habits that make life better.

OBTAIN A YIELD

PEST-PROOF YOUR GARDEN

Whether you're growing a few herbs on your windowsill or a heap of veggies in a sprawling backyard patch, discovering that critters have munched through and devoured almost every leaf is decidedly unfun – and can seriously dent your motivation.

So in the name of obtaining a yield (and avoiding frustration), it's useful to find ways to maximise your harvest and minimise your losses. No chemical sprays needed, though: we've found exclusion works best to save our veggies from the jaws of critters, while also preventing us from swearing more than is ideal.

But first, don't forget the permaculture ethic of 'fair share'. These so-called 'pests' are only after your yield because they're hungry or quite possibly starving. In many cases, humans have removed their habitat and food sources, and squeezed in on wild areas until animals have nowhere left to go, or are out of balance.

So why not include some of your ecosystem neighbours in your garden design? This could look like planting some native forage away from your veggie patch, or attracting owls to help deal with rats, or advocating with your neighbours and the local council not to use poisons that can kill predatory insects, birds and other wildlife.

With all that in mind, the best way to get started is to write a list of what's eating your harvest (besides you and your family) and where they are getting in. Depending on where you live, your local critters might be birds, bats, foxes, insects, possums, gophers, rats, bears – or a combination of these and more. If you're not sure who the culprit is, try taking photos of the damage and sharing with other gardeners, or going out at night to see what's happening under the cover of darkness.

Once you've identified your garden's main pests, consider appropriate ways of excluding the critters. You could also go for the 'guardian' approach, as we do in our garden: our small dogs who sleep outside are on patrol each night to chase the possums back over the fence.

Thinking beyond physical factors, you can also get to know the life cycle of your particular 'pest', because sometimes interrupting the life cycle is even more effective than exclusion. For example, you might check the leaves of your broccoli plant every couple of days, and pull off the caterpillars before they turn into cabbage moths and lay more eggs.

Do whatever suits your circumstances and remember to look up and beyond your own fenceline. Plan for the rest of your ecosystem's needs along with your own. Work with your ecosystem, not against it.

Excluding pests from your garden

So, you have a 'pest' problem: let's get that sorted.

1. What's eating your harvest? Where are they getting in?

2. How can you exclude them? For example, you could try:

- electric fencing, or for urban areas, a low-voltage electric line
- bagging crops
- chicken wire mesh
- fox-proof fencing
- building an anti-aviary – to keep birds out, not in! The wire tops of old birdcages will protect plants from birds and small animals.
- fruit tree netting: dome or tube
- limiting access to compost (rat-proof the base with mesh)
- putting shadecloth or a mesh enclosure over seedlings.

3. Look at pest life cycles and get involved that way. You could:

- pick off caterpillars and larvae
- build a snail/slug trap.

Apply self-regulation and accept feedback

✳
Locavore
challenge

✳
Rehome all
that stuff

✳
Use your privilege
for purpose

✳
Learn how to
communicate well

✳
Get water wise

Apply self-regulation and accept feedback *is an important principle that we can all learn. If* Catch and store energy *and* Obtain a yield *are 'power principles' that encourage positive feedback from our actions, this principle is about that other essential kind of feedback: the not necessarily positive kind.*

Negative feedback isn't just bad news, however; it's a constraining force that helps us set limits, and allows things to be better for everyone. Every bicycle needs a brake, as well as the leg-power to cycle it forwards.

If we look around us, all levels of our ecosystem are self-regulating: they're receiving feedback all the time and adjusting accordingly. Field mice flourish during a bumper year of grass or seeds, and populations dwindle during less productive years. And in turn, as the mice die, their bodies become an abundance for other life in the ecosystem, sending the regulation, feedback and abundance back around. Different types of plants occupy different niches in the forest, in the canopy and the understorey. They are constrained by the growth of other species, and nurtured by a myriad of interspecies relationships. These patterns in our ecosystems are a basic fact of life on Earth; we need to learn from these patterns too, in our own actions and behaviour – in how we decide what is 'enough' for each of us, and how we accept feedback on our actions and choices.

On a personal level, it's a lot easier to accept positive feedback than negative, but negative feedback can be empowering, and it's absolutely crucial that we heed it, and act upon it.

On a large scale, our planet is providing undeniable feedback that the burning of fossil fuels for energy has negative consequences for all, and must stop. On a small scale, we can consider what we can do to behave in a way that confronts this huge challenge – as an individual and as part of collective action, too.

At home, you can use this principle to consider what 'enough' looks like, for you. It's an invitation to cultivate, accept and even celebrate the necessity of limits, at all levels, to enable a fairer distribution of resources and a minimisation of harm. Can you get by with less, in order to create more abundance elsewhere? This might mean accumulating less stuff, consuming less of a damaging thing, or altering your habits to create more goodness for those around you, and all the life in your ecosystem and beyond.

LOCAVORE CHALLENGE

It's strange to think that in most places, if you go back just a couple of generations, everyone was a locavore to some degree. Sure, some foods and ingredients still came in from far away, but the majority of what folks ate was grown locally by necessity.

Most of us now shop and eat within an industrial food system operating at a global scale, even though it may not say that on the packet. Basic food items are often grown in one country, shipped to another country to be processed and packaged, and then shipped via a third to a fourth country, where you pick them up off the shelf at your store.

Thinking like a locavore challenges this system in a quietly radical way. Can we eat well from what is around us? Can we minimise our impact by choosing local alternatives to common foods, forging new connections where necessary to ensure local supply, or even occasionally going without something (gasp!) because we can't find a local, ethically produced version?

So here's a challenge: can you apply self-regulation and accept feedback on your current diet, and source your food as locally as possible for three whole days?

The point of this challenge is to look – really look – at what you eat and have a good think about how the impact of the foods you choose affects your ecosystem, and what it does or doesn't do for your local economy.

You are taking back your 'foodshed' – your local food region – and allowing the possibility for a local food economy to thrive. This kind of thinking is fundamental to permaculture, and also to having a habitable planet for everyone.

Food deserts

Many folks live in what are called 'food deserts': places where very little food is grown (such as cities) or where there is very little affordable local (or indeed nutritious) food. Chain stores and packaged foods from far away may be all that people in these communities have access to for their food shopping.

Exploring your local foodshed

Is it possible to eat local where you live? Let's find out! The purpose of this three-day challenge is to explore whether you can, in fact, eat from only your local foodshed.

By beginning to understand your local food system (or lack thereof), you will be in a position to advocate for local food sources, find and support local producers, and figure out how to source more good-quality food locally, which can help erode the injustice of these food deserts for everyone in your community. Supporting local food systems creates more resilience for everyone.

So, by the end of the three days, regardless of whether or not you were able to be 100 per cent locavore, you'll have a much better sense of your local food system and economy. You'll be in a better position to apply

self-regulation and accept feedback about your current diet, and you'll have found new ways to source your food as regeneratively and locally as possible. Eating and shopping locally can lead to increased community resilience, an improved local economy, sustainable livelihoods for local growers – and fresher food for you and those around you.

Research and use your nearest food co-op or store that stocks local produce; you will learn about what grows near you and what doesn't.

How local? Choose your radius

The first step for this challenge is choosing your radius: the distance from home that you're aiming to source your food from. The area within this boundary makes up your local foodshed. You might choose 200 kilometres (125 miles) as your radius, or 1000 miles (1600 kilometres). Or the boundaries of your country: this will depend on where you live. If you're in the city or not near an agricultural area, you may need to make your radius wider and expand your foodshed to ensure you have enough to eat. If you live in a farming area, maybe you can tighten this radius to be more challenging.

This is all part of the 'accepting feedback' part of this permaculture principle and thus all part of this experiment. Figure out what you've got to work with and set yourself some reasonable boundaries.

Starting your three-day challenge

List your foods

Make a list of the everyday foods you'll want to eat during this three-day challenge. This might include milk, bread, fruit, eggs, vegetables, herbs, fish, fruit juice, olive oil – and what about salt and sugar? What about snacks, flour for cakes, or tea and coffee? Write it all down.

One of the first things you might notice is that, based on what you know about your local ecosystem, some of your foods come from very far away. Maybe you live in a cold temperate place, but you love coconut sugar and bananas. Or you live a long way from any grass-fed dairy country, but you love lots of butter on everything. These items might need to be set aside for the duration of the challenge. If it ain't local, it ain't happening.

Research local suppliers

Now it's time for some research to determine what local food sources are available to you. You might consider things such as:

- Do you have farmers' markets nearby? How about a local greengrocer? Ask them where they source from.
- Do you have any farms nearby? Can you buy direct? Call them and ask.
- Is there a local food box scheme you can sign up to?
- If you eat meat, do you have a local butcher shop? Go in and ask them where they get their meat from. It's more likely to be sourced locally than meat from supermarkets.
- Have a look at the eggs you normally buy. Where are they from?
- Can you swap to local honey instead of sugar during this challenge?
- Do you have a friend with a veggie garden whom you can ask for some herbs or salad greens for the sake of this challenge?
- Can you supplement with a few local wild greens, as identified in Habit 1 (see page 20)?

Get cooking and eating

Once you know where you can source local food, it's time to make a menu, do a shop, and go for it. Three days of a locally sourced diet: what will you discover? New tastes, new relationships. Probably a fair bit of self-restraint. It may leave you wondering what a functional local foodshed would actually look like in your area.

This challenge is also about being creative. What tasty things can you make from local ingredients to replace the faraway foods? There will probably be a bunch of things that are really difficult to source locally, such as bread, salt and pepper, oil, fruit, or whatever else. That's okay. You decide how deep you go in this. Maybe you go hardcore and don't eat any of them for three days, which will be pretty illuminating for you. Or maybe you decide that spices, sugar, coffee and bread are exempt from the challenge. It's up to you.

More ideas for eating locally

Once you complete the three-day challenge, you'll have a heap of new knowledge and skills around how to find local food. Some of this knowledge might be sobering, but we hope some of it is exciting, too! From here, engage with your local food movement any way you can – as an eater, supporter, organiser or whatever. In this way, your weekly groceries become a tool for increasing local resilience on every level possible – and you might save money, too.

Your whole community stands to benefit from a local food economy. Here are some ways you can help support yours.

Follow the seasons
Start to understand what foods grow in your area and when things are in season. Those midwinter tomatoes? They're probably not grown near you. Now you know, you can adjust your eating habits accordingly.

Support local producers
Sourcing food directly from farmers and growers creates an alternative economy outside the mainstream food system. Search your area and you might be able to access veggie boxes, Community Supported Agriculture (CSA) schemes, farmers' markets or farmgate stall sales. But a lot of farmers don't sell directly to the public anymore, which leads to our next point …

Join or start a food co-op
Many a food co-operative has begun with a few families getting together to order bulk beans and potatoes, or whatever, from a great-quality source that doesn't deal with smaller orders. It's cheaper, you can choose a local producer, and there's far less packaging and food miles. Maybe there's already a co-op in your area? Check it out. Or gather a few friends and start your own (Habit 53; see page 250).

Consider hyper-local (often free) options
By which we mean foraging! Green weeds for your salads, your neighbour's lemon tree, that rosemary hedge by the school, seaweed down at the beach (Habit 54; see page 252).

Grow some of your own
Even growing just a few greens or veggies can help reduce your reliance on faraway foods. Remember, you can grow sprouts and microgreens on your kitchen windowsill (Habit 11; see page 64) – no garden required.

Forage local greens such as dandelion leaves. Local food doesn't just have to come from the shop or garden.

Three days of a locally sourced diet: what will you discover? New tastes, new relationships.

REHOME ALL THAT STUFF

We've all got it: stuff, things and a multitude of bits and pieces that we just don't need anymore, unused and gathering dust. Meanwhile, someone else who could be using that thing is buying a new one.

This isn't about chucking things in landfill and then replacing them. It's about considering what you've accumulated and then making some decisions about what isn't needed anymore, and how best to rehome it. This habit is about learning how to thrive with less, considering what comes into your home, and fixing and cleaning up stuff so that other people can use it – giving new life to old things.

First, figure out what you do and don't need, by assessing what you have. Go through your entire wardrobe and lay it all out on the floor to both reconsider and imagine new combinations of the clothes you already have, and identify what you no longer need.

For the 'pile of stuff' parts of your life (we have them too!), start small: choose a drawer, a bookshelf or a cluttered tabletop that needs dealing with, and focus on that one area first. Once you've done that, move on to the next area. We don't want you tearing the whole house apart, only to feel overwhelmed! Take it one step at a time.

Thoughtfully rehoming all that stuff you find will not necessarily be just putting it all in a big bag and taking it to your closest charity store, although that's a good start for some items. Take the time to consider the best path out of your life for each thing. Because once you do this, you'll start thinking a lot more about what that thing actually is – the resources that went into it, how it was made, where it was made and what the options are for passing it on based on its quality of manufacture, its actual 'usefulness', its age and other factors.

In turn and in time, becoming honest and aware of what you've brought into your home – and what the options are for responsibly passing that thing on once you're done with it – may well give you pause in your future buying behaviour.

Once you take on this habit, goals such as 'buy it once, buy it right' may start becoming part of your purchasing rules: resolving to save up and invest in a good-quality item that will last 10 years (or a lifetime!) instead of just 12 months. Or for an item that you need, but you know you'll only use once, how about looking at the local thrift stores before heading straight to a big-box store and buying a low-quality new one to use that one time that you need it?

Good books are gold, but you can have too many! Who would like to read your 'excellent, but ready to pass on' stack?

What to do with your stuff?

Give it away

Consider a clothes swap party, post it on a swap/sell group, ask on online forums if your friends would like it, or donate it to charity or the tip shop. For more significant items, could your local school use it? What about your local domestic violence shelter? Call them and ask. Consider giving good things away as birthday (or unbirthday) presents to friends.

Repair it

Ask a friend who has the know-how, or check if there's a repair café in your area. Then decide if you still want it, or if it can go off to charity, or even be sold.

Upcycle it

Make it into something else useful that you, or someone you know, needs or would like: for example, seedling tray? Rag rug? Indoor plant pot?

Sell it

Clean it up, take photos, and register with your local swap and sell, online marketplace or community group, or have a garage (estate) sale.

E-waste

Unusable tech items can (and should) be recycled, so take them down to your local e-waste recycling centre. Check with your local council, or search for your town and 'e-waste recycling' to find out where.

If it all seems too much, ask around: a friend may be only too happy to spend a weekend organising your shed in exchange for first dibs on your unwanted gardening tools, or maybe a case of beer. Just make sure that they're on board with sending your things to good homes wherever possible: chucking it all into landfill is not a good option.

And, yes, some bits will end up in landfill. While this is the least-great option for your unwanted stuff, it's also part of our current reality, which is full of single-use or low-quality stuff that ends up broken. Dispose of these items as thoughtfully as you can, and if it doesn't feel great to do this, there's some extra feedback for you.

Because the point here – more than finding the perfect home for every single unwanted thing – is that you're self-regulating and accepting feedback. If, through clearing out your unused stuff, you see that you tend to buy what you don't use, then take on that feedback. This is a great opportunity to reassess your buying habits and make changes, and better choices where you can.

Upcycle chipped and broken coffee cups into planters for your windowsill succulent garden.

Throwing a swap party

Hosting a swap party is probably one of the most fun ways to rehome stuff. We highly recommend getting together with some friends and holding one of these.

You can make your swap party on a specific topic – a clothes swap, a garden equipment swap, a book swap – or you can go for the whole 'bring things that you reckon others would love' attitude and see what happens.

This kind of party is simple but awesome. Get everyone to bring a plate of food to share, as well as their swaps. Set up some tables so there's plenty of room for all the precious stuff that needs rehoming. You can take turns in a 'one choice at a time' approach, or just let everybody dive in: it's chaos, but the best kind. Everybody gives and everybody gains!

USE YOUR PRIVILEGE FOR PURPOSE

We use our privileges all the time; we just don't realise it, for the most part. Learning how to understand, acknowledge and act upon our privileges – in a way that reduces disparity and helps create more equity for others – is definitely a lifelong process. It's really necessary for cultivating a just and equitable world, as much as we can.

I'm speaking specifically of your 'unearned' privileges here, at least to begin with, until you get the hang of this habit. These are the privileges that you just have – because of who you are and where you live. Things like your skin colour, your ethnicity, your gender, your abilities, your sexual orientation, your literacy level or your age might all afford you unearned privilege where you live and, conversely, some of them may not.

Your privileges consist of simple truths, but also exist in relation to other people: everything is connected, as always. The fact that you do not have certain privileges does not cancel out the ones that you do have, even though it may feel this way, at times. Your privileges also exist in relation to each other, so they not only add up, but may collaborate to amplify your overall privilege.

Privilege is intersectional

Intersectionality signifies the many ways that a person may be either advantaged, or disadvantaged, and how those ways come together to create overall privilege. It's a word that was coined in 1989 by Kimberlé Crenshaw to highlight how our attributes relate to each other.

Intersectionality can highlight your privilege; for example, if you are white, this will intersect with your other privileges to amplify them in most scenarios. So how can you act upon your privilege in a positive way?

Can you speak up when folks with similar privileges to you are being racist, misogynistic or homophobic? Your inherent privileges will make a difference here: when we are called out by folks we identify as similar to us, it makes a deeper impression. Can you use intersectional privilege to help out in community scenarios or direct action where those with more privilege are likely to experience less intimidation or harm?

I highly encourage you to read up on this idea and learn how to recognise and acknowledge the mycelial matrix of your intersectional privilege and, once you understand it, how you might utilise it most effectively to do good in daily life. Even if you think you know already, this process will be eye-opening.

Reading list

On Intersectionality: The Essential Writings of Kimberlé Crenshaw (The New Press, 2019)

Me and White Supremacy: Combat Racism, Change the World and Become a Good Ancestor by Layla F. Saad (Quercus Books, 2020)

Sister Outsider: Essays and Speeches by Audre Lorde (Crossing Press, 1984)

The Intersectional Environmentalist: How to Dismantle Systems of Oppression to Protect People + Planet by Leah Thomas (Souvenir Press, 2022)

Holding Change: The Way of Emergent Strategy Facilitation and Mediation by Adrienne Maree Brown (AK Press, 2021)

Steps to get you started

- Acknowledge the privileges you know you have.
- Learn more about the concept of privilege, to better understand privileges that you may not have thought of.
- Practise deep listening to marginalised voices from people who do not have your identified privileges, to understand how their lack of privilege affects them.
- Identify and confront your own internal biases – we all have them – and understand how these internal biases can cause harm to others, even if unintentional.
- Name your privileges in discussion with others, when relevant to the discussion. It will help frame your thoughts, and help others better identify and frame theirs, too.
- Use your voice to speak up on disadvantage and to call out discrimination wherever you see it, focusing on others who share similar privileges to you.
- Show up, in whatever ways you can, to use your privileges to assist others who do not have those privileges. How can you level the playing field? (Note: this does not mean 'speaking for' marginalised groups; it means holding yourself, and others with more privilege, to account for disparity.)
- Be accountable: you will sometimes get this process wrong! Be honest with yourself, apologise if necessary, and keep learning and moving forward. This is how we learn, and help out, and rise together.

APPLY SELF-REGULATION AND ACCEPT FEEDBACK

LEARN HOW TO COMMUNICATE WELL

In a world out of balance, the need for us to communicate effectively, clearly and kindly with one another has perhaps never been more urgent. Even though it's often a tricky or even scary process to engage in, seeking to create consensus and understanding with others helps us all move forward, and closer to one another. Yet some days it can feel like we are spiralling further and further away from each other, aided by online platforms and misinformation campaigns that only seem to amp up the snark and disconnection.

The good news is that effective communication is a skill you can totally learn. There are many techniques you can investigate, and what might land best for you is a combination of different methods. One method I love for beginners is the Nonviolent Communication process, created in the 1960s by American teacher and author Marshall Rosenberg as a tool to aid in conscious communication.

'Nonviolent Communication shows us a way of being very honest, but without any criticism, without any insults, without any putdowns, without any intellectual diagnosis implying wrongness,' Rosenberg (who passed away in 2015) said. So, if you find interaction with some people in your life unsatisfying (to put it mildly), your communication and listening styles may need a bit of TLC. How much energy do you spend watching TV, scrolling social media, sitting in traffic or waiting in line at the shop? Now compare that with how much time you spend focusing on conscious communication. If the answer is 'not much time at all' for the latter, it might be worth having a play with some new communication strategies and skill-up.

Rather than assigning blame or labelling (for example, 'it's your fault' or 'you are messy'), nonviolent communication asks you to objectively explain what happened; to identify the feelings this brings up for you and needs that aren't being met; and then to be clear about what the other person can do to help resolve the situation. It's an excellent way to apply self-regulation in your interactions with others, and to accept feedback, too, by learning to deeply listen to the other person's point of view.

In short, nonviolent communication uses consciousness, language and communication skills to create a framework from which you can:

- express your feelings and needs with clarity and self-responsibility
- listen to others' feelings and needs with compassion and empathy
- facilitate mutually beneficial outcomes for all parties involved.

It may feel a little clunky at first, but it does become more natural with time. And this is a habit that is pretty essential if you want to do a good job at life, and take the best care you can of yourself and others.

In a world out of balance, the need for us to communicate effectively, clearly and kindly with one another has never been more urgent.

Getting started with nonviolent communication

First up, see if you can get your hands on a copy of Marshall Rosenberg's excellent book *Nonviolent Communication: A Language of Life* (Puddle Dancer Press, 3rd edition, 2015). It's a bestseller, so your local library might have a copy you can borrow. The Center for Nonviolent Communication website (cnvc.org) has links to order it and also a bunch of videos and resources you can access for free.

Essentially, nonviolent communication is about structuring your sentences following this specific pattern: 'When A happens, I feel B because I need C – would you be willing to D?' For example, 'When there are papers all over my desk, I feel frustrated because I need to have a clear space to work. Would you be willing to put your papers on the shelf?'

Here's a bit more detail about each of those elements:

A = Observations – what you see, hear, remember or imagine, which does not contribute to your wellbeing. You'd start this sentence with: 'When I see/hear/remember ...'

B = Feelings – an emotion or sensation rather than a thought, which does not contribute to your wellbeing. You continue your sentence with: '... I feel ...'

C = Your needs or values – what you require to feel better, without stating a specific action just yet. So you continue your sentence with: '... because I need/value ...'

D = Your request – the concrete actions you would like taken. Now it's time to clearly request (without demand) what would make this situation better, from your point of view. So try ending your sentence with: '... would you be willing to ... ?'

This framework can be used in all kinds of situations: in your personal relationships, when parenting or communicating with family members, in schools, at work, in stressful situations, for conflict resolution. And a whole lot more. It is about clearly expressing how you are feeling without blaming or criticising. And when someone uses nonviolent communication to raise an issue with you, it can allow you to empathically receive how you are feeling without hearing blame or criticism, which is a very good thing indeed.

GET WATER WISE

It's pretty easy to see drinking water flowing freely from your household taps, where and when you want it, and therefore take this precious resource for granted. So it can be astounding to discover that only 0.4 per cent of the Earth's water is usable and drinkable – and must be shared among eight billion people (not to mention all the rest of life that relies on clean water). Plus, in many developed countries we use this precious drinkable water for crazily inappropriate things, like *flushing the toilet*. Wait – what?

It's clear that water is a precious resource; slowly, we're all becoming more aware of its value. And so we should, as water's central role in our lives and the planet's life cycles cannot really be understated.

In any country, the users of the majority of the water are not households like yours and mine, but industry and agriculture. So part of becoming water-wise is not just about what comes out of your taps; it also involves familiarising yourself with the systems of food production and manufacture you choose to support and advocate for (and against).

However, as with the macro, so with the micro. Your relationship with your tap water is a part of your relationship with your ecosystem. So what does your water use at home look like? How do you steward this precious resource, while it's inside your home, until it leaves your household boundaries and flows onward and downward through your catchment?

Part of your responsibilities are downstream (so to speak), with what you put in the water while it's in your household. But part of your responsibilities are upstream, too. The less water you use in your home, the less burden on your local water reservoirs, and also on your surrounding community and ecosystem.

By incorporating small reminders into your life, you can become much more conscious of how much water you're using, and can then more easily take steps to reduce your usage if needed.

For context, the average person in Sydney, Australia, uses nearly 300 litres (80 gallons) of water a day across their home and garden. Your personal 'water footprint' is much, much more than that if you count the water that goes into producing all the food and other stuff purchased and brought into your home. It adds up quickly, but once you start to pay attention, it can be relatively simple to start reducing your own personal water use.

Being conscious about your water use allows you to make changes where you can, identify where you can't make changes right now, and plan for how you could steward your water better in the future.

Read your meter

So now you might be wondering: 'Hmm, but how much water do I actually use in my household each day?' If you have access to your water meter, this is relatively easy to figure out. Read your meter at, say, 8 am. Then read it at the same time the next day; the difference between the two readings is how many litres of water you used. Try this simple check at different times of the year, to see how seasonal changes impact your water usage; for example, watering your garden more in summer will cause a seasonal spike, which could prompt thought on how to make your veggie patch more water wise.

Mulching plants can save up to 70 per
cent of the water that would otherwise
be lost through evaporation.

Some simple changes

Use the meter method outlined on page 97 to figure out how much water you're using right now by taking a couple of readings. Now that you have a baseline figure to work from, you can compare it with others in your community and around the world and get creative about how you could reduce your usage. Consider setting a goal for your household to work towards as you become more water wise.

Usually, it's baths, showers and toilets that consume the most household water; as much as a third of your daily use, according to some estimates. Showering uses between eight and 20 litres (2–5 gallons) of precious water *a minute* (depending on your showerhead), so cutting back on shower minutes is a great first step to conserving water. You can also install a water-saving showerhead. We've done this showerhead swap-out in rentals we've lived in: it's pretty straightforward, and we just took the water-saving showerhead with us when we moved out, and reinstalled the original one! While you're at it, install a half-flush on your toilet, too, if you own your home.

Gardens and outdoor areas are often the second biggest household water consumer, potentially accounting for another third of your daily water use. But a few small behavioural changes can help. Applying mulch 7–10 cm (2¾–4 inches) deep around your plants can save up to 70 per cent of the water that would otherwise be lost through evaporation. You can also skip things such as washing down pavements and simply sweep instead, and wash your car on the lawn so the runoff waters the garden.

In the kitchen and laundry, wait until you have a full load before turning on the dishwasher or washing machine. Keep an eye out for dripping taps and stay on top of maintenance. And consider collecting water in a big bowl or tub whenever you're running the taps and waiting for the water to heat up or cool down, then pour this onto your garden. We use this technique in our shower also, with a bucket that lives in the bathroom for that purpose.

Beyond that, start thinking about your greywater – the water that exits your house from your washing machine and so on – and how you could safely reuse that water in your garden before sending it on its way downstream. There are ideas for this in Habit 36 (see page 170).

Principle 5

Use and value renewable resources and services

✳
Make natural home cleaners

✳
Start a worm farm

✳
Cook with sticks

✳
Reuse your wee

✳
Reuse your packaging

We're all familiar with renewable energy: solar panels that capture the ongoing (and therefore renewing) resource that is sunlight and turn it into electricity, wind turbines that capture the natural cycles of weather, and so on. But that's not all there is to renewables. Far from it.

What else can be regenerative and enduring, if managed carefully, consciously and well? Things like soil, plants, animals, your own energy, the seaweed on the beach and the wrens in your garden. Things that are both renewable and useful are all around us. And they *are* us. So how can you consciously and carefully **Use and value renewable resources and services**, to make life better for yourself, your household, your community and your ecosystem?

By 'use', I don't mean 'use up'. I mean consider, steward, learn from and practise gratitude for – with an attitude of reciprocity. Because to be renewable, a resource needs to receive something back from you, in order to be renourished, and flourish into usefulness again.

Consider the tree: an inherently renewable resource. It's a living thing that grows, making its own food; providing a habitat for other species; interacting with fungi and soil microbes; dropping useful sticks and leaves; and producing flowers, fruit and seeds that can nourish other organisms. Not to mention the big one: oxygen. The cycle of growth, harvest and regrowth can be virtually infinite. And yet these renewable products and services are by-products of what the tree 'does' while it's just living. It simply exists in a reciprocal relationship with the Earth and the organisms that live around and within it.

Now, here's the thing – the more we each commit to using and valuing renewable resources and services in our daily lives, the more we find ourselves moving away from the immediacy that comes with our culture of endless consumption. When we're working with renewable resources and services, we can't just have it all, right now. Sometimes we have to wait.

And that can be okay, as long as we become more adept at planning, sharing and working with what's available. Because if we expect to have everything we want, all of the time, our Earth will not be able to carry us for much longer. But if we're prepared to work in rhythm with these renewable resources and services, we can sustain ourselves and others in a way that gives back and ensures renewal.

Your most immediate renewable and regenerative resource? It's you! Your energy, your wonderful brain, your body, and all the things that you can do. That's not to say you're inexhaustible, because I know you're not. But you are an amazing renewable resource. So use that energy of yours like it matters.

MAKE NATURAL HOME CLEANERS

Cleaning products probably aren't the first things that spring to mind when you think 'renewable resource'. But when you get into the habit of making your own home cleaning products out of simple things you probably already have – or even 'waste' products, such as apple cores – you're taking a fundamental step away from a swag of non-renewable and possibly questionable ingredients, chemicals and single-use packaging entering your household. This new habit is an easy win.

It can be a bit overwhelming sometimes to work out whether something is truly renewable or not, because there's so much tied up in this concept! Often, the easiest approach is just to go for the simplest non-toxic thing that you can find, or make, that does the job. Take a store-bought window-cleaning detergent, for example: look at the bottle and you'll see a whole bunch of different ingredients – some of which are potentially toxic – and there may be even more that aren't listed.

On top of that, it will be wrapped in plastic. And then there's all the manufacture and transport to get that product from wherever it was made to the shops and then to your house. *All up, that's a lot of resources used up and gone, just so you can have cleaner windows.* Instead, you could switch to something really simple: vinegar and water. This works just fine, is super-cheap and not harmful to your health, and you can even make the vinegar yourself (see page 107).

You can apply this same kind of thinking to lots of household cleaning products, so we've gathered a few methods and recipes to get you started. While these cleaners aren't equivalent to 'hospital grade' disinfectants, for many households that's absolutely okay. At our house, we're not actually trying to sterilise benches and floors to remove all microbial life from our home, because we know it's partly the balance of microbes in our air and on everything (including on us, and inside us) that helps keep us healthy in the first place.

We are, however, into ensuring things are clean and safe to cook with, eat off and play on. And for many things that need cleaning, this means that cleaners made from basic household ingredients will work just fine.

You could start by investigating one of the cleaning products you use often; check the brand against an online chemical list, such as the Guide to Healthy Cleaning issued by the US-based Environmental Working Group (ewg.org). You might be surprised by some of its ingredients. You can use this information to help you choose another brand that is better for the ecosystem and for your health. Or, even better, you can have a go at making your own.

The beauty of homemade cleaners is that one all-purpose mixture can often do the job of multiple products, which means less packaging. Plus you can reuse your containers over and over.

Simple swaps and DIY cleaning hacks

Happily, you can make a heap of seriously good cleaning products out of the same two or three basic ingredients – simple everyday items that you may already have at your place.

These ingredients are the building blocks of many ace DIY recipes.

- **Vinegar** is surprisingly powerful and can cut through grease, remove stains, kill some bacteria, dissolve hard-water deposits, remove mildew and more. White vinegar is best diluted in water, to cut down the acidity. Apple scrap vinegar (see recipe opposite) and other fruit vinegars can usually be used straight, as their acidity is much lower.
- **Bicarbonate of soda** (baking soda) is a really cheap and accessible mild abrasive, great for scouring and dissolving dirt and grime. It also reacts with boiling water or vinegar, which can unblock drains or lift away baked-on food in the oven.
- **Soap** can clean just about anything, from your dishes to surfaces and so much more. Basic soaps, such as Castile soap, are biodegradable. Check the ingredients: avoid soaps that contain petroleum distillates.

Other helpful hacks

A suds-maker or soap saver can be great for washing up: it's the classic invention of a wire cage that you put a soap bar inside and shake around as you fill the sink. It's especially great for loading up with odd soap ends.

If you don't like the smell of vinegar (it really gets to some people), add aromatics such as citrus rind or a sprig of rosemary to your cleaning products: steep for about a week before using and the smell will be much more pleasant. Adding a tiny dash of essential oil is another idea.

USE AND VALUE RENEWABLE RESOURCES AND SERVICES

Apple scrap vinegar

You can make this vinegar with all kinds of fruit scraps – from citrus peel to pineapple or banana peel. Where we live, apples are what we use. The length of time needed for the ferment stages will vary depending on the room temperature.

What you'll need

1 kg (2lb 4 oz) apple scraps, such as skins, cores and pips

A wide-mouthed jar

1 litre (4 cups) water

4 tablespoons sugar

Muslin and an elastic band

1. Put the apple scraps into a wide-mouthed jar (the wide mouth means a larger surface area on which natural yeasts can work their magic).
2. Boil the water, stir in the sugar, and set aside to cool.

3. Pour the cooled syrup over the apple scraps to cover, leaving 5 cm (2 inches) of space at the top of the jar, for bubbling. The syrup should completely cover the apple scraps, so if they are floating to the top, find a small dish or something to weigh them down.
4. Cover the open top of the jar with muslin and secure with an elastic band; you want air to circulate over the top.

Ferment 1: Chunky stage

5. Check each day for changes, smell it, mix it. Foam will form on top and it will bubble.
6. After 1–4 weeks the bubbling will stop and the apple scraps will sink. Strain and pour the liquid back into the jar. Replace the muslin and elastic band.

Ferment 2: Liquid stage

7. After 2 weeks, check on it. When it tastes vinegary and delicious, it's done. If it's still sweet, wait another week or two, up to 6 months.
8. When you're happy with the taste, seal the jar and store it in a cool, dark spot. It's now ready to be used for cleaning or eating.

All-purpose cleaner

Imagine having just one bottle of homemade cleaning liquid with which you can clean almost your entire house. And it couldn't be simpler to make, from just vinegar and water.

1. In a jar with a lid, pour in 1 part white vinegar to 1 part water. Using fruit scrap vinegar? Pour it into your jar neat.
2. Add any of the following (or similar) to make your nose happy:
   - lemon rind
   - rosemary sprigs
   - essential oils such as peppermint, eucalyptus, citrus
3. Close the lid tight, shake, put it aside, and let it steep for about a week.
4. Filter or strain out the solids.
5. Use a funnel to transfer the cleaner to a spray bottle, and use as a surface cleaner pretty much everywhere. Make this in big batches if you like, or a small amount at a time. It keeps for a long time.

Window cleaner

This simple recipe builds on all-purpose cleaner with the addition of alcohol to help remove streaks from your glass and windows.

1. Mix 1 part vinegar (fruit scrap vinegar or white vinegar), 1 part water and 1 part alcohol (methylated spirits, isopropyl alcohol or ethanol) together in a spray bottle – and that's it, you're ready to go!
2. Label the bottle with 'glass cleaner' so you remember for next time.
3. This will last in the bottle indefinitely but does have an alcohol smell, so save it for glass only, not general purpose cleaning.

Tip

Scrunch up old newspaper and use this to clean your windows. It gives a streak-free finish and can be reused as an excellent firestarter when you're done.

Dishwasher detergent

You don't need those little plastic-wrapped tablets.

1. Fill the dishwasher powder compartment with washing soda (soda ash). You can even make your own washing soda from bicarbonate of soda (baking soda): preheat the oven to 200°C (400°F) and spread the bicarb soda on a baking tray. Bake for 30 minutes to 1 hour, then cool and store in an airtight container until you need it.
2. Grate a little pure soap over the top. Keeping a jar of grated soap for this purpose is handy.
3. This will clean your dishes really well, but can leave a little residue, so pour white vinegar into the 'rinse aid' compartment – it will make your glasses shine.

habit
22

START A WORM FARM

A worm farm is a great way to use and value your own renewable resources, in the form of food waste. By the time you're done, you will be turning your food scraps into worm castings, which are solid (and liquid) gold for your garden or pot plants.

You don't even need a backyard to run a worm farm: they work well on balconies, on back steps, or even inside your home. They're great for just about any situation, anywhere in the world.

If you just throw your food scraps in the bin, they will create methane in your local landfill as they break down – a greenhouse gas that's contributing to our climate crisis. By feeding your scraps to your worms instead, you can make free fertiliser for your garden, reduce household waste, avoid landfill, reduce methane emissions and make the most of the resources you have around you. Wins all round.

In fact, you will be converting your kitchen scraps into nutrient-dense, bioavailable plant food of the highest quality, with zero waste and zero emissions. Good stuff.

Which worms?

Compost worms are the lifeforms doing all the work here. Sometimes called red wigglers, brandling worms or tiger worms, compost worms are a slightly different species to the normal earthworm you'll find in your garden soil. Compost worms are typically smaller and redder and they specifically eat organic material and the microorganisms that live among that material. In a forest ecosystem, they're the worm species living in the top layer of groundcover, especially where there are leaves or other material to munch. Earthworms, on the other hand, take their food and tunnel downwards into the soil, aerating as they go; they are typically bigger, longer and browner than compost worm species.

Another thing about compost worms is that they eat a lot. Once your worm farm is working well, you can expect your worms to eat up to half their own bodyweight in scraps each day. That means if you start your worm farm with a kilo of worms, they will soon be able to eat half a kilo of scraps per day. This is seriously awesome food waste processing.

You can source compost worms from a hardware store, community garden, sometimes your local council, or a generous worm-farming friend.

You can expect your worms to eat up to half their own bodyweight in scraps each day.

How to set up a worm farm

Worm farms don't have to be fancy to be functional. There are some good shop-bought worm farm designs, but you also don't need to spend hundreds of dollars in order to create an efficient, happy and healthy worm farm that will eat all your kitchen scraps.

The most common type of worm farm that you can make or buy is a series of boxes, stacked atop one another, which the worms can pass between. Those boxes could simply be polystyrene ones (the kind used to hold veggies), which you can collect free from your local supermarket. Or reused plastic storage crates with holes drilled in the bottom. Whatever works for you. Make sure the bottom layer doesn't have any holes that you don't want, as this is where the 'worm wee' liquid will collect.

Once your boxes are sorted, it's time to make lasagne layers of all things delicious to worms. Start your first layer with a bedding of carbon, such as shredded newspaper that has been soaked in water. Make that layer about as deep as your finger. Now, add a few vegetable scraps on top – not too much, just enough to cover the paper – then add your worms. Lastly, put a wet hessian sack or an old cotton T-shirt on top to keep moisture in. Add a lid, then wait a few days for your worms to adapt to their new home before adding more scraps.

Each time you visit, peel back the hessian cover and note whether the worms have processed the scraps from last time; if there are still heaps of uneaten scraps, wait a day or two before adding some more. Slowly, the worms will build up their abilities to chow through your food waste at an impressive rate. And once that first layer of the box tower is full, you can add a few food scraps to a box above: the worms will climb up there when they're hungry and ready for more food scraps.

The idea with this type of system – and all worm farms, really – is that the worms will slowly continue to travel upward in search of food, leaving behind trays and trays of rich worm castings, with the worm juice dripping out the bottom. As part of this process, they breed like crazy, making more worms and increasing the efficiency of your worm farm.

Once you have a few trays of castings below your food scraps, you can start harvesting them to sprinkle on your garden, or to swap with your neighbours for their gardens. Just remember to use in moderation: it's potent stuff.

The leachate (or 'worm wee') that drips out the bottom of your worm farm can be collected and used as a liquid fertiliser, too – but do dilute this goodness 1:10 with water before using.

Worms can eat half their body weight each day, so it won't be long until you're stacking up the layers of worm castings. Collect the worm wee too, to use as a liquid fertiliser.

Your worms will make short work of kitchen scraps, eggshells and paper bags, turning them into a renewable resource.

The dos and don'ts of worm farming

Worm farms come in all different shapes and sizes. But to succeed, they need certain features for your compost worms to thrive.

- **Good drainage:** as the worms eat through your scraps they produce castings – their poo – and also liquid, which needs to be able to drain off effectively so that the worms don't drown. This also prevents your worm farm from going all stinky and anaerobic.
- **The right temperature:** ideally, keep your worm farm somewhere that won't get too hot, or too cold, and that you visit every day. Worms like the same temperature range as humans – so they will be most productive at around 15–30°C (59–86°F). Below that range, your worms will slow down and eat much less food. Above that range, they will head for a cooler spot at the bottom of your farm, leaving your food scraps up top to rot. Somewhere close to the house that's out of direct sunlight is ideal, or even on your back porch or inside your laundry.
- **A regular supply of carbon:** things like leaves or shredded newspaper will fulfill your worms' carbon needs. This helps balance the high-nitrogen kitchen scraps you'll be feeding them, so your worms have a balanced diet. And, again, so your worm farm doesn't go all sludgy and stinky, a good ratio to stick to is 50 per cent carbon and 50 per cent food scraps.
- **Food in small chunks:** remember that worms have small mouths! This means that although they can eventually break down big chunks of scraps, like whole cabbage leaves, they much prefer smaller bits. If you're putting big bits of stuff in your worm farm, chop them up a bit first and your worms will be super-happy.

Worms will basically eat veggie scraps of most descriptions. A small amount of bread is okay, but not heaps. But there are some things that compost worms do not like to eat.

- Citrus – skip the orange peels
- Alliums – things like garlic or onion ends
- Meat scraps, as the worms don't much like them, but flies do (and a maggoty worm farm is no fun for anyone)
- Fats and oils
- Dairy products
- Spicy food

If a bit of this non-ideal stuff ends up in your worm farm, it's not going to immediately poison your worms; they just won't be keen to eat it, which means that food will rot instead of being turned into castings. Some of the other microbial life in your worm farm will likely deal with it, but generally feed your worms (like anyone in your household, really!) things that they can eat and that are good for them.

You will need:

A piece of 150 mm (6 inch) diameter plastic pipe, about 50 cm (20 inches) long

A drill, to make holes in the pipe

Newspaper

50 compost worms

A terracotta pot (or similar) to fit over the end of the pipe

1. Wash the pipe and drill random holes that are at least 5 mm (¼ inch) in diameter.
2. Choose a spot in your garden bed for the worm tower. Allow for easy access (for adding organic material) and maximum benefit.
3. Dig a 30 cm (12 inch) deep hole, a bit bigger than the diameter of your pipe, in your chosen spot. Place your pipe in the hole, and fill in around it so the pipe stands steadily upright. There should be 10–20 cm (4–8 inches) of pipe above the surface.
4. Put a thick layer of dry carbon material (straw, dry grass, etc) in the bottom of the pipe, to a depth of 10 cm (4 inches).
5. Tear newspaper into strips and soak it in water (or use more straw, dead grass, etc). Make a 15 cm (6 inch) thick bedding of this wet carbon material in the bottom of the pipe.
6. Add your worms!
7. Add another layer (5 cm/ 2 inches) of wet newspaper to bed the worms down.
8. Place the terracotta pot on top of the pipe as a lid, to exclude rain and keep critters out of the worm tower.
9. In a couple of days, start adding handfuls of organic matter, and off you go!

Make a worm tower for your garden

A worm tower is essentially an in-garden worm farm, which allows the compost worms and their nutrients to interact directly with the surrounding garden bed. It consists of a vertical pipe with holes drilled in it, half-submerged in a garden bed. Simple stuff.

You place a bunch of compost worms inside the pipe and periodically feed them handfuls of organic matter, such as kitchen scraps, leaf litter and weeds. The worms eat the lot, converting that organic matter into rich worm poo and worm juice. This leaches out of the pipe holes and into the surrounding garden, bringing increased soil moisture, microbiology and fertility, which, in turn, takes any garden bed from average yield to gloriously abundant. And this system works well in every climate.

COOK WITH STICKS

Wood is a renewable resource in that it grows back, unlike gas, which many folk use for heating and cooking. If well-managed and stewarded, some types of firewood can be sustainably produced, unlike fossil fuel alternatives.

Using wood-power to heat and cook is an age-old technique that *can* be done sustainably, but it comes with caveats in our modern world. Sourcing sustainable firewood can be tricky, and there are considerations of woodsmoke and air quality for your wider community. It is possible to use wood stoves in a hyper-efficient way, with very little smoke, and there are some excellent, nearly smoke-free wood heater designs out there; however, in the balance, the best outcome for many of our homes and communities is to use electricity instead, wherever we can.

With that being said – how well do you know sticks? And what they can do for you on a Sunday morning, to make a hot cuppa while you sit outside and greet the day? This is an exercise in smallness, and the immediacy of tactile, renewable resources, and using them well.

Here's the thing: generally speaking, the smaller the diameter of dry wood you use, the better its combustion and energy efficiency. And the humble stick is an amazing renewable cooking resource which will give you just about the hottest, cleanest flame there is.

Added to that, stick wood is arguably the most sustainable type of firewood. Sticks grow fast, can be harvested without damage to the larger tree, are plentiful in any woody area, and don't need a truck to transport a load of them, because they're relatively light. Added to that, in places like Australia, you're often doing your closest wooded area a favour by gathering the sticks and reducing the fuel load of that area's undergrowth, which helps protect against bushfire.

All hail the stick.

Cooking without gas

If you have access to efficient electric cooking and heating options – awesome. As a society, we need to ditch all natural gas and coal usage and electrify everything – from our cars to our cooktops – and importantly, have that electricity be powered by renewable energy sources.
In the meantime (and also when electric cooking and heating isn't an option), bring on the stick wood.

Rocket stoves

Stick wood isn't an infinite resource so – like any resource, renewable or otherwise – it's essential to use it as efficiently as possible. If you've ever made a campfire you know that dry sticks burn really well, and fast. So in a regular fireplace or wood stove, you would need a huge amount of them to actually cook anything, and most of the sticks' heat energy will be lost.

But with clever stove design, the power and energy of the stick can be turned into super-efficient cooking heat. There are lots of traditional cooking stove technologies that harvest the power of the stick beautifully, and one of the designs that has emerged from this thinking is the rocket stove.

Rocket stoves may forever change the way you cook breakfast on the weekend. They are super-simple, wildly energy efficient, can be built by almost anyone out of 'rubbish' (a few old tin cans, or bricks) and result in far more usable heat and far less smoke than nearly any other wood-burning system we've come across.

This design originated with Dr Larry Winiarski, of the Aprovecho Research Centre in Oregon, USA, where the focus on low-energy, low-tech, super-efficient cooking techniques has created a worldwide community that continues to use and refine the rocket stove. Search online for 'rocket stove' and you'll find heaps of easy-to-follow methods of making your own.

Rocket stoves rely on maximum heat energy, from minimum inputs.

How rocket stoves work

Unlike normal fireplaces, rocket stoves are designed to maximise the combustion of the wood they use. So, rather than emitting smoke, soot or creosote out a chimney, all those compounds travel through the stove's insulated burn tunnel and are recombusted – releasing even more heat. You can actually hear the air roaring (rocketing!) through the system, supercharging the fire as it goes.

So you don't need much wood at all to run a well-made rocket stove: a handful of sticks will be enough to generate a hot cup of tea, and a second handful will be enough for your scrambled eggs. Which is better for you, the stick gatherer, and for the forest being gathered from.

The humble stick is an amazing renewable cooking resource which will give you just about the hottest, cleanest flame there is.

REUSE YOUR WEE

Got a garden? Time to think about a renewable resource literally all of us have access to: our own wee. Yes, seriously! Here's this sterile, nutrient-dense urine, which we flush away with clean, drinkable water, thereby causing pollution downstream. Meanwhile we purchase manufactured, imported chemical fertilisers of similar composition to urine ... to put on our gardens. A bit nuts isn't it? Many a pragmatic gardener has thought so too, and implemented the 'wee bucket' system of fertiliser production.

With a few basic caveats, using this 'liquid gold' on your garden is entirely safe, and a darn good way to use a renewable resource that you create every day of your life.

If you're not familiar with this age-old technique, don't worry; once you know the basics, it's not a big deal. You'll get used to it, especially once you watch your veggies thrive. Because wee is not just for the lemon tree, it's a potent fertiliser for all food plants. 'Ew,' you might say, 'I'd never want to put that on something I eat.' And that's okay, because I'm not talking about pouring urine straight onto your lettuce. What you can do is use a diluted mix of wee on whatever bits of your garden make sense to you – add a bit to your compost or around your fruit trees while you're at it.

Urine is not called liquid gold by many traditional cultures for nothing. In fact, it has been said that one person's urine contains all the nutrients needed to grow an ongoing supply of food for one adult. Urine includes phosphorous, which is critical to plant growth, thus eliminating the need for superphosphates, which are mined in faraway places, packed in plastic and transported for many miles. Urine also happens to be packed with nitrogen, which is another major agricultural input for depleted soils to promote plant growth.

So, take responsibility for your own outputs and fertilise your veggies at the same time. Like any garden fertiliser that's concentrated, less is more: urine contains lots of nutrients, but also concentrated salts, so don't overload your garden beds. A little, though, is fabulous. If you can do only one nutrient-cycling technique at home, let it be this.

Urine as fertiliser

At our place, some of our urine goes into a small outdoor bucket and is then diluted to be used around plantings that need a nitrogen boost. Yes, we wash our veggies before eating them. No, urine is not gross to use if you dilute and use it within a day of making it.

How to collect and use your wee

Find a bucket with a lid and clearly mark this as your 'wee bucket'. Keep this in a private spot in your backyard, or in a corner of your bathroom, and wee into it as often as you remember, over the space of a day.

After you've got a day's worth of wee, it's time to dilute one part urine to a minimum of 10 parts water. This diluted mix can be used directly around fruit trees, added to your compost pile, or tipped into a watering can and distributed around whichever garden beds need a nutrient boost. If using on veggie beds, stick to just the soil around your veggies, not directly onto the leaves. Stick to one application per bed per month, as a good rule of thumb, so you don't overload your garden with either nutrients or salts.

After you've emptied your wee bucket, rinse it thoroughly so it doesn't start to smell. Urine is sterile when fresh, so there's no need to worry about pathogens as long as you empty your bucket daily.

Got a busy week? Just use your wee bucket for collection on the day before you know you'll have some time in the garden. On gardening day, you'll have fresh wee to use – then rinse the bucket and set it aside till next week.

This liquid gold doesn't need to be smelly; it's free, it's easy, and it supercharges your veggies and garden with organic nutrients. Try it out: your garden and your water bill will thank you.

Things to consider

If someone in your household is sick, or on lots of medications, don't include their wee in this routine. Wash your veggies when they come into your kitchen, as you would do anyway.

There are plenty of plants that will love a free nutrient boost and reward your efforts to recycle your wee.

Salinity

If you have a very small backyard or balcony garden, this habit might not be suited to you on the regular. Our mate Kat Lavers from The Plummery in Melbourne, Australia, calculated that five wees per square metre per year was the maximum her garden could handle before she started to get issues with salinity. So in a small space, use this renewable resource sparingly.

habit
25

REUSE YOUR PACKAGING

The single-use packaging we all use will continue to exist in our ecosystems for many thousands of years to come, and also does great harm in the here and now. Single-use plastic is endemic in our societies: it's in every industry, manufacturing process, supply chain, supermarket and coffee shop. It's true that we cannot solve this massive challenge with reusable coffee cups alone.

However, we *do* each have the power to choose how we participate in this problem, and one essential action is demanding that distributors and manufacturers take responsibility for their packaging and do better. On the everyday level, though, we can also commit to reducing and reusing some of the packaging that comes into our homes. This new habit invites you to see single-use packaging as a reusable resource.

Though we don't like to think of single-use packaging as part of our ecosystem, it is, unwelcome as that may be. So how do you live with this resource, and in relation to it? By pretending it's not in your house at all, and outsourcing your impact by adding it straight away to landfill? Or by considering how you could reuse it now that it's here, to make the most of the resources that are with you, before it leaves your care?

By making a habit of reusing whatever packaging we can, we are acknowledging the resources it took to make that packaging, and aiming to make the most of it, eyes wide open. This helps us better comprehend our personal impact, as well as the impact of the packaging and the systems that create it, on our societies and ecosystems.

Happily, reducing and reusing packaging can be done in every single household to some degree, by tweaking your daily habits and your buying choices, and via your advocacy, too. If this all feels a bit overwhelming, focus on just one thing you can reduce or reuse, and take it from there, one step at a time. You will get better and better at this as you go.

Got plastic bags? Honour them as the reusable resources they are. Wash and dry as needed, and use them again and again. Opposite page: Cut plant tags from old plastic milk containers and write on them with a permanent marker.

A word on recycling

Recycling soft plastics, hard plastics and other packaging is a good first small step towards reducing waste in your household. But often this just outsources your impact, by making the plastics in our household go 'away' into another industrial system that may or may not recycle those resources effectively.

We would like to propose to you that *reduction and reuse* of your waste stream, wherever possible, is a more powerful household habit to actively cultivate. And about those plastics ...

While in many ways plastics are the bane of all our lives, they are also an incredible material. Plastic packaging, with all its embodied energy – made of oil from ancient forests, then manufactured and shipped around the world before reaching your kitchen bench – would best be treated as a valuable resource in your house.

Because what we value, we look after. And most plastic packaging can be reused many, many times, for all sorts of important and useful things. So – now that it's here – how about viewing that sea turtle-choking plastic bag on your bench as the robust reusable resource that it is (stewarded properly by you) and treat it accordingly.

Tips to get you started

Reduce what comes into your home

It's pretty simple: the less packaging that comes into your home, the less packaging you need to be responsible for reusing. So check out your local food co-op or bulk foods store, and take your own bags and jars when you can. Is there a local veggie box or CSA scheme you can join, and get a weekly box of unpackaged veg? Can you get together with other families and do a bulk order of something you all use regularly (potatoes, toilet paper, whatever) to reduce packaging in the process?

Keep packaging in mind when you're choosing products. Does one option come in a cardboard box, while the other is in an 'eons of responsibility' plastic packet? Is there a way to pick up that item from the store, rather than have it sent to you in a packaged sea of styrofoam?

Reuse as much packaging as possible

Enter the revolutionary nanna-technology of washing packaging out, drying it and using it again! And again, and again. This works for plastic bags, tubs, some cans, bottles and more. Yes, even the thin plastic bags. Wash them if necessary, hang to dry, fold up and reuse.

A note that how you open your plastic bags can make all the difference: if you can't open the bag cleanly, snip along the top neatly with scissors. This makes for a much more useful reusable bag.

Upcycle packaging into something new

The DIY and crafting world of packaging reuse is vast: crocheted bags made from all your leftover plastic twine, garden signs and tags made from old milk containers, mushrooms grown in empty yoghurt buckets (Habit 51; see page 240), plastic bottle planters and mini greenhouses, Ecobricks made from plastic bottles stuffed with small plastic pieces, fashion items, useful shopping bags and all the rest.

Advocate for better options

The responsibilities for plastics manufacture and impact belong primarily to industry – it's not all on you, the end user. Manufacturers are responsible for how they create plastic, companies are responsible for how much and why they use plastic and single-use packaging. Advocating for better practices, alternatives or redesign – as well as alternatives for communities and folks who cannot afford not to buy things in single-use plastics – are all a part of this complex web.

But the fact remains – if you are able, given your privilege and access to alternatives to make changes, do it. Reuse everything you can. Vote with your dollar. Question your favourite suppliers. Small steps can lead to big changes, when we each make them, talk about them with others, collectively make better choices, and shift worlds as a result.

Most plastic packaging can be reused many, many times, for all sorts of important and useful things.

123

Principle 6

Produce no waste

✳
Commit to a
five-day no-waste
challenge

✳
Learn
to mend

✳
Eat real
food

✳
Learn to love
second-hand
things

✳
Compost
everything

Produce no waste *is a goal, rather than an arrival point. This principle provides so many opportunities for us to make powerful, positive change in our lives and in our wider communities, too.*

While 'waste' is simply an output of something – which could, in theory at least, be a valued input for something else – it's the excess of it, and our ecosystem's limited ability to reabsorb that excess, that makes it waste.

On this finite planet, with its amazing but not unlimited capacity to absorb waste in the form of carbon dioxide, plastics, heavy metals and all the other potentially life-choking products that we create, we need to adopt a bunch of strategies that make moving towards a low-waste life – and maybe even one day a zero-waste life – a normal and possible state of affairs.

We also need a lower-waste lifestyle to be possible for everyone, not just those who can afford it. When access to lower-waste solutions is limited it can lead to reduced health outcomes for communities and for their ecosystems.

Is it all up to you to fix the destructive and awe-inspiring volumes of waste that have been created by capitalism and consumerism? Nope. As I outlined in the introduction of this book, you have – and always will have – responsibilities to your ecosystem and community. But that's not the same as being the cause of this enormous mess that we're all in, or bearing the guilt for it all – that is not on you.

So this principle is about creating efficiency and cultivating responsibility for whatever waste we can within our daily systems – as an individual, as a household, as a member of a community. We can think in terms of the idea of a circular economy, where things go round in a loop: the discards from one part of the system are the resources for another part. Of course, that's exactly how ecosystems work: every output nourishes something else as an input – there's no waste.

The idea of producing no waste is partly about minimising actions that are wasteful, but it's also thinking differently about what we regard as waste. This is a change of mindset; for example, how might your town sewage be processed into useful fertiliser for nearby farmland? (Heads up: this is totally possible.) How can we transform the outputs around us and repurpose them as inputs that nourish and give life to other things? And if we cannot use that output as a useful input for something else, how can we avoid creating the output in the first place?

We can each make individual changes to produce less waste, but we must collectively take action to make this happen within our larger social, power-driven and profit-driven systems. And we can also examine and reframe our relationship with waste to reduce it still further, wherever we can.

COMMIT TO A FIVE-DAY NO-WASTE CHALLENGE

Single-use plastic items infiltrate our everyday lives, and it's really quite difficult to avoid them even when we make a conscious effort. If it's not lunch wrapping, it's the packet of pasta or the shopping bag you're given at the checkout.

Where does all that plastic go? Most often, it's into the bin, then into landfill and eventually into our ecosystems – our rivers, lakes and oceans. Where that plastic never, ever actually goes is 'away'. It breaks down into smaller and smaller bits, to cycle around our ecosystems as microplastics, possibly choking turtles, seabirds and other wildlife in the process.

Buying less single-use plastic is a very good idea, but not acquiring any can be a difficult goal to reach. This five-day no-waste challenge is an achievable time frame – no overwhelm here – for looking deeply at your daily habits and figuring out what changes you can make, on an everyday level, as you shoot for the ultimate goal of producing less waste.

It's important to remind yourself straight up that many traditional cultures and Indigenous peoples and the 'make-do' sectors of society are the original no-waste crews. As in every other aspect of permaculture thinking, we owe a great debt to these communities for stewarding this knowledge that we all can benefit from.

This challenge is not only about limiting, or eliminating, the single-use plastics that come into your hands. Another aspect of the challenge is building on the habit of reusing your packaging (Habit 25; see page 120). You don't need to spend money on shiny glass jars and metal lunch boxes so that you can look like you've never used plastic in your life. In fact, I encourage you to do the opposite: use what you have. As tennis player and AIDS activist Arthur Ashe is reported to have said, 'Start where you are, use what you have, and do what you can.'

Plastic bags and containers you might already have in your house? Commit to using them again and again. Once they break, figure out how to responsibly deal with them. Small bits of plastic can be pushed into plastic bottles to make a building material called Ecobricks. Larger items can sometimes be responsibly recycled.

This challenge is about taking responsibility for getting real about plastic and waste in your household and daily life. Once you are aware of your plastic use, you may find yourself shifting – in many ways – when you're making new purchasing decisions and choices of all kinds.

'Start where you are, use what you have, and do what you can.'

Privilege comes into this, big time

It's a simple truth that some folks' privilege (Habit 18; see page 91) will make this particular challenge easier than for other folks. Your level of income, your proximity to fresh-food stores and farmers' markets, your available spare time, your ability to choose where you shop and lots of other factors all help to smooth the way.

And it's important to consider these kinds of disparities when we 'get the feels' about household waste, and who seems to care about it and who seems not to; who can change things and who can't.

That said, if you do have the privilege to be able to give this no-waste challenge a shot, I encourage you to do so. Even if it turns out not to be 100 per cent possible for you, you will learn a lot about yourself, your daily habits and the justice of your local food system in the process. And that is all useful knowledge that can be used for good.

In addition to this point, if you *do* have the ability to go no-waste for five days, you probably also have the ability to use your purchasing power beyond that five days to vote with your dollar for less waste and packaging. This ongoing action is a powerful individual act which, when others do it too, can influence your local options and bigger companies. Which will benefit you, your friends *and* those in your community who are not able to make the choices you can, but who would benefit from readily available, affordable, less-packaged options, once your collective advocacy has brought those options into your local area.

How to get started on your no-waste challenge

Plastic-free basics

- **Water bottle** – how many times have you been caught out buying water, because you didn't bring a bottle? A clean glass jar or plastic bottle works just as well as a fancy metal water carrier, though metal ones are often easy to find secondhand.
- **Reusable cup** – these are everywhere these days and also at thrift stores, so find one you like and take it everywhere. (Or make one: instructions on page 131.)
- **Reusable bag** – find one you can roll up small, or that has its own pouch, and keep it in your handbag or daybag at all times. Don't leave the house without at least one.
- **Lunch box** – finding a lunch box that you love and that works for you can be a gamechanger when it comes to reducing waste. I love the bento-style ones with little compartments so I can have different bits of food and snacks all in the one place, but separated, preventing things getting mushed together.

Household-level things

- **Groceries** – is there a bulk-food store near where you live, or near where you work? Can you buy pasta and sultanas in bulk from there, and bring your own jars or bags?
- **Meat** – if you eat meat, can you source it from a butcher rather than prewrapped supermarket portions? And will they put sausages directly into your reusable container, rather than in a single-use plastic bag? It never hurts to ask. Your feedback may encourage them to offer this as an option for everyone. This goes for your grocery store, too.
- **Veggies** – is there anywhere you can get your veg from where they don't come in packets or bags? Sometimes the solution is as simple as taking lightweight fabric produce bags to your supermarket.

Remember to reuse

- **Plastic bags** – wash them out if you need to, peg them on the clothesline to dry, and use them again. And again and again. The same goes for any plastic containers you have: figure out what they're most useful for, and get to it. Use what you already have, take care of it, and make it last as long as you can.

There's no such thing as 'away'

When it comes to plastic (and most rubbish, really), there is no such thing as 'away'. By throwing that wrapper in the bin, we're just putting it somewhere else – and, nearly always, that somewhere else is doing damage to our planet. Which is why challenging yourself to use less single-use plastic is such a powerful habit.

My best-ever reusable cup

If you love a good coffee, tea or other beverage on the go,
a good habit is avoiding disposable cups – Australians throw
literally millions of these into landfill every single day – and
although it's a small action for lil' you, collectively these choices
can add up. Happily there are bazillions of reusable cup options
available these days (also – ahem – actual *cups* can be used for
this, depending on your context), and often secondhand reusable
takeaway cups are easy to find too. Or you can make your own.

*Shoutout to Erin O'Callaghan,
owner of RAD Growers, who
said to me (in the dinner line
at a Deep Winter farmers'
conference, years ago),
'Just put that jar in a stubby
holder and you're there, mate.'
(Mind. Blown.)*

1. Find a glass jar, with a good lid,
    that's about the dimensions of
    a beer can.
2. Find a stubby holder (a koozie
    for US folks). We source the
    neoprene ones from thrift stores
    – sometimes they have bonus
    souvenir vibes.
3. When you get to your local café,
    hand over your clean glass jar, so
    your barista can make your drink.
4. Then slip your jar of hot-beveragey
    goodness into your stubby holder,
    screw on the lid and away you go:
    smashproof, leakproof (when the
    lid is on) and cosy warm for as
    long as you'll be sipping.

LEARN TO MEND

To mend, rather than to make, is to call things worthy of repair. And to name things as worthy of repair – the Earth, ourselves, our relationships, our shoes – has far-reaching implications for renewal, gratitude and transformation.

We all know that it's not great for the planet when we buy more 'stuff'. This is contrary to what most advertising tells us every day. It's really hard to not get sucked in by the promise of the new shiny thing as a way of making our lives that bit better, or ourselves feel more worthy. Because you do deserve comfort, and beauty, and to have fun. You really do. But buying a new thing is not the only possible path to that happiness, or to making the hole inside you a bit smaller.

Taking care of the stuff you already have, and reimagining it, is also taking care of yourself and your savings. And one way to lessen the 'need' for new stuff is to start really taking care of the things you already have. Because often, *the most sustainable T-shirt, shoes, bike, dress, computer, or whatever, is the one you already have*. Even if it needs a touch up, or a new screen, or a few stitches. So: let's make fixing stuff awesome again.

This habit has some side benefits too. You will save money by not buying as much, you'll get more creative as you figure out how to fix the things you already have, and as you reconsider your relationship to your things you'll feel less 'need' to purchase more. This changes your relationship with consumer culture and can, in turn, free up a bit more spare time ... and I hope, by this stage of the book, you've got a few ideas about what you'd like to do with that!

When you do need to buy something, consider going second-hand instead of new, which extends the life cycle of products. You could try deciding on the hiking boots you want in the store, then accessing them second-hand online. For significant items, research it first and ask yourself: 'Do I really need it?' If the answer is yes (and sometimes it just is), look to buy durable products that are well made and have readily available spare parts for ease of repair.

Learning how to fix simple things such as clothes or shoes is a great first project. Mending is fairly easy to get your head around, can be done at home with minimal equipment and can have a wide-reaching environmental impact. Each year, the average Australian throws out more than 23 kilograms (50 lb) of clothing, contributing to a whopping 800,000 tonnes (880,000 tons) of textile waste being sent to Australia's landfill sites each year. You can reduce your impact by taking care of your clothes, extending their life cycle and getting closer to the goal of producing no waste.

Make it a regular habit

Mending is a skill you will build up over time, so committing to having a go regularly is a good idea. What will make this work as a habit for you? Can you start a Fix-it Friday or Sew-day Saturday, once a month? Perhaps you could set aside 30 minutes each week to mend and maintain?

Visible mending is an awesome style trend and it means you don't have to be an expert stitcher to make basic repairs on your clothes.

Things that are (mostly) simple to mend yourself

If you're just getting started with mending, it's best to start with the easiest fixes, so you can build your skills and confidence and chalk up some wins. The satisfaction of a newly hole-less sock might just give you the motivation to keep going with bigger projects. Here are some ideas on where to start:

- Maintain your boots with a bit of polish
- Sew a button back on
- Hide a snagged thread by pulling it through to the other side
- Hand-stitch over torn seams to keep everything together
- Depill your woollen jumpers with a razor (or a depiller thingy)
- Tighten the screws on your glasses and sunglasses so they sit better on your face
- Sew up a hem
- Learn how to darn holes in your socks (very simple, once you know what to do)
- Patch up a hole in your jeans using visible mending
- Cover a stain by dyeing a T-shirt a new colour (be sure to pick a non-toxic natural dye).

Four easy visible mending stitches

Clothes can usually be fixed in completely invisible ways, so no-one ever needs to know that a repair has been done. Or you can get awesome, and try visible mending instead. This growing movement is all about highlighting imperfections in artful and eye-catching ways, while sparking conversations about repairing and valuing our clothing.

Running stitch

One of the easiest stitches to learn, running stitch useful for repairing seams or stitching two layers of fabric together. Using a needle and thread, create straight stitches in a line, where the stitches are the same length as the gaps between them, or slightly longer than the gaps.

Satin stitch

This embroidery stitch is great for covering tiny stains or mending small holes and rips. The area you're mending should not be much wider than 6 mm (¼ inch). Draw an outline of a shape around the stain or hole, then stitch from one side all the way to the other, completely covering the problem area.

Start with the easiest fixes, so you can build your skills and confidence and chalk up some wins.

Blanket stitch

Great for blanket edges, jumpers (sweaters) and patches. To get started, wrap your thread around the edge of the fabric and go back through the same hole to make a loop. Pass your needle through that loop. Now continue sewing stitches a short distance apart, passing your needle through the loop of each stitch. When sewing on a patch, blanket stitch over the edges of the patch and through the fabric behind.

Cross stitch

Another embroidery stitch that is great for repairing small holes and rips. Make a row of slanted stitches in one direction, then sew another row of stitches over the top, slanted in the opposite direction to make an X.

How to get help fixing trickier items

Ready to look beyond clothing and figure out how to fix some of the other rickety items around your home? If you're low on time, tools or know-how, you might prefer to seek out your local fixer-people and organisations for some help. Ask around and see what's available in your community: your local library or community noticeboard may have some suggestions, too.

- **Repair cafés** are free meeting places that are all about repairing things together. You'll usually find tools, materials and people to help you. These spaces are especially handy for repairing trickier items, such as home appliances and computer or tech gear.
- **Libraries of things** are starting to pop up, sometimes run by councils or sustainability groups. You can borrow all sorts of functional tools and items, which might fill a gap that was preventing your own repairs.
- **Banks of time** allow you to exchange your skills for 'credits': blocks of an hour, which you can redeem for the skills of someone else, possibly someone handy at building or fixing the very thing you need.
- **Bike kitchens** are community groups of cycle-loving folk who kit out a space with all sorts of bike-repair equipment and often also accept donations of second-hand bikes for repairs and spare parts. Take your bike in and get help from folk happy to share their skills and knowledge. Some cycling shops have a corner dedicated to this, too.
- **Local tailors and dressmakers** can sort out more complicated clothing repairs or alterations, such as replacing broken zippers.

There's a wealth of knowledge in online communities, such as ifixit.com.

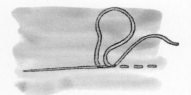

Running stitch

Satin stitch

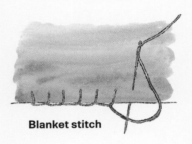

Blanket stitch

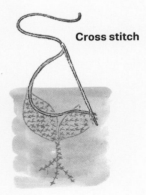

Cross stitch

Four simple, sturdy and decorative stitches that can help you mend your clothes so they are wearable again.

habit
28

EAT REAL FOOD

Highly processed foods can become a go-to in our homes quite easily, especially when you are knackered from work, or have a household to feed or a hectic schedule and little time to prepare. These foods are also delicious – just the right combo of sweet and salty to make your brain say 'more please' – especially when you're stressed or tired. But that convenience and taste often come with downsides: the food is packed with things that aren't great for your health, such as sodium, fats, sugar, preservatives, colourings and flavourings. Plus, there's the impact of industrial processes that went into making these processed foods: the energy, water, transport, packaging and more.

Buying and making 'real' food doesn't have to be a big deal. The basic idea is this: stick with simple foods and ingredients that contain minimal preservatives and additives. These foods can be healthier and produce less waste.

If you're keen on this habit but starting to feel a bit overwhelmed – especially if cooking isn't your strong point – start by choosing just one thing that you normally buy in a packet and learn to make it from scratch instead. This trick has been eye-opening for me, especially with less-wholesome-but-so-delicious family favourites, such as ice cream. It was inspired by the idea that if we had to make our treats from scratch we might make them differently and, probably, eat less of them.

The new household deal was that if you wanted ice cream, you had to make it yourself. And – with only a few tears – we got there: with a second-hand electric ice-cream maker and a few failed experiments we eventually developed our Family Standard Base Recipe for ice cream that everyone liked (flavourings variable).

It's got simple ingredients: yoghurt, cream, sugar, vanilla, a pinch of salt and flavouring – usually fruit such as frozen berries or whatever fruit is in season. We now make a batch every Friday night while we're making pizzas, and it's the only ice cream that's regularly in our house.

It's been a good experiment that we've been able to turn into a habit, because it works for us, has a weekly rhythm to it and is delicious, simple and achievable, even when we're tired.

Once you've got your game on making one usually-packaged-and-processed favourite thing from scratch, you can pick another, and try that. Pasta is another great choice of food to make yourself: it's cheap, easy and tastes amazing (see my recipe on page 138).

Do you need to make it from scratch Every Single Time? No, you do not. Go easy on yourself, friend – every household should have a few packets of dried spaghetti for those days when it's All Too Hard. But if you're curious and up for trying, give making your own a go.

Our family ice-cream recipe is a simple weekly favourite that we've perfected over the years to our own tastes.

How to make your own pasta

You will be amazed at how different this tastes from packaged pasta: prepare to be converted. Just three simple ingredients are needed: flour, eggs and salt. And you don't necessarily need a pasta-making machine: a rolling pin and a sharp knife will do just fine, if that's all you have. You can add other flavours once you get the hang of it – there's a whole world of pasta experiments waiting for you out there.

You will need:

375g (2½ cups) plain flour, plus a bit extra for dusting

½ teaspoon salt

4 eggs, at room temperature

SERVES 4

1. Clean and dry your kitchen bench, then sift the flour and salt together directly onto that surface.
2. Make a well in the centre and crack the eggs into it, then lightly whisk the eggs with a fork.
3. Next, gradually blend a little flour into the eggs, using your fingertips, slowly working more and more flour in until you have a ball of dough. Check it's the right consistency by pressing one finger into the centre of the ball: if your finger comes out clean, you're ready to roll. If it's still a bit sticky, add a little more flour.
4. Now it's time to knead the dough. Lightly flour the work surface before getting started. Use the heel of your hand to push down into the dough, away from you.

Lift the dough and fold it back on itself, then half-turn it and knead again.

5. Continue kneading for 6–7 minutes until the dough feels smooth and has some elasticity. This step is really important, as it develops the gluten in the flour.
6. Divide the dough into quarters, cover with a damp tea towel (dishtowel) and set it aside to rest for 10 minutes; this will make your pasta easier to roll out.
7. If you have a pasta machine, flatten one section of dough into a rough rectangle and feed it through the machine a few times, gradually compressing it until you have a thin, flat piece of dough. Don't have a machine? Use a rolling pin.

8. Now you can slice the dough into thin strips (fettuccine) or whatever pasta shape you like. Dust it with a little more flour to stop it sticking together. Or use a cookie cutter to slice pasta circles, add a yummy stuffing (cheese and herbs, maybe?) and fold in half, crimping the edges together to make half-moon shapes (*mezza luna*). Yum.
9. Cook the pasta in boiling salted water for a few minutes; it will take far less time to cook than dry pasta. When it floats to the surface, test it to see if it's *al dente*. Then drain and enjoy it with your favourite pasta sauce.

LEARN TO LOVE SECOND-HAND THINGS

Choosing second-hand whenever possible is a great way to produce less waste – and, though I've mentioned it already, I want to look at this purchasing ethos as its own habit, because it's quite a big one.

When you choose to refuse new products (even the pretty 'no waste' ones), you avoid using your dollars to vote for the mining, manufacture, transport and disposal of so much stuff.

In our family, when we committed to buying the things we needed second-hand, our rate of purchasing slowed hugely. Firstly, we needed to plan ahead: if new shoes (or whatever) were required, finding the right ones might require multiple trips to op shops or hunting online. Secondly, no more impulse purchases: *Do we actually need that? Can we be bothered to source a good second-hand one?* If not, that was that; no purchase needed.

And then, of course, there's the hugely reduced environmental impact of sourcing an existing item, rather than buying new. The second time around, this item costs nothing to make, because it already exists. No footprint. No production. No slave labour. Better for every living thing, including us.

Buying second-hand is all about getting creative with ways to source necessities and trying to find as many things as possible from society's waste stream. This can apply to almost everything in your home: clothes, homewares, toys, games, books, jars and even car parts. It's surprising how many great things can be found with a good rummage or two at your local charity op shop, garage sale or tip shop – often at a fraction of their original selling price.

Some items might prove more challenging than others. Sometimes it's just a matter of having patience and waiting for the right thing to appear. Perhaps you have a friend who frequents second-hand stores and can keep an eye out for what you want. For larger items such as furniture, bikes or electronics, online swap-and-sell sites are a goldmine, as are estate sales, antique stores and flea markets.

Practise the art of sourcing second-hand enough, and this way of living may well become a lifelong habit. Folks who live without buying new end up with a keen eye for rare items, such as stationery and socks that don't come up all that often in second-hand stores, so they stock up when they can. Familiarise yourself with the stuff-foraging options in your local back lanes: this just may become your new favourite hobby.

Like any practice that involves a not-insignificant time investment on your part, committing to second-hand can also be tricky, especially if

Practise the art of sourcing second-hand often enough, and this way of living may well become a lifelong habit.

you're time-poor because of other commitments. I've been there, too. Sometimes the best thing for your family's mental health is to buy the kid's shoes new, even though he'll grow out of them in six months and you suspect they were made somewhere with awful labour practices. Such is the world of late-stage capitalism we live in, and that's not on you. But if you do have the bandwidth to take on this habit, it's got lots of goodness to share with you.

Tips for buying second-hand

If you've avoided buying second-hand in the past because you can never seem to find what you need, here are some tips to help hone your thrifting skills. Like any new habit, your abilities will grow and develop over time, so stick with it: treasures await.

- Discover the options for buying second-hand in your area: where are the local charity shops, op shops, tip shops and fleamarkets? Even antique shops can be worth a look sometimes, although they may be a little pricier.
- What about garage sales or community noticeboards listing items that folks have to sell?
- Where is information about estate sales and auctions posted, so you can go along next time?
- Is there a local online 'buy/swap/sell' you can join? You can also request specific items in these groups – I've had that work well in the past.

You can often find what you need at op shops and garage sales.

Train your eyes to spot the items you need.

- Keep a list of things that you need, and run your eyes over it before second-hand shopping, so your requirements are front of mind.
- Visit your local op shops regularly, maybe as part of your shopping run. Stock is usually replenished weekly and sometimes even daily. Ducking in regularly with your list is the go.
- Browse through all sections of the store. Sometimes the great stuff is tucked in a back corner, or has accidentally been put in the wrong spot by a volunteer.
- Check tags on clothing and other items: prioritising natural fibres and good-quality brands that are more likely to last can help cut down your choices so you don't get so overwhelmed by all the options.
- Small household items can be some of the easiest things to find in op shops, where there are mountains of excellent plates, glasses, cutlery and whatnot waiting for you.
- Don't be immediately put off if something is a bit broken. Could it be mended easily by you, or cheaply by a professional?
- Share the load, by sharing your wishlist with op-shopping friends! I often pick up particular items (for example, size 5 workboots) if I know they're on a friend's wishlist. It all goes around.

COMPOST EVERYTHING

Committing to composting your food scraps is a major win for your garden, your soil, the veggies you'll grow – and the health of our planet. You can set up a compost system suitable for most situations, whether you have a big backyard or just a balcony garden.

Why is this such a good thing for our planet, beyond the nutrients it brings to your garden? When buried with all the other stuff in landfill, food matter is forced to break down without the presence of oxygen – a process known as 'anaerobic digestion'. This produces methane gas, a powerful greenhouse gas. About half the emissions from waste come from food rotting in landfill.

So an excellent habit to develop is not to send any organic matter to landfill. Imagine if this was the total norm in all our suburbs, properly supported by local councils? We'd be contributing to healthier, more biodiverse soils, bountiful gardens and healthier people.

Compost is rich in nutrients, improves moisture retention, adds plenty of good microorganisms, and gives plants (and therefore, in turn, you) the food they need to thrive. All in one hit. Some gardeners call it 'black gold'.

To make really good compost, you need to get the right balance between materials: adding only food scraps is a recipe for disaster. You want to add carbon materials (dried leaves, newspaper, paper towel, tissues and cardboard) at a rate of about double the proportion of your nitrogen-rich food scraps. It's these two elements that feed the bacteria and fungi to make compost. Yes, compost is actually a process of actively feeding a huge number of microorganisms the right stuff in the right amounts, so that they munch and breed and munch some more, converting your pile of leftovers, paper, poo, green stuff and whatever else into a rich soil additive. Consult a good home composting guide for your climate (we have a general one at milkwood.net) before you get started.

As you start to develop this habit, set yourself up for success: perhaps a label on the bin that instructs: 'Landfill – NO VEGGIE SCRAPS'. Dedicate a bucket – with a lid that fits firmly but is easy to remove – to food scraps and add them to your compost.

If you don't have a compost bin or pile yet, now is a good time to start one. Or, if you're tight on space, start a worm farm (Habit 22; see page 110). Another option is to make friends with someone who composts, or start leaving scraps for composting at your community or school garden. Check with your council, too: some allow food scraps in the green organics bins, or have community composting schemes. Always ask! Or start your own.

However you decide to do it, make it a goal to let no food scraps from your house go uncomposted. And good luck making some black gold.

Turn over a compost pile with a garden fork to aerate it and speed up the process. You get a free workout while you co-create an amazing resource!

Solutions to common composting problems

When you're first getting the hang of composting, some things may not go exactly to plan. That's okay! This is a new skill you're developing, so give yourself time to learn. To help you on your way, here are my best solutions for common composting issues.

Help! My compost is ...

... really smelly: mix in more carbon materials; add lime.

... breeding maggots: remove meat or excess food; sprinkle with lime.

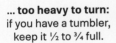

... infested with ants: add water and cover the top with hessian.

... too heavy to turn: if you have a tumbler, keep it ½ to ¾ full.

... taking ages to break down: add more nitrogen (food scraps, green waste) and water.

... swamped with vinegar flies: cover the top with a layer of carbon material.

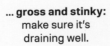

... gross and stinky: make sure it's draining well.

... home to rats and mice: reduce the amount of food you're adding; add vermin mesh.

However you decide to do it, make it a goal to let no food scraps from your house go uncomposted.

Principle 7

Design from patterns to details

*

Make a base map

*

Start a garden or nature diary

*

Write a Will – and talk about it

*

Learn about your local climate

*

Get to know the soil beneath your feet

Like a lot of these thinking tools, the principle of **Design from patterns to details** *encourages us to look beyond some of the cultural tendencies that we may have inherited.*

One of these tendencies in Western culture is to focus on the details, sometimes so much so that we are not even aware of the larger whole. The scientific method often pulls things apart to try and understand the properties of living things by understanding their DNA or their molecular structure. And although there's an enormous amount to learn from looking at such details, it's also essential that we zoom out and look at the greater whole and beyond: to see that whole thing in its larger context.

This idea is not limited to permaculture, that's for sure. But it can be an incredibly useful thinking tool when you're deciding where to begin, and what to focus on, when designing your permaculture system.

We've all seen parks with 'desire lines' in them: those spontaneous but well-trodden-over paths that are *not* the officially mapped-out path but cut across the grass or up the hill, because they reflect someone's (often multiple someones') desire to get from here to there, overriding the park's allocated pathways.

Anticipating how things or places that we design will be actually used, as opposed to how we expect they should be used, is not just for parks. When designing a backyard permaculture system, for example, can you anticipate the desire line you will take, again and again, from the veggie patch to your kitchen door? How can you make the most of this desire line, and design more usefulness around it?

Patterns come in all shapes and sizes: where the sun falls, the prevailing winds, seasonal cycles, life cycles and more. How can you design things at your place, thinking first about these larger patterns and how to make the most of them, before you dive into the details?

Because that's the thing about details; while they're super-important, they also have an emergent, self-organising aspect. If you can design for the larger patterns well, and first, the details are often much easier to figure out. Some details may even figure themselves out, if you're lucky.

Patterns also exist in the smallness of our daily lives, and choosing new habits can help support the patterns we want to cultivate.

MAKE A BASE MAP

Permaculture is a regenerative design system for both living and land use, and so far we've focused a lot on the 'living' part of that definition. But we also want to give you a start at designing the physical place where you live. This is where a base map comes in. It's not a full design, but rather a tool that allows you to collect a wide range of observations and interpretations, so you can do a better job of designing from patterns to details at your place.

A base map is always minimalist, containing only the permanent and immovable features currently on your site. This helps you to see the big patterns of your site before you drill down into the details of where you will place new elements and what will fit where. You'll use this bird's-eye view of your site for further investigation, brainstorming or even to make an idea book in which you can collect images and ideas that inspire you. Base maps are simple yet powerful, because they allow you to:

- record your observations and interpretations of your site
- provide a canvas for drawing up more detailed designs for your place
- be accurate – you can measure how many veggie beds will fit in this or that space, rather than guessing (and being way off, because optimism)
- reduce the time you spend redrawing permanent elements of your site each time you make a plan
- ensure consistency between different plans and drawings you might show to other people or contractors
- free up your creativity to experiment with how to fit in all the fruit trees or reimagine your whole place.

When you create a base map, you're documenting how your site currently is with a simple diagram.

Making multiple copies of your base map will make it easy to collect information and sketch out plans quickly. For example, you might want to install a new veggie garden. After creating a base map and then making multiple copies, you can sketch your patch dimensions into several different spots, and see how that affects things such as human access, sunlight, visibility and the path to your kitchen. This makes it easier to get your design workable before you get to the building stage.

Collect ideas

A base map also makes it easy for the whole household to be involved in the observation and design process: give everyone a blank base map to imagine on, and collect their ideas.

Drawing up your base map

Most folks don't happen to have a good-sized, to-scale drawing of their home or site. So let's go through how to create one yourself. Remember, your base map is a plan; a bird's-eye view of your site. To make it more useful and easy to read, stick to these rules and well-accepted conventions when you draw it up:

- Make it big enough. Small-scale plans are fiddly and don't have a lot of space to record information and explore ideas. Make it at least A3 size (297 × 420 mm/11¾ × 16½ inches), or preferably A2 (420 × 594 mm/16½ × 23½ inches).
- Draw an arrow indicating north. This will really help when you are working out where the sunlight falls during different seasons. Aligning your site so north is at the top of the page is ideal, but if that doesn't work for your map on the page, just draw an arrow.
- Use a friendly scale. By making your base map a to-scale drawing of your site, you will find it so much easier to measure distances on your plans and add new features to your design at the right size.

How to work out your scale

Scale is simply a number that you divide your real-world measurements by, to fit your drawing onto a piece of paper. The scale you use will depend on two things: the size of your piece of paper and the approximate size of your site.

An easy metric scale to work with is 1:100, where 1 cm on the plan equals 1 metre on the ground. Or perhaps 1:50, 1:100 or 1:200 will work for your site. If you're using imperial measurements, you might choose 1 inch = 6 feet.

Let's say you have an A3 sheet of paper measuring 297 × 420 mm (11¾ × 16½ inches). Measure the longest length of your site: you can do this with a tape measure or an online map. Let's say that your longest side fence is 12 metres (40 feet). The next thing is to convert all your dimensions to the same units – let's go with centimetres. An A3 page is 42 cm; your site's length is 1200 cm.

Now you need to work out a useable scale (with a number that's easy to divide and multiply by, such as 1:25, 1:50, etc). You will divide the real-world measurement by the scale number to work out the size of your drawing. In our example:

- If you use a scale of 1:25, you will get a drawing of 1200 cm ÷ 25 = 48 cm wide. This won't fit on an A3 page.
- If you use a scale of 1:100, you will get a drawing of 1200 cm ÷ 100 = 12 cm wide. This drawing would be way too small to be useful.
- If you use a scale of 1:50, you will get a drawing of 1200 cm ÷ 50 = 24 cm wide. This is just right; your drawing will fit neatly on your page with room to spare. So 1:50 is a good scale for this base map.

Now you've decided on the scale, it's time to start gathering information and transferring it onto your blank piece of paper.

A bit of blank space around your drawing is good, as it leaves you lots of room later to make notes or add extra information.

Now you've decided on the scale, it's time to start gathering real-world information and transferring it to your blank piece of paper. This should include all the long-term things that are currently on your site: property boundary lines, fixed buildings and structures such as fences and access paths, significant vegetation and any large structures or trees just outside your site that could affect your design. Avoid adding items that are temporary or may change, and avoid text. The simpler the better.

You can gather and record this information in several different ways, depending on what resources you have available to you. A ruler comes in very handy regardless of what technique you use.

Method 1: Use an existing scale drawing
Can you access a professional plan drawn up by a surveyor? Your local council may have plans if a development application was ever submitted. Double check the plan is still accurate and then get a photocopy made. Trace over important features to make them stand out and use correction fluid to remove any extraneous information.

Method 2: Trace off a screen
Grab a big piece of tracing paper, a marker pen and the largest computer screen you have access to, and bring up your place on an online map that shows scale – preferably with a satellite view. Now put the tracing paper over the screen (adhesive tape is good to hold it in place) and carefully dot the boundaries of your place, including structures. Unstick the tracing paper, rule in the lines, then go over them all again with the marker. From there, you can put this plan under a thin sheet of paper and trace the lines to make the base map.

Method 3: Use a projector
If you have access to a video projector and a ruler, this is the easiest method to produce a base map. Set up an online satellite overview of your site and project it onto the paper. Then move the projector or adjust the zoom until the scale legend on the image matches the distance on your ruler. Trace the important features onto your drawing.

Method 4: Measure your site
This method uses trilateration or the offset technique to collect your site measurements and transfer them onto your drawing – go look up those techniques if this sounds like what you want to do! Make a rough sketch of your site or print a satellite image or aerial photo. Then go around your site measuring the distances between important items and mark down the measurements on your sketch. You can use those measurements to accurately draw the main features of the site onto your base map.

One method is to use a projector and trace the important features onto your sheet of paper.

Make lots of copies
Whichever method you use, you'll want to make multiple copies of your base map so you can sketch and experiment with new ideas. Always keep the original safe so you can make more copies later.

habit 32

START A GARDEN OR NATURE DIARY

Observing and recording what is happening around you also connects you to place and to your surrounding ecosystem. So keeping a garden or nature diary is a great way to start thinking from patterns to details, while building your connection with your garden and deepening your knowledge of your ecosystem.

If you have a garden, or are thinking of starting one, a garden diary is the perfect place to chart what grows when – and how well – from year to year, helping you plan and make good decisions in seasons to come.

Being connected with the large patterns of the seasons and also the smaller patterns – such as which particular bugs visit the yellow flowers in your window box – helps us make better design decisions. Because when we're designing – whether it's deciding where to put your favourite pot of herbs, plant a garden, position a house or add on a sunroom – reading the natural patterns around us is everything.

For example, if you've made a commitment to record descriptions of all the bugs you see visiting your tomato plants, you're much more likely to learn their names and figure out which are helpful to your garden. Then you can find out how to encourage them, whether as pollinators or as predators of garden pests.

A garden diary also serves as a reminder of what we've learnt and how far we've come as food producers – it's a beautifully never-ending learning curve. Plus, it's fun! As adults, we sometimes lose that permission that small folk have, to draw and record the simplest of everyday things. A garden diary can help you kick-start that again.

No garden? No worries

If you don't have a garden, or not much of one, you can definitely still keep this kind of diary: it's all about observing the seasons and your ecosystem around you. So try keeping a nature diary. Observe the spaces around you, or a park where you walk often, to flex your pattern recognition and start building more connections with the art of designing from patterns to details, and just getting to know the bees, birds, trees and other life.

This sort of knowledge and observation is what our brains are for. It is how we learn to deeply relate to spaces and places that, in turn, enable us to effectively design, and live, in a harmonious way. And a nature diary can be a beautiful and important pathway towards strengthening our relationships with place.

Getting started

You might like to get a blank notebook and just go for it, or use a notebook with tabs and columns for different types of information, or create a bullet journal. Grid notebooks can help when sketching planting or seeding layouts in various garden beds.

Straight-up day-to-day diaries can be good for easy organisation, but you may find you need more space on some days than others.

Different-coloured pens, pencils or highlighters might also be handy to highlight specific themes, so you can easily find what you're looking for when flipping back through your diary.

And a reminder: no-one is going to judge your wonky bug drawings or misspelt cloud formations. This diary is a personal practice to cultivate your connection with your ecosystem, so just have fun with it.

Find a local 'sit spot' where you go regularly to observe, reflect and record what's happening around you.

Things to observe and record

Observations increase pattern recognition and relationship to place. We're storing up this knowledge to help us design better, from patterns to details.

In a garden diary

A record of your seasonal tasks is a useful observation from year to year, especially when you're planning next season. You might like to record:

- When seeds get planted and then pop up in the garden, or when seedlings are ready for planting out.
- What is planted where? This is helpful for planning crop rotations.
- What you harvested, when, and how much you got.
- Weather events, such as rainfall, frosts, heavy winds, really hot days.
- The types of insects you see, both predator and pest.
- Things that grow really well – and things that don't.

In a nature diary

Keeping a diary of the local spaces around you could be as simple as committing to going to the park or your local wild space each week and spending half an hour observing and recording. Ask yourself:

- What are the trees doing?
- Which species are here?
- What is flowering?
- What is that bug I always see in the bark under the big tree?
- Which way is the wind blowing today?
- How much rain has there been this past week?

Elderflower fizz season begins!

Chickweed

Cardam

{ Spring Equinox }

- Predominant winds: N – NW
- Rainfall: 423 mm – so so wet this season!
- Sunrising about 6:06 am
- Sun setting about 6:03 pm
- Avg. temp: 7.8 – 16.9 °C

Some cute fungi coming up in the woodchip paths

← we saw a brandnew tiny blue-tongue lizard! I thought it was a huge earthworm until I saw the legs!! :)

The quince blossoms are really catching my eye this year

WRITE A WILL – AND TALK ABOUT IT

Writing a Will can affect, enhance or change the lives of many people for years after you're gone.

As much as we avoid thinking about it, we all must pass through the cycle of nature: birth, life, ill health, decline and eventually death. Death is just part of living. We can try to stay healthy as long as possible, but when it's our time we've all got to go. And it's wise to be prepared for this most certain of events, for yourself and also for those who live on.

Writing a Will can affect, enhance or change the lives of many people for years after you're gone, so it's worth doing properly – and talking to your next of kin about it. Ideally, Wills aren't the sort of thing you write once and then forget about, either. Committing to updating your Will regularly (every three years or so is usually recommended) is a prudent habit to cultivate, to ensure it remains legally sound and your estate is handed down as you intended.

Part of this planning may also be about who can make decisions for you, when you no longer can. Think about power of attorney and enduring guardianship documents, and talk to your close loved ones about such scenarios. What would you ideally like to happen if your health fails and someone has to make a decision about your treatment? What do you want to happen when you die?

So now you have the high-level view mapped out – the overall patterns – it's time to look at the details. Talk to your next of kin and family about your intentions for your estate. Perhaps certain items are of sentimental value to a certain person? Perhaps one person has made certain sacrifices you wish to repay after you're gone? Think on those things of value to you: the photos, the memories, items that capture something of import. It may not even be a monetary thing.

It might feel uncomfortable when you're getting started, but it's good to get these issues out in the open. Too many families have been split apart by ill-thought-out Wills or nonexistent estate planning. We should plan for death the way we do other aspects of our lives, to make the most of our legacies once we're gone, and ensure a better life for those who keep living after us. Where there's a Will, there's a way!

The basic steps of writing a legal Will

It's best to check the laws in your state or jurisdiction; they vary on what is required, although some commonalities usually exist. Depending on your skills and situation, you might be able to use a free or low-cost Will kit to help as you write your Will. Just note that they're not really suitable for complex situations and you'll need to make sure you fill out every section properly, without overlooking any bits, to ensure it's binding. Considering how important your Will is, it might be best to seek legal advice, whatever route you choose.

A few things to note:

- Wills are usually only legally binding when written by someone 18 years or older, or by someone who is married.
- Your Will needs to be written down.
- It's important to be really clear. So rather than writing 'my daughter', make sure you write out their full name.
- Make sure you circle back to your Will and give it a refresh whenever your circumstances change (new significant relationship, new baby, separation, that kind of thing) or every three years or so.
- Seek legal advice to ensure everything is as it should be.
- Think carefully about where you'll store your Will: make sure it's in a safe place.

Some basic steps to get you started:

- Include your full name, address, identification details and the date.
- Clearly state that you're of 'sound mind' or in good mental health, and that you revoke all other Wills you may have executed before.
- Name your beneficiaries: the people who will receive your assets, or guardianship of your dependants. Be clear about who gets what.
- Appoint an executor: this is the person who, after your death, carries out your instructions and administers your estate. This can be a time-consuming role, so chat to the person beforehand. It's wise to appoint a substitute executor, too; a solicitor might do the trick.
- Once you're done writing, your Will needs to be witnessed by two people (not folks who stand to benefit from your Will or are married to you), who sign it in your presence. It's prudent to also get the witnesses, along with yourself, to sign and date each page.

We should plan for death the way we do other aspects of our lives, to make the most of our legacies once we're gone.

LEARN ABOUT YOUR LOCAL CLIMATE

In this age of abundant air-conditioning, heating and all the rest, it can be easy to get a bit disconnected from seasons and weather patterns. Part of reconnecting with the place you live is about understanding more about your climate and what that means – for your landscape, for your community, for all the life downstream and for you as an inhabitant of your ecosystem. Once you start to understand the big patterns, you might start recognising the smaller details where you live.

We all live in different climate zones. Some of us live in tropical areas, some in cold or warm temperate areas, others in drylands. Each zone has its own pattern of weather that influences not only how we grow food and do stuff outside, but how we live, fundamentally.

Where to start? You might look up and learn the broad brushstroke statistics on your local climate first: annual rainfall, temperatures, prevailing winds. Note the extremes – highs, lows – and averages. From which direction do winds generally come? When does the most rain fall and how much? What is the hottest month?

Beyond general climate zones, many smaller areas fall into what are known as 'microclimates'. These are places that differ slightly from the normal climate around them, for whatever physical reasons. One microclimate might be the sunny side of the hill which is warmer than the rest of the valley throughout the year (just slightly! But it can make a difference to frost patterns, flowering times and life generally). Or the nook beyond the big industrial sheds and the small pine forest, which is protected from the spring winds. How much sunlight do you get in certain areas of your garden or home? On the summer and winter solstice, where does the sun shine in and where do the shadows reach, at your place?

Understanding your local climate, and looking out for microclimates, can sharpen your pattern recognition, and your understanding of place and help train your design eye, too. And thus you might gradually start to notice the smaller details, the smaller-scale microclimates within your garden or space. What shadows are cast by the sun? Is there a cooler area that never gets sun? Where does the water always fall and pool? Where is the sunniest patch? What areas are protected by harsh winds? Which ones are most exposed?

Becoming familiar with your local climate will also help you understand how your climate is changing. Look for the broader patterns, especially over the past two hundred years, and compare them to recent years. How you use this information is up to you, but as a life member of your ecosystem, the more you understand about where you live, the better for everyone.

Aspects of climate to notice

There is so much to learn about your climate – so much information and data available – that it can feel a little overwhelming at first. Start with just one area to focus on and delve into: rainfall, maybe?

Once you've got your head around that topic, take a look at another aspect. Take it slow, and remember to keep an eye out for how these wider patterns create smaller details in your own space and place. The following list will give you some ideas to get started.

- Research Indigenous weather knowledge and ways of understanding climate. The Bureau of Meteorology in Australia has some excellent Indigenous weather resources online.
- Rainfall, wind and temperature for your local area and wider region.
- Some of the larger-scale factors that influence weather near you; for example, ocean currents, mountain ranges, seasonal trade winds.
- Severe weather events and significant weather summaries: your local Bureau of Meteorology will usually keep this information and data.
- Historical weather patterns for your area or country.
- The basics of weather: clouds, atmosphere, upper air, wind, pressure charts, and so on.
- The sun patterns in your area – where the sun rises and sets, and when – as well as solstice and equinox data, and geodata (latitude and longitude).
- Cultural burning approaches for helping reduce major fire risks. Look for resources in your area to learn more.
- The major patterns of climate change over time. NASA has lots of good scientific evidence on this.

The sunny side of a hill can form a microclimate that is different from the rest of the valley around it.

GET TO KNOW THE SOIL BENEATH YOUR FEET

Considering that all plant life grows out of it, and everything from our diet to our clothes to our future depends upon it directly, developing a Significant Relationship with your soil seems only right. We all have responsibilities to the soil, and this plays out in how we eat, how we advocate and lots of other big-picture ways. But there's also the soil in your home patch, which you can care for directly. How can you better tend and care for the soil right beneath your feet?

The first step is learning about your soil as an amazing ecosystem – this is called the 'soil food web' – and how you may assist it to create a nourishing foundation for your garden, if you have one. You'll increase your household's resilience, show up for your responsibilities to your ecosystem, and, if you're stewarding some soil personally, grow great veggies, flowers and other plants. Because healthy soil means healthy plants, gardens, waterways, wild spaces and people.

Beyond the backyard context, there are lots of ways to connect with the soil in your area. Learn a bit about the soil types where you live; advocate for regenerative approaches to weed management (as opposed to toxins that damage soil life); support local growers; and educate yourself about the amazing ecosystem that is the soil food web.

Your soil's physical properties

Composition: the DIY jar test

You will sometimes hear gardeners refer to their soil type as 'sandy clay' or as 'silty clay loam' or maybe even just as 'clay' . . . but what exactly do they mean? These terms refer to soil composition – something that's really helpful to know when figuring out things such as how often to water your veggie patch. The texture of your soil is determined by the specific ratio of sand, silt and clay.

Grab a large glass jar – about 1 litre (4 cups) is good – and half-fill it with soil from your garden, collected from at least 5 cm (2 inches) below the surface. Top up the jar with water and add a drop of dishwashing liquid. Set it aside overnight, so the soil settles into layers.

The next day, measure the layers: sand settles to the bottom, then silt is the second layer, clay the third, and you may also see some organic matter floating on the top. Measure the depth of each layer and you'll have a good understanding of the basic make-up of your soil: is it mostly clay, or perhaps 60 per cent sand? You can also look up the 'soil texture triangle' online to see precisely which textural class your soil belongs to.

Getting to know your soil is another step towards reconnecting with the earth on which you stand.

The pH test

Another basic soil test is pH, which measures how alkaline or acidic your soil is. This simple test can be purchased at hardware and gardening stores: it only takes a couple of minutes to do, and anyone can do it. Most plants are happy at a pH of between 6 and 7.5, so if your pH is a lot higher or lower, you might want to look into ways to gently rebalance your soil.

Laboratory testing

If your plants aren't growing as well as they could be, or if you're unsure what was on your land before you lived there, it's a good idea to get your soil tested for things like heavy metals by sending a sample to a lab, especially if you'll be eating a lot of produce from your garden. Find out if there are any free, cheap, or subsidised soil-testing labs in your area. For example, if you live in Australia, VegeSafe – run by Macquarie University (360dustanalysis.com) – will check your soil sample for heavy metals. Or you can opt for a thorough soil analysis, listing the mineral levels and contaminants of your soil.

Caring for your soil

After you've learned about the physical properties of your soil, you'll want to get your head around the many excellent ways to feed your soil using organic systems and sustainable approaches, rather than synthetic fertilisers (which can lead to an immediate flush of growth but will deplete your soil over time, and may damage the wider ecosystem while they're at it). Our favourite soil-friendly approaches include green manures, where you grow a cover crop only to chop it down and turn it over into the soil; liquid fertiliser teas, made by soaking nutritious plants such as comfrey and seaweed in water; and, of course, all the goodness that comes out of your worm farm or compost heap (see Habits 22 and 30; pages 110 and 142).

In this jar, there are three approximately equal layers of sand, silt and clay, then some water with clay dispersed through it and organic matter floating on top.

If your soil pH is not great

- Add more biology to your soil in the form of good compost and green manure crops.
- If your soil is very acidic (pH of 5 or less) you can carefully apply a little lime or dolomite to your soil.
- If your soil's pH is very high (pH of 8+) apply a little garden sulphur, or more compost. Always carefully check application rates for these soil-fixing additives before you begin!

Principle 8

Integrate rather than segregate

✳ Reuse your household greywater

✳ Keep chickens

✳ Engage with the commons

✳ Support a local person in need

✳ Eat with friends and family

Integrate rather than segregate *is all about making functional connections, so each part of your system can work more closely with, and benefit from, other parts.*

Connections come in many guises: between biological parts – the plants and animals – and between the built parts – your home and your veggie patch – as well as the behavioural connections between your household, community and ecosystem. The actions and habits you can choose from this chapter will help you to build connections that will make you more resilient and productive.

We know from whole-system thinking that keeping elements separate increases the effort and energy inputs we need, while if these same elements are integrated with each other – one flowing into the other, every output an input for something else – efficiency is increased.

In our neighbourhoods, this integration can mean using street trees as cooling devices, reducing the heat-island effect that comes with paved surfaces and making summer more comfortable for everyone. While they're shading the pavement and making life more beautiful, these trees are also breathing out

and blessing every passer-by with fresh oxygen; increasing biodiversity in your street; providing food for all types of bugs, birds and bees; and possibly even providing a bit of extra food and therefore resilience for the street's human residents, if the trees are fruit or nut bearing.

In our built environments, we can integrate all kinds of community-building and life-enhancing elements into our designs when we centre reciprocity and integration as design goals and ways of being.

At home, you could use a grapevine to shade the sunny side of your house in summer: it will lose its leaves and let sunlight in during winter to help warm your home. And that grapevine, tended with care and love to meet its needs, can also be part of your food system, with leaves for vine leaf-wrapped dishes and pickles and grapes for eating fresh, drying and maybe even making into wine. Top-notch integration and reciprocity, on a small scale.

habit
36

REUSE YOUR HOUSEHOLD GREYWATER

Although most folks understand how precious water is as a resource, somehow we tend to think that only pure water is worth using or conserving. Water that's already passed once through our kitchen sink, washing machine or shower often goes straight down the drain with barely a second thought. Yet greywater is a resource that can increase your household resilience, especially in dry times.

The benefits include a more abundant garden: trees and plants thrive from extra water inputs. Plus, using your greywater leads you toward being much more conscious of what you're putting down the drain – soaps and detergents, and whatever else – and the impacts these substances have on your ecosystem and your watershed.

You can start this super-simple habit right now by just putting a bucket in the shower. Or you can decide to make a whole system, using mulch pits or reedbeds and worms: it's totally up to you. Either way, you'll be learning how to catch and reuse your household greywater, allowing you to integrate rather than segregate this valuable and awesome resource that would otherwise go down the drain.

Safe greywater reuse

The principles of effective and safe DIY greywater reuse are endearingly simple, contrary to what you may have been told. The first is turnover: *let it go*. Get your greywater out onto your garden the same day that it exits your house. It's best not to store greywater for prolonged periods.

Why do we do this? Because of the second principle of greywater reuse: *let the biology do the work*. The moment your greywater hits the stable ecosystem that is your garden soil, it starts to be used in all the right ways and, if distributed thoughtfully, it won't be stinky or problematic. The little bits of food, hair and everything else in your greywater will quickly get eaten up by the biology of your garden, the water will infiltrate and the soil life will start to break everything down into useful components.

The third principle is *share the love*. Move this resource around to different places within your garden, because pulses of this resource will be best for any one garden bed, and it will benefit your whole system. Moving the output of your raw greywater around ensures you don't overload one garden bed or fruit tree with the residual salts and other substances that may be in there from your dishwashing or shower.

You can start this super-simple habit right now by just putting a bucket in the shower.

Think of greywater as a powerful but ephemeral resource: it is awesome, but needs to be used immediately and diversely, so that it can do its best work, rather than becoming a problem.

Know the difference between greywater and blackwater

So you're ready to try catching and using your greywater to create a more liveable home and surrounds. Great! But before you get started, you need to know exactly what greywater is, and separate it from blackwater.

Greywater is commonly defined as the water that exits your sinks and washing machine: water that may have soap in it, and maybe small bits of food, fat or dirt. This kind of water is perfect for watering some garden plants, especially if you use greywater-friendly soaps.

Blackwater is defined as the water that exits your toilet when you flush. It's full of substances that are not suitable for going straight onto your garden; that is, poo. You can deal with this output on a home scale. Most people who want to close this particular loop (rather than using drinking water to flush their poo to a faraway treatment plant) do it with composting toilets. But that's another conversation entirely. Look up 'humanure' if you're interested.

Shower water and bathwater exist in a hazy zone that blurs the line between blackwater and greywater. Technically, and depending on your household plumbing, your shower water and bathwater will probably be defined as blackwater. The thinking is that this water may possibly contain poo or urine, depending on what you get up to in your shower or bath. So the plumbing links up with your toilet and away it goes. Now, you could choose to take some responsibility here. If you keep your shower and bathwater clean and do your toileting elsewhere, this can become valuable greywater; in fact, it's one of your largest greywater resources.

Consider soaps and other inputs

When reusing greywater, avoid putting certain things down your sink. Choose natural soaps and detergents that are greywater safe. Don't let salts and vinegars go down the drain. Fats are a lesser concern, but still good to avoid when you can, because fats have the potential to clog up whatever greywater hose system you're using.

If you're not sure, just think about your garden soil: is adding something that's very salty or highly acidic likely to contribute to healthy soil and plants, or is it more likely to kill things? There's your answer. Just use your common sense.

Keep a bucket in your shower, and place it under the flow while you're getting the water temperature right.

Four ways to reuse greywater

The simplest ways to start collecting greywater involve just leaving a bucket to fill up incidentally in the corner of your shower, or finding a sink-shaped bucket and using that in your sink when you're rinsing dishes and other things. Then empty it outside on a garden bed, choosing a different bed each time. The manual nature of these two super-basic techniques helps give your body a sense of your water usage, too. Every time you heft another bucket outside, you're physically connected to your impact on your watershed. These are also great jobs for kids to be in charge of, helping them learn the impact and value of water reuse.

Next, take aim at your washing machine: can you divert the outflow pipe? Can you attach a longish hose to it and run it outside to some plantings or garden beds (not veggie beds), and move the end of the hose each weekend? Remember to be mindful of your inputs: perhaps all those softeners and brighteners aren't actually necessary?

Check your sink pipes: you may be able to divert this water. This could be as simple as a hosepipe to outside plantings, the same as your washing-machine water. Or you can get into more advanced branching drain systems, or a mulch-pit system: there are lots of great books on greywater reuse to help you get started (see the reading list below).

Put a bowl in your sink, or two, if you wash and then rinse. Fill it up as you're using the sink. When you're done, empty it into the garden.

Three-bathtub greywater worm system

A slightly more involved – but still rather simple – DIY greywater reuse option is a continuous-flow gravity-fed worm farm system, made using three bathtubs. While this design won't suit everyone, it can be a cheap and effective way to make the most of a small household's greywater.

Tub one – worms
- The water inlet pipe is open at each end, and has a series of small holes along its length to allow for even distribution of water into the tub.
- The tub is filled with compost worms and straw, with more straw regularly added on top, as the previous layer beds down and gets eaten by the worms.
- Worms appreciate the regular moisture and eat all the solid bits coming out of the sink water.
- Needs to be well-drained to prevent worms from drowning, so water drains straight through to tub two. Wire mesh raised on bricks sits in the bottom, with shadecloth on top to act as a sieve, keeping worms and their solids in the top tub.

Reading list

Resources on greywater and stormwater harvesting and use.

HarvestingRainwater.com

Create an Oasis with Greywater by Art Ludwig (Oasis Design, 2000)

RetroSuburbia by David Holmgren (Melliodora Publishing, 2018); retrosuburbia.com

This three-bathtub system (based on a design at Melliodora, Victoria) is set up on a slope and works with a continuous drip-feed of water through the material in each tub, draining into the garden.

Tub two – reeds

- Contains scoria (a rock similar to pumice, with lots of cavities for microorganisms) and wetland plants.
- Water comes in at one end and is slowed down by being pushed under tile baffles in the middle of the tub, before exiting at the other end.
- Water is filtered by the rocks and their resident microbiology, and the plant roots.

Tub three – holding pond

- The water comes out of tub two and into the holding pond.
- It overflows gently to a shallow earth drain, which deposits a trickle of outgoing water into a large garden bed that is used for summer crops such as corn, wheat, etc. Green manures are grown in this bed over the winter months.
- The output of this third tub could alternatively go to a forest garden, to water shade trees or similar.
- Because of the biological activity in all three bathtubs, the water is clean enough to be used in the same patch continuously without a build-up of salts.

KEEP CHICKENS

Chickens can be such a great addition to your backyard, if they fit in with how you live and you have the space. They are friendly, hugely entertaining, affectionate and playful. They have truly individual personalities and are just so loveable, once you get to know them. All this and they're highly productive, in lots of different ways.

Treat your chickens well and in return you'll receive an abundance of fresh eggs, plus manure for fertilising your garden – and even meat, if you're that way inclined. Given the chance, your hens will also turn over organic matter and help keep problematic insects under control.

But before you race off to find some new feathery friends, think deeply about how you'll integrate them into your system, rather than segregating them to a small out-of-the-way pen that hardly provides for the chickens' needs or mental wellbeing, and may turn all the awesome yields of a chicken – manure and so forth – into a problem rather than a solution.

If you're going to keep chickens, do it well!

One of the first big decisions is which type of chickens to keep: there are more than 500 breeds to choose from. Hybrid laying chickens are often the easiest to get, either at 'point of lay' (which means they are young and about to lay their first eggs), or as older rescue hens from commercial egg farms. But keep in mind that hybrids are a cross between two other breeds, usually chosen to maximise their egg-laying for industrial production situations. So they will produce the most eggs per year, but the strain of laying so much can mean they stop laying earlier in life or encounter health problems.

In contrast, heritage breeds might not lay quite as many eggs, but can be really unusual and may keep laying for many years. They are often hardier, healthwise, too. So we'd recommend choosing a heritage breed wherever possible; your local poultry club might be able to help.

Consider your space, too: if you only have a small yard or young children live at your place, bantam chickens or some other small breed might be best. Smaller hens will be gentler on your soil and are often very friendly as well.

Whichever breed you choose, make sure you spend some time preparing your coop and run, and planning how you will integrate your new friends into your home system. Happy chickens are healthy chickens, so plan to meet their needs and give them a great life at your place.

Treat your chickens with love and care, and you'll get more eggs as a side-effect: wins all round!

Must-haves for happy and healthy chickens

Friends for your chickens

Hens are social animals and need companionship, so ensure you have at least three birds in your flock.

A safe coop for night-time

Your chicken coop can be beautiful or basic, but it must provide a dry place that keeps your girls out of the wind and rain. It should be fully enclosed and able to be shut tight against any night-time predators. And it needs sturdy, wide perches for the chickens to roost on at night.

Nesting boxes

Have about one nest box for every four birds. The best spot is inside the coop. Chickens like to lay in a dark corner, so provide them with space that is dark, dry and cosy, and easily accessible (from a back hatch, perhaps?) for egg collection.

A regular cleaning regime

Cleaning out the coop regularly keeps pests and diseases at bay, while ensuring you collect your yield of manure. You could go with a slatted floor where the poop falls through and you rake it out from underneath regularly; or a solid floor with a layer of sawdust or straw that is cleaned out every month; or some other system. Or use a portable chicken tractor to move the coop around so their manure is not concentrated in one spot.

A daytime pen for roaming

Chickens need a place to stretch their wings. They can be surprisingly destructive to many plants that you'd rather they didn't attack, so don't give them free run of your veggie patch. Start with a secure pen attached to the coop, with at least one square metre (3–4 square feet) per chicken. Allow your chickens free access between the coop and pen during the day.

Good food and clean water

Good food is critical: a laying hen needs a lot of energy and protein to produce an egg almost every day. Feed all your kitchen scraps and garden weeds to your chickens, but don't expect them to give you lots of eggs on scraps alone! A high-quality, organic, commercial laying pellet is a good choice to ensure your girls get all the protein, vitamins and minerals they need. Automatic waterers are a good idea, too, to keep their water clean and always available. These can be simple and super-cheap.

Dust baths

Chickens love a regular dust bath to keep their feathers clean and healthy, and prevent mite build-up on their bodies and legs. If there's an extra-dry area in your chickens' run, you'll see them doing this. Choose a dry and sunny spot in the run and add a barrowload of sandy soil. You can also add powdered charcoal, fine rock dust or food-grade diatomaceous earth.

Shell grit

Chickens don't have teeth, so they need some shell grit to help their gizzards grind up food. It also gives them calcium. They won't go through this quickly, but it's essential to their diet.

Integrating chickens into your life

Ideally, your chickens will be able to be integrated into your life in a harmonious way, where their needs are provided for and their amazing yields are appreciated. But you do need a plan for the outputs, so you don't just create sources of pollution.

Permaculture works on recognising the connections between inputs and outputs and using them accordingly. As permaculture co-originator Bill Mollison described, it's 'a design system involving the placement of all the elements of the landscape, of the living system, in the right relationship to each other'. If we don't fully consider all the inputs and outputs, especially in a small system such as a backyard with chickens, there's a possibility of problems and pollution.

Consider first the chicken and her need for food, a resting place, shelter, companionship and safety, as well as a happy life that allows her to express her innate chickenness. Think also of her yields: feathers, feather dust, eggs, chicken manure and so on.

So your goal is not to add chickens as a segregated backyard element that requires work and produces pollution, but rather as an awesome element that helps create abundance in many ways, through both inputs and outputs. Integration is the key. At its most basic, your integrated system might look like this:

- Your kitchen scraps (and any suitable garden offcuts) are a great addition to your chickens' diet – and it's another waste stream that you're diverting from landfill.
- The hens will give you eggs, manure and free pest-eradication services.
- You eat the eggs (then crush the shells and put them back into the chook scraps).
- The manure fertilises your garden – age it in a compost bin first, or dilute it and make a slurry as liquid fertiliser – which helps grow more vegetables.
- Some of the chicken manure goes into a black soldier fly farm (look this up – it's so cool). Black soldier fly larvae breed in the farm and can then be fed to your chickens as a homegrown source of protein.

Consider first the chicken and her need for food, a resting place, shelter, companionship and safety, as well as a happy life.

177

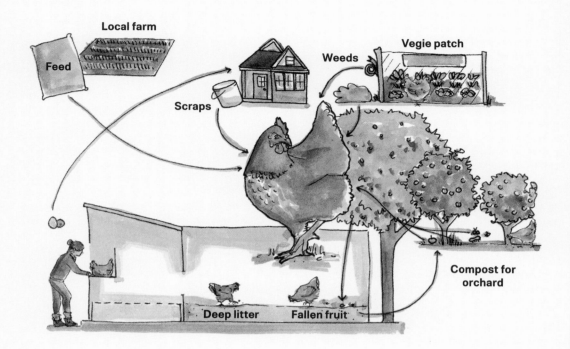

Local farm

Feed

Scraps

Weeds

Vegie patch

Compost for orchard

Deep litter

Fallen fruit

Chickens can create a positive loop of waste reuse and productivity in a permaculture garden.

What an awesome positive loop you've created! Here are a couple of other ways to integrate and close the loop:

- Bugs of any kind are a great high-protein addition to your chickens' diet. Get rid of any caterpillars, grasshoppers, slugs and snails in your veggie patch by feeding them to your chickens.
- Got a local café or bakery that you can source scraps from regularly? Deliver a good bucket with a sturdy lid, and swap it out each week. Your chickens will love the results.
- Green plant material is crucial for really healthy chickens: try growing a range of edible greens and herbs just outside the wire of their run so they can pick off any tips that poke their way in. Or make a 'herb cage' inside their run, with plantings that they can peck at the edges of without damaging the plant. Plant a mulberry tree inside your chicken yard (if you have the space) – the chickens will love the fruit and the leaves, and will help fertilise the tree.

INTEGRATE RATHER THAN SEGREGATE

ENGAGE WITH THE COMMONS

The concept of the commons is something that has come to mean many things to many people, but in this case we're talking about the assets used by all members of an ecosystem, such as air, water and land – especially the land that is 'public space', or should be.

The history of the commons as land that benefits the whole community is the history of us all. It's also a history of functional community and reciprocity, and how we as communities have recognised the importance of that and fought for it time and time again, even in the face of emerging industrialisation and capitalism. Look up the European 'enclosure of the commons': there's some wild history there, both sad and inspiring. Indigenous histories of dispossession are even worse examples, and an ongoing and important part of current and future reparations. See Habit 3: Pay the rent (page 29) for ways you can get involved in those.

In the age of private ownership that we live in, you may not immediately know what functions as the commons in your area, but these spaces and resources are there, even if they're mediated and not currently very wild.

The air we all breathe is part of the commons. Oceans are the commons. So is the water that flows through your watershed and in your local waterway. Your local park or wild space where folks go jogging or walk their dogs. The street outside your house. Engaging with the commons can take many forms: learn the names of the trees and plants; get involved with cleaning up your local waterway; advocate for watershed restoration; and lobby against pollution in that place.

Become a guerilla gardener

Guerilla gardening, in an urban context, can be collaborating with your local street plantings to better benefit local pollinators. Or it might be more about you choosing to weed a patch of local green space, to prevent the council spraying it with toxins. Plant species that are helpful to your ecosystem, poked in around the edges of public spaces where you think they have a chance of surviving.

Of course, there are considerations here: don't plant things that could be a problem for native vegetation in your area and 'go weedy'. And, yes, by the very nature of this practice, it is not officially approved; however, your streets and your 'hood are your local ecosystem. What are your responsibilities to it? How can you help it thrive, while creating more beauty and hope for all the life that lives in it? Even just a tiny bit? I know you'll find a way.

Make seed balls to grow things in unlikely places

Seed balls are really simple to make and are an excellent everyday guerrilla gardening technique that can be used in cities, on farms and even in bush regeneration settings. They're nothing more than a ball of moistened clay and compost, with seeds inside, that is dried until hard then lobbed into whatever spot needs more plants. The seed ball will patiently wait until just the right amount of rain comes, then dissolve, allowing the seeds to germinate and get growing.

When choosing seeds for your balls, it's best to prioritise local native plants that grow well in your area, as they'll have the best chance of survival. You could also choose other flowering plants to help pollinators, but avoid varieties that are potentially weedy in your area. And, of course, don't throw seed balls where they're not welcome. Use your brain and your heart – and choose species to grow that work for everyone.

1. Mix all the ingredients together.
2. Add water in small increments, until you can form a tight ball that holds together.
3. Roll balls about the size of a truffle or half the size of a golf ball: smaller seed balls are generally more successful.
4. Place in a warm spot to dry completely.
5. Throw your balls into an area that needs more plant life and then wait to see what happens.

SUPPORT A LOCAL PERSON IN NEED

One of the core permaculture ethics is *people care*, because we are all so much more resilient and happy when we are connected and supportive of one another. So, here's a really tangible way to put that into action in your own community, by identifying and supporting a vulnerable person who lives near you and who might be doing it tough. This is integrating rather than segregating marginalised community members, something that can be exceptionally rewarding for everyone involved.

This habit is about forming relationships and identifying how to take thoughtful, empathetic and appropriate action; all great skills to cultivate, though it can be uncomfortable until you get the hang of it. Just keep going!

If you already know a single parent, a recent migrant, an older person, a family struggling with a medical condition or someone who seems isolated in some way, start by gently aiming to cultivate a relationship with them. If you're not sure how to connect with vulnerable folks in your neighbourhood, it's worth keeping in mind that you can meet a surprising number of people simply by going for walks and saying 'hi' to those walking their dogs and watering their gardens. Introduce yourself and be ready to listen.

Once you've built rapport and some gentle trust, be sure to check in on them during big events such as heatwaves, or give them your number in case they really need to reach out to you when they're in need.

You can also check in with local charity groups and see if they can connect you to someone or, even better, get involved as a regular volunteer and make connections that way. Offer a specific way in which you can help, such as weeding a garden, setting up email, helping someone learn a new language, sharing spare eggs or lemons, or taking people who need medication to the chemist when you're next driving into town.

All this integration is great for building communities of care and it also leads to safer neighbourhoods for everyone.

Don't force it

It can be hard for some people to accept help, for all kinds of very valid reasons. Don't be offended if this happens; take it as feedback. Keep thinking about – and trying out – ways to help that could be appropriate and non-confronting; when in doubt, volunteer your time with a crew that already has people coming to them for help. This is a great place to start, and also hones your understanding of what help is needed, appropriate and actually helpful where you live, for a person like you to contribute.

Simple ways to offer help and support

Once you've connected with a vulnerable person in your community, one simple but powerful way to help is simply by checking in regularly to see how they're going and offering a listening ear. Stop by their house, make a phone call or just leave a card in their letterbox. The key is to maintain regular contact and then listen for tangible ways you can offer more help, as your capacity allows.

If you're not sure where to start, adding some good books to a local free stand or 'little free library' is a good way to contribute to those around you.

This might include things like:

- offering excess fruit and veggies from your garden, or dropping off a care package at their front door
- bringing over a meal that you've cooked yourself or giving some extra groceries you have purchased for them
- offering to help with minor home repairs, if you're handy with that kind of thing
- starting a carpooling group for things like taking children to school
- running small errands, such as picking up a prescription or collecting a parcel, which you can do while ticking off your own to-do list
- helping to set up digital bits, such as a new TV, the local library's app, video-call technology, podcasts apps, etc
- dropping off your already-read books and magazines for them to read
- lending boardgames
- starting an honesty stall or free food pantry in front of your home and encouraging your local community to share their bounty with others.

EAT WITH FRIENDS AND FAMILY

In this world of ours, we're all so busy that sometimes the important things – like meaningful social connections – can start to slip. Happily, food can help rebuild these connections, because we all have to eat, every day. So a great habit to cultivate is integrating with, rather than segregating from, the people in your life by organising to get together regularly for a meal.

This simple act yields so many positives that it's actually kind of mind-boggling. For starters, when you sit down and eat together with loved ones, it's very likely that you will consume more healthy foods and eat more slowly, which is better for your digestion and helps prevent overeating. You might learn a few new recipes, too, as you either expand your own repertoire to cater for various dietary requirements, or try new things that other folks have made.

Shared meals are also really great for our brains. Eating together can help improve communication skills and self-esteem, and might even help prevent serious psychosocial issues in young people, such as depression, eating disorders and alcohol abuse. Eating together also helps foster better dietary habits and increases fruit and veggie intake, especially among adolescents.

Then, of course, there are all the excellent social elements. Sitting down for a meal with friends or family draws you away from screens and digital communication and brings you back into the space of face-to-face conversation, where things like body language and tone of voice give you so much more to work with. All of this helps strengthen community bonds and build up your friendships, which just feels really darn good.

And depending on how you choose to run your shared meals, they can be a great way to meet new people, use up what's growing in the garden and keep your community strong. We're big on communal get-togethers, where everyone in our little community is invited. In winter we stoke up the fire and bring things to cook over the flames, and in summer we picnic on the beach by the river. It really does help to create a sense of belonging, shared experience, friendship and support. And all simply because we choose to eat together.

An outdoor meal shared with friends and family is a great way to keep things simple and relaxed.

It really does help to create a sense of belonging, shared experience, friendship and support.

Creating opportunities for shared meals

This habit is one to create as you like, depending on how you live and what you feel most comfortable doing. The main thing is that you're integrating with your loved ones and your community, and having fun.

If your family tends to eat in front of the TV, or perhaps at different times or in different rooms, organise a family dinner at the table (with the TV off) for one or more nights a week. Or why not wander down to the local park for a dinner picnic during the warmer months?

If you and your partner hardly spend any time together, then perhaps try setting up a weekly date night where you hang out. This doesn't have to be exclusively at dinner time either; breakfast can be just as much fun, if that's a timeslot that works better for your schedule.

Or maybe you've been meaning to catch up with friends for a while. Invite them over and ask everyone to bring a plate of food. That way you get more time to enjoy their company instead of wrangling the whole menu, and everyone contributes in a meaningful way. In the community where we live, these kinds of get-togethers are a regular thing, and they create so much meaning from this simple act.

Opportunities abound for shared meals with folks just outside your friendship circle, too. Perhaps you're part of a yoga group or sporting club or guerrilla gardening collective. You could try suggesting a pot-luck dinner (where everyone brings something to share) at the conclusion of your next get-together, providing a space for folks to chat about their wider lives. Or drop a note in your neighbours' letterboxes inviting everyone to a shared dinner at the local park, or a front-yard barbecue. Or get really brave and send a text to that person you met briefly and would rather like to be friends with, and get them along to your next picnic.

Try a few options, see what feels good and keep going. Your heart, your belly and your sense of connection will be happier for it.

185

In winter we stoke up the fire and bring things to cook over the flames; in summer we picnic on the beach.

Principle 9

Use small and slow solutions

*

Start a home seed bank

*

Make your own sourdough

*

Walk or ride there

*

Take your lunch

*

Plant a tree and take care of it

This principle is all about thinking deeply and then taking small actions as a result; however, that doesn't mean that these small actions will only have small effects.

Use small and slow solutions is a pretty radical principle in disguise as a gentle one, because it flies directly in the face of consumerism, capitalism and many of the systemic messages that we're bombarded with daily, telling us to want more and to do it now.

Crafting a life in which it's possible to choose less can have a powerful effect on the way you experience and interact with your ecosystem, and, potentially, on your entire community's health and happiness.

In this world there's often a sense that unless something is big, it's not important or useful – but that's just not true. Small habits, systems, ideas and projects are usually less complex and easier to get happening, and they often avoid the many problems that come with greater size and complexity. When we start things at a small scale and then consolidate that activity, we can build from and grow that idea or solution. When many people do small individual actions, the collective effect can be so big that it shifts lives, worlds and futures. In addition, a small decision that leads to a small mistake or misstep in a design is not a disaster, whereas when we invest big time in a large, fast, all-encompassing (and often expensive) approach to whatever it is we're trying to do or design, the consequences of getting it wrong can be huge. The bigger they are, the harder they fall.

This principle is also about simplicity and elegant design. How will you simplify some of your everyday actions while making them powerful forces for good? How can you shorten supply chains or participate in your ecosystem with small and slow solutions?

Do all of your solutions need to be small or slow? Heck, no. There's a time and place for everything. And yet, when we keep this principle in mind, we may be just that bit more likely to choose a simpler, more elegant solution to the challenge at hand, rather than choosing the big one simply because it's fast and shiny. Because, sometimes, all you need to do is plant a seed, and wait. The soil, mycelium, water and sunshine will all come together to do the rest.

Yes, it will take time. But that's time you can spend doing other things, while your small, slow solution – hand-in-hand with your ecosystem – grows like an oak tree, bigger and more beautiful than anything you ever could've constructed by yourself.

START A HOME SEED BANK

Learning how to save seeds is a community service of the highest level. By saving and stewarding locally adapted varieties for the future, you increase the resilience of your entire community. A small and slow solution with the largest effects imaginable: good food and nutrition for all, for generations to come.

Seed saving costs next to nothing and potentially means a lifetime supply of seeds: a powerful symbol of independence and renewal. And it's a great way to get to know your ecosystem better, through working with, and caring for, some of its small yet significant elements.

There are lots of practical advantages to saving your own seeds, too. You'll help preserve great-tasting and traditional varieties of food plants. And, by collecting the seeds from your best garden plants, year after year, you are actively creating locally adapted varieties. This means plants, flowers, fruit and vegetables that are better able to deal with your local soil and climate, as well as conditions such as late frost or early heat, than packets of seeds bought from far away.

That we learn to steward locally adapted varieties of the food plants we eat is just so important, in these times of climate crisis. Seed savers across the world are being called on to share their knowledge (and their seeds) as more folks realise the value of locally adapted seeds to help our gardens and communities thrive.

Saving seeds is a task and a stewardship that stretches waaaay back into your past, too – we're talking many thousands of years. Each and every year, farmers and communities have carefully selected and saved the seeds of all the plants that you know and enjoy as vegetables today, which is literally why we have them now.

Seeds are our communal history and also our combined future.

Just think of that: these seeds have all survived revolutions, genocides and the downfall of societies, and have crossed continents and oceans, in the hands of seed-keepers who have stewarded them from year to year, from our ancestors all the way to you today. Seeds are our communal history and also our combined future.

Indian activist Vandana Shiva refers to this worldwide system as the 'living seed bank': a network of seed-keepers and seeds, the seeds kept safe by the cycle of being continuously planted in the ground and passed among the hands of the people, rather than being kept in big, centralised seed vaults, under copyright and multinational companies' control.

There is no reason why you can't be a part of this, and become a seed-keeper, no matter how small or large your garden might be. Every home with a garden can benefit from a small seed bank.

The basic principles of seed saving

To start your seed bank, you can save seeds of any suitable plants growing in your garden now, or you can plant seeds purchased from a local seed company, and save the next generation of seeds.

But first up, let's walk through some information about seeds, so you can give your home seed bank the best chance of success.

Save open-pollinated seeds, not hybrids

Some seeds will save better than others, because of their plant breeding. A whole wide world of plant breeding exists out there, but to simplify: keep open-pollinated varieties of plants, not hybrid varieties. 'Open-pollinated' simply means the plants have been pollinated out in the open – with *only* other plants of that variety – rather than in a lab.

A hybrid seed, on the other hand, will grow well and produce lovely fruit or vegetables in its first season, but its seeds will not be suitable for saving. Hybrid seeds are a cross of different varieties combined to give special traits or 'hybrid vigour'. The next generation of that plant will not necessarily grow true to type. You don't want to go to all the trouble of saving seeds from your favourite tomato only to find that the seeds grow into a different and possibly less tasty or resilient variety. To identify a hybrid variety, look for an F1 or F2 on your seed packet or seedlings, or look up the variety's name on the internet.

Be aware of cross-pollination

Generally speaking, you want to keep your plant varieties pure and not have them cross-pollinate. This doesn't have to be a big deal. Do some research on your plants and find out what their potential for cross-pollination is, and whether you need to be careful where you plant them.

Different varieties from the same plant families will cross-pollinate, if given a chance; for example, broccoli, kale and some other brassicas will all cross-pollinate if they're flowering near each other at the same time.

'Save your best and eat the rest'

Wanting to save seed at the end of this season, from the plants or seedlings you're growing now? This little saying will help you choose which seeds to save, when the time comes. Select the most perfect, well-shaped ripe fruit or veg from your patch, then get seed saving.

Other ways to access your first seeds

Perhaps you need to acquire some seeds. Check with your local community garden, online gardening group or even local classifieds, to see if anyone is swapping or selling locally grown seeds. Look up your local seed company; wherever possible, support your closest seed-keepers! At a pinch, your local supermarket will have some seeds that may be suitable: try coriander seeds, fenugreek and unhulled buckwheat.

Tomatoes, top, and broad beans are some of the easiest seeds to save.

Do your research

Get yourself a good seed saving book and keep experimenting with more varieties. It's not confusing once you understand the basics, and this stuff is essential for any seed-saving gardener to know.

Getting started with two easy plant types

We recommend you start your home seed bank with just a few varieties. Go through the entire seed-saving process with only one or two plants and really get the hang of it. Once you're comfortable with this new knowledge, add a few more varieties.

Peas and beans

Possibly the easiest place to start: the flowers of both these plant families are self-fertilising, so you can be fairly sure they won't cross-pollinate with anything else. A broad bean will beget more broad beans, and a purple pea will produce more purple peas. You simply grow the plant, allow it to flower and watch as those flowers turn into seed pods, which will slowly dry out. And then you remove the seeds from the pods for storing. A great place to start building your seed bank.

Tomatoes

Tomatoes need a little more care, but are still pretty simple to save. Tomato flowers are also self-pollinating, as each one is what is called a 'complete flower' with both male and female parts. But they can cross-pollinate with other tomato varieties if grown next to each other, as pollinators such as bees visit multiple flowers in your garden. The simple solution is keep your tomato patches apart – all your climbing cherry tomatoes over here, and all your beefsteak tomatoes over there. This way, the flowers will most likely be pollinated by plants of the same variety, and consequently the seeds will remain true to type.

To collect tomato seeds, you can use the fermentation method, which removes the seed coating and protects against some seed-borne diseases. Scoop the seeds from a few very ripe tomatoes and put them in a jar with a little water for a few days. Once a foamy skin forms on top, add some more water and stir: the seeds will settle to the bottom. Pour off the gunk, then rinse the rest through a sieve. Spread the seeds on newspaper and leave them to dry for a few days, then store them in a labelled envelope for next season.

USE SMALL AND SLOW SOLUTIONS

Passing seeds to other hands

Good labelling and storage is important. Two jars of well-stored seeds are better than ten random bags that you never get around to processing properly. Again, this doesn't need to be fancy or complicated: your seeds just need to be kept cool and dry, in a dark place that's free from pests.

Some people store their seeds in jars, some in tins, some in seed envelopes inside a larger container. Clear labelling is crucial; write down the plant type and variety, and also the year of saving. Many seeds are most viable in their first three to five years, so knowing how old they are will help you make choices on what needs to be planted next.

Share your seeds

Once you're a seed-keeper, it will soon be time to replant, and you will also have an opportunity to share your bounty with your community. Seeds make great gifts for friends and family. You might be able to join a local seed-swapping network in your community. Maybe you could start a seed library at your local school; sometimes local libraries have them too.

Or go online and find out what online community groups swap seeds in your wider area: you may well uncover a whole quiet world of seed-keepers, hiding in plain sight.

Apply the seed-saving rule of thumb: save only the best, and eat (or compost) the rest.

MAKE YOUR OWN SOURDOUGH

Baking bread as a regular practice is an ancient tradition that will still be around long after you are gone. It involves patience and intuition, so it's one of the best and yummiest small and slow solutions. A home-baked loaf, fresh out of the oven, is warm comfort and happiness, and is more effective than a dinner bell or a call to 'come and get it'. It's also often a more healthy option than store-bought bread, and can save you money, once you get your bread game on.

Whether you choose to use store-bought yeasts to get your bread going, or go the sourdough route with a homemade 'starter' instead, making your own bread has many layers of goodness to it. Yes, it does take longer than buying bread at the shops, but you get to choose exactly what goes into it – no artificial additives or flavourings. You can use any type of flour you like: something local or organic, or you can even mill it yourself, which ensures you keep nutrients that are otherwise lost in the first few days after milling.

Baking bread at home allows you to get creative with flours. Think outside the box with corn, rice, barley, oat, buckwheat, millet, kamut, quinoa, chickpea (garbanzo), wheat, rye, pea, mung bean and lentil flours. You might decide to add nuts, grains and seeds on top. Or choose your favourite flavours, such as pumpkin (squash), sweet potato, spinach, olives or cheese. Go sweet if you prefer, adding cinnamon, sultanas or chopped fruit. It's one giant, ongoing, deeply delicious experiment.

But let's home in specifically on sourdough here. This involves first creating your own pre-ferment, also known as a 'starter' or 'mother'. It's something you can make at home. It's this starter that makes your bread rise.

Why bother with a homemade starter when you can buy yeast easily at the shops? Well, sourdough is said to be easier to digest and more nutritious, plus who doesn't love the idea of harnessing their own biodiverse wild yeasts? And in our opinion, it's far more delicious.

This slow and steady solution will link you to the ancient art of breadmaking, as well as your immediate environment and its yeasty cultures, and thus your own health and wellbeing.

A sourdough starter is easy to make.

Understanding your sourdough starter

A sourdough starter is essentially a wild-caught, homemade yeast culture that helps your bread to rise. All you need is flour, water and a bit of time and soon you will have created a symbiotic community of lactic acid bacteria and wild yeasts (these are present in the air all around us). Together, these two types of microbes release gas as they eat the carbohydrates in your jar of flour, providing air, life and fermentation for your future bread.

Creating your own starter at home is usually pretty easy. Basically, you mix the ingredients and then allow bacterial and wild yeast processes to take over for seven days. By the end of the week you should have a living bread starter that you can keep replenishing and using for years. It's a gift that keeps giving.

How to make your starter

1. Find a large glass or ceramic jar. Put in 2 cups (300 g) of unbleached plain flour and 500 ml (2 cups) of unchlorinated water and stir well. Cover with a tea towel (dishtowel) and place it in a warm spot, giving it a stir each day.
2. When you notice small bubbles forming in your mixture (usually after about three or four days), it's time to start feeding your starter. If no bubbles have formed, you might need to find a warmer spot for your jar.
3. Each day for about three days, feed your starter. Firstly, remove most of the existing starter, leaving only a couple of tablespoons (you can add discarded starter to your next batch of pancakes, or put it in the compost). Then, stir in 2–3 tablespoons of flour and the same amount of water. It should have a pancake-batter consistency, so add a little more flour or water if you need to.
4. Soon, you will notice your starter rising each day after its feed. It's ready to use when it's bubbly and active and rising to at least double the size (it will fall back down again each day).
5. After baking, replenish your starter by feeding it again. If you used a lot of starter, you might need to give it a big feed. Use a 1:1 ratio: if you add 1 cup (150 g) of flour, you will also add 250 ml (1 cup) of water.
6. If you bake regularly, keep your starter on the kitchen bench and feed it daily. Otherwise, store it in an airtight container in the fridge and 'wake it up' by feeding it daily for a day or two before you want to bake.

No-knead (lazy) sourdough

There are LOTS of great sourdough recipes, but this one tastes amazing, while being easy to fit into a busy schedule. It's a combination of techniques we've learned over the years (hat-tip to Su Dennett at Melliodora for introducing us to this sloppy sourdough world) and it gets made on the weekend in our household, depending on our needs. It produces a really moist, firm bread with lots of little holes.

This is a 24-hour recipe, but the total work involved is less than 10 minutes. The method below is good for one loaf of bread. It will store well as a whole loaf for over a week, but like any bread, it is at its best when it's fresh.

You will need

6 cups (900 g) wholegrain flour (I love emmer or spelt; wheat is fine)

1–2 cups sourdough starter – or as much as you have

Whey (the watery bit off the top of plain yoghurt will do), optional

2 teaspoons salt

Seeds, nuts, fruit or spices, optional

MAKES 1 LOAF

Day 1 – evening

1. Combine half the flour with all of the sourdough starter in a big bowl, and slowly add enough whey (if using) and water to make a sloppy dough – too wet to knead, but not a complete soup. Pancake-batter consistency is good. At this stage the mixture is *very* forgiving, so the amount of starter you use is not crucial.
2. Cover the bowl (we use a dinner plate for this) and let it stand at room temperature overnight.

Day 2 – morning

3. Remove a portion of the mixture from the bowl – this will become your ongoing sourdough starter. (I take out about 3 tablespoons to put in a separate jar, add a little new flour to feed it, then set it aside.)

4. Add the remaining flour plus the salt to the bowl and stir well. You may need to add a bit more water: you're going for a slightly firmer consistency this time – just a bit too wet to knead. Add any seeds, nuts, fruit or spices, if using, and stir to combine.
5. Set the bowl aside, covered, and leave it at room temperature for several hours.

Day 2 – evening

6. About 2–3 hours before you want to bake, grease a loaf tin well (sprinkle semolina or oats on the bottom and sides of the greased tin if you are worried about it sticking), and pour in the dough. The dough will collapse, so cover the tin and leave it somewhere warm until it has doubled in size: a few hours should do it.

7. Preheat the oven to 180°C (350°F) and bake for 40–50 minutes, until the top is nicely browned and the sides pull away from the tin a little.
8. Turn out onto a rack to cool completely before slicing.

Tips

This is a very adaptable method, so vary it at will.

If I have a bit of whey left over from cheesemaking I'll replace half of the water in the first ferment with that.

Caraway seeds in and on the bread are very good, as is fruit.

Don't forget to feed your starter between bakes to keep it alive.

habit 43

WALK OR RIDE THERE

If you aspire to be fit and healthy, this habit can be powerful. It's also great for your mental health, and will shift your relationship with your local ecosystem, even if it's just the bit between you and your corner store.

It is easy to just jump in the car instead, we know. But what if you tweaked that habit, just for *one* place that you regularly go, and got used to walking (or riding your bike) there, each and every time, rain, hail or shine? Okay, maybe not hail. But every other time.

There are a few things happening here, with this kind of habit. First, you'll be less reliant on your car to do every tiny trip and this is a good thing, if you have the capacity to walk places.

Cultivating the regular habit of walking or riding there may also reconfigure how you approach your body's capabilities. A body with legs that work, and an empty backpack ready to be filled with groceries, is a beautiful thing – a powerful thing, even. These days, there's a lot of standing and sitting in our daily lives. Flip that script and move that body of yours. It will thank you for it, and the results can be far-reaching.

This habit is not about going car-free; although, if you're up for that, and you live somewhere that it's possible, great! This habit *is* about *choosing one place you go regularly* that's suitable to walk or ride to – because of its distance, and because whatever you do or get from there can be reasonably carried home – and doing that.

Along the way, you'll re-map your ecosystem in your head, as you watch the seasons change and notice new things (a mulberry tree on the corner, a bird's nest, a new neighbour moving in). You'll also interact with your neighbourhood in a way that's not possible if you're zooming by in a car, plus it's one less car trip in your local streets and community.

Cultivating the habit of walking or riding there instead is powerful for your community, too. The more of us who do this, the more 'walked' our communities become, the more human-scale our interactions become, and the more folks are out on our streets, living in relation to each other instead of cultivating a life of transiting from private space to car to building and back again.

Yes, this is one tiny action. But it will reshape your relationship with where you live, and your place within your ecosystem, quietly and slowly, for the better.

USE SMALL AND SLOW SOLUTIONS

Walking instead of driving can completely change the way you experience a short journey and help you cultivate all kinds of connections.

Our walk-there-instead rule

Our family has a (loose, but mostly effective) rule that if something we want for cooking didn't make the list for the weekly shop at our local supermarket, we walk there to get it instead. The local shopping strip is a five-minute walk down a steep hill from our place. We are fitter for it.

We've met the (frequent, especially when we're tired) mental response of 'Uuugh, it's too much to carry' with a decent backpack. And met rain with a good raincoat. While this habit is not rocket science, we've found that having the right gear and knowing we'll be back in less than 20 minutes, because we do this all the time now, really works for us.

Along the way, I always meet other ecosystem residents (there's a shortcut through a patch of bush on the way), smell the earth, see the sky and hang out with the place I'm a part of . . . just that little bit more. I see people in my community as I walk: nodding an acknowledgement, sometimes a quick chat to see how they're going. Every time, I come home more grounded than when I left the house, even if I left annoyed because we'd run out of something that *should* have been on the shopping list.

I never, ever regret taking this walk, even when it's raining. And all these tiny advantages just wouldn't happen if I scooted down to the shops in the car every time. Thanks, body and ecosystem: you're the best.

TAKE YOUR LUNCH

Taking your lunch means the world is your restaurant: the train, the park, the harbourside, up a tree, you name it. With a small thermos and a good book, I have become firm friends with the public spaces of my city.

As the old saying goes, you are what you eat. So, *what will you choose* to eat for lunch each day? Maybe you buy your lunch from a café or fast-food place. How much does that cost you each week? If you spend just $10 a day, five days a week, 50 weeks a year, that adds up to $2500 a year. *How many extra days are you working each year just to pay for your lunch?* Habits that cost you money each day ultimately cost you working time as well.

So, how about making a habit of taking your own lunch to work, to school or whenever you head out for the day? It seems like such a small thing, but a big part of living a permaculture life is establishing positive habits that help get you where you want to go, bit by bit.

And the actions you take every day, such as the way you choose to source and eat your lunch, are like all the other parts of life: you can ignore them and just do what you do (and hey, if this habit is too hard at the moment because of other life factors, leave it – no-one needs to do everything) or you can consider shifting that habit, just a bit, and see what happy flow-on effects that has.

Beyond the impact to your hip pocket, what does that takeout do for your health? When you have a whole range of lunch options to choose from, it's pretty easy to end up making an unhealthy or unethical choice based on your frazzled brain and delicious smells.

Then there's the packaging: take-away containers, disposable cutlery and plates. While more places are shifting to compostable packaging, which is a positive move, remember that the most sustainable take-away plate option is not to need one in the first place. On top of all this, buying takeout supports industries that throw away mountains of uneaten food each day.

Remember, as in so many parts of our modern society, the adverse impacts of our wider food system are not your sole responsibility as the end user with your little takeaway container. We all have so much work to do, at the consumer level all the way up to national governance, in how we hold the multinationals that profit from these destructive products, supply chains and systems responsible for the damage they do.

Bringing your own is a small and slow solution, and every time you do it you create a little less waste, and disengage a little bit more from a system that doesn't have your interests, or those of your ecosystem, at heart.

Planning ahead makes it much easier to quickly throw a lunch together when you're about to head out the door.

Lunch box planning tips

A small amount of planning ahead makes it much easier to quickly pack a lunch box when you're about to head out the door. Here are our best tips for planning and packing your own delicious lunch.

Storage

- Get yourself a nice container: one that seals properly so the lid won't pop off and spill stuff everywhere. Second-hand shops often have good options, or you might choose to buy a new metal one that has compartments for keeping different food types separate without the need for individual containers or wrapping.

Ways to jog your memory

- Connect preparing your lunch with something else you already do every day. Maybe in the evening when you clean up the dishes after dinner, instead of putting away your lunch container use it as a trigger to prepare your lunch for the next day.
- Keep the fruit bowl on the breakfast counter, so you remember to take a piece of fruit with you on the way out of the house.

Simple lunch suggestions

- Leftovers are the easiest next-day lunch, so cook an extra portion the night before, if you can.
- Wraps are delicious and can be thrown together with whatever salad, protein and condiments you have in the fridge.
- A thermos of soup is magic on a cold day.
- Homemade fruit leathers or dried fruit is a great sweet snack.
- We bake cookies or a cake once a week, usually on a Sunday afternoon, so there's a sweet treat for each day of the week.
- Other quick snacks include popcorn, pickles, hardboiled eggs and raw veggies such as cherry tomatoes, sugar snap peas and celery sticks.

PLANT A TREE AND TAKE CARE OF IT

Tree planting is surprisingly powerful. In the simple act of placing a seedling into soil, we create a small and slow solution that draws down carbon, cools and shades the surrounding area, and provides habitat, fruit, flowers and seed for people, animals, birds and insects. This future tree may well be climbed by children whose parents haven't even been born yet. What a gift!

There are many ways to get involved in tree planting. You might have a friend with a big rural property that needs revegetating, or you could volunteer on a similar project through a local environment group or charity. Or, you can start much closer to home: in your yard, on your front verge or even in a local wild space.

Wherever you choose to plant your tree, it will benefit everyone nearby. Over time, your tree will soak up carbon dioxide and filter out pollutants such as dust and smoke, releasing clean air. It will help capture and sink rainwater into the soil, reducing the risk of flooding and preventing erosion. Depending on the species you choose, your tree – just one single tree – could end up being home to hundreds of insects, fungi, animals and plants. It might even help boost the mood of folks in your area, because spending time in green spaces can help reduce stress and anxiety.

So you plant a tree. And then there's step two, the one that sometimes gets forgotten: caring for the tree. This might be something as simple as removing the tree guard once the plant is old enough, so it doesn't hurt the tree by being left on. Perhaps you need to commit to regular watering in the first couple of years as it becomes established, and prune it every now and then. Perhaps in year three you notice it's growing a bit crooked and could use a stake to straighten it back up again. Checking in on your tree regularly will ensure it grows big and strong for future generations.

Once you've planted your first tree, think about where the next one will go, and the next. Get the street and your neighbours involved. Maybe each person can adopt a tree, and dedicate theirs to a special person. Encouraging community involvement helps share the load of caring for your trees after planting, and gives everyone ownership of – and the chance to feel proud about – this beautiful life-giving project.

Where and how to plant a tree

Before you plant a tree, it pays to plan a little, especially in urban areas. You don't want your future tree to shade someone's solar panels or veggie patch, or cause weed issues near sensitive bush regeneration sites.

Consider the type of tree you'd like. Perhaps you have a local nursery that focuses on local endemic and indigenous plants; varieties native to your specific area, and therefore likely to be better adapted to the climate. Endemic plants can be easier to care for in the long run, and you're putting biodiversity back into your neighbourhood, which is great for native birds, butterflies, bees and other lifeforms that perhaps can't feed or breed on the exotic ornamentals that many people choose to put in their gardens. Or you might instead go the food-producing route, and choose a fruit or nut tree that will feed your family and community for decades.

Next, research how wide and tall your tree will become and choose appropriately if you have space restrictions. Don't forget to plan for its needs: water, light, etc. (No point planting a tree and then having it die in the first heatwave.) If you're not sure, head down to your local nursery or ask neighbours for advice on what grows well in your area.

Head down to your local nursery or ask neighbours for advice on what grows well in your area.

General steps for planting

- Dig a hole twice as deep and wide as the pot of the seedling you're planting. This creates a loose soil zone around the root ball for easy growth and good water-holding ability.
- Mix compost with the soil you removed from the hole, at a ratio of about 1:5. As an optional extra, you can add a handful of trace mineral dust or mycorrhizal tree starter, if you have some. For clay soils, you might also sprinkle a small handful of gypsum into the hole, which can help break up the clay so new roots can penetrate outwards.
- Return a few spadefuls of that soil mixture to the hole.
- Loosen the roots of your potted plant a little, especially if tightly bound. Place the plant in the hole and push the remaining soil mixture in and around, pushing down firmly with your fingers.
- Water the tree in as you backfill with soil mixture. This will help things settle properly without air pockets. Water thoroughly to ensure the soil is fully wet.
- Mulch around the planting hole and surrounds (using materials such as pea straw, autumn leaves or bark chips), ensuring the mulch doesn't touch the tree trunk.
- Water every week or so for the first month. You may need to water intermittently after this for the first couple of years, until your tree becomes established.

Principle 10

Use and value diversity

✳

Support your local pollinators

✳

Make your own probiotic drinks

✳

Install a gate in your side fence

✳

Make a lizard hotel

✳

Share a garden

Diversity is one of nature's strategies for building resilience in systems. Diversity creates stability.

Use and value diversity is a principle drawn from the living example that is biodiversity, with myriad life forms creating stable systems with their integrated differences. Whether we're making gardens, participating in land restoration, or keeping our personal biome on track, diversity is at the heart of everything.

You can look at different ways of achieving the same function, for the sake of stability. Using and valuing diversity can act as an insurance policy, so to speak; a backup for when the main way doesn't work. The proverb 'Don't put all your eggs in one basket' reminds us that people before us understood the insurance value of diversity.

In our homes, this can mean creating stability in essential things such as the drinking water supply.

You may have access to town water, but you might install a small rainwater tank – just enough for drinking, not for all the water your house needs – as a backup and alternative to the town supply. This simple retrofit to your home builds resilience, so you're not just relying on one source of drinking water and therefore being entirely dependent on that supply.

We can *use and value diversity* to build resilience, in our homes, our ecosystems and our communities. Diversity of opinions, gender identities, partnerships, food, plants and people: all these elements combine to create a stronger, more inclusive, resilient community.

Whether it's in your local neighbourhood or your own body, by using and valuing diversity you can ensure each system is more resilient and capable of dealing with the stress and shocks that life delivers.

habit 46

SUPPORT YOUR LOCAL POLLINATORS

Pollinators are all around us – mostly insects, yes, but also birds and bats – and all these beings are crucial residents in our food production and wider ecosystems. You will be familiar with honey bees, but there are also native bees, beetles, butterflies, wasps and literally millions of other pollinators helping keep our ecosystems fertile and functioning. These creatures carry pollen on their bodies as they travel from plant to plant, flower to flower. The pollen bears a plant's male sex cells and so forms a key link in the reproductive cycle of many plants.

Alarmingly, our pollinators are increasingly threatened by industrial agriculture and chemical use, with species loss escalating on many continents. Concrete and other hard surfaces placed over soil aren't helping: these remove habitat for pollinators that nest in the ground as well as key pollinator food sources. This is deeply worrying because an estimated 75 per cent of our food supply benefits from the presence of pollinators. Many staple foods, such as apples and pumpkins, rely entirely on pollinators to produce fruit. Without pollinators, where will we be?

Our collective food security rests on the good work of pollinators all over the world. So what can you do to safeguard our collective future and help pollinators thrive? You can use and value diversity by becoming a pollinator steward: get to know your local insect and bird species, plant a heap of flowers for pollinators or support local beekeepers and farmers.

Insect hotels are excellent, too: we have one that lives by our back door and has multiple occupants. Pollinators and good bugs just showed up over time, co-opting this safe haven for themselves. They will do the same at your place, if you provide the right conditions. All over the world, we can help house and feed pollinators.

So make a list of how you could support your local pollinators, given your personal context, and get building, researching and planting. Take on multiple actions here, if you can. Pollinators deserve and require all the support we can give them

An insect hotel provides living quarters for diverse species and helps keep your garden in balance.

Ways to support pollinators in your garden

Pollinators are a gardener's best friends: they help supercharge the vegetable garden's abundance and resilience. In our ecosystems, and also in the smaller setting of a garden, diversity begets more diversity. So the more flowers and pollinator food you can pack in – no matter how big or small your space might be – the better for attracting more and more local pollinators.

- Provide a safe and chemical-free haven in your garden. Use zero chemicals that may disrupt or harm pollinating insects.
- Grow lots of different flowers to increase diversity and bring in beneficial insects, which will help control pests organically. Flowers are also pollinator food, particularly blue ones, such as borage, blue salvias, lavender and nigella.
- Plant herbs such as dill and fennel that have umbelliferous flowers – a bit like the shape of an umbrella – as many pollinators love these.
- Include good habitat plants in your garden; for example, dense, low plants will attract small birds, some of which are pollinators.
- Don't forget flowering perennials and trees! All of these plants are amazing pollinator supports.
- Provide a body of water, large or small, for pollinators to drink from.
- Make an insect hotel – an 'air-bee-and-bee' – where pollinators such as burrowing bees and small wasps can make their homes and nests. This could be as simple as a short bundle of sticks or reeds, tied with some wire. Or it might be a more involved affair.
- Become a beekeeper yourself. As Simon Buxton, author of *The Shamanic Way of the Bee*, wrote, 'The future of beekeeping is not in one beekeeper with 60,000 hives, but rather 60,000 people with one hive each.'
- In some places in Australia, keeping a small hive of native *Tetragonula* stingless bees is an option too: look up 'stingless beekeeping' to see if this is possible where you are.

Adding a small pond to your garden gives local insects, birds and other residents somewhere to drink, as well as being a mini-ecosystem itself.

Pollinators are a gardener's best friends; they help supercharge the vegetable garden's abundance and resilience.

Types of pollinators and where they live

All the bees

You know about honey bees, but most places in the world have lots more types of bees. Many native Australian bees are solitary (like the blue-banded bee), but some are hive-minded (like the *Tetragonulae* of eastern Australia); some look like small flies; some are big and some are truly tiny. Look up a local bee guide and find out what lives near you.

A lot of the solitary bees live in cracks, such as in walls, and some burrow into the ground. The more 'social' bee species (those that live together in hives) are most likely to be found a metre (3–4 feet) or so up inside a tree trunk, or wherever they can find a suitable spot.

Wasps

Lots of wasps are pollinators, too. So if you have a wasp nest near your house that you're assuming is bad news, identify the species first! It might be an amazing pollinator friend and no threat to you.

Butterflies

All the butterflies (and moths) of your area are pollinators, so look up the types of flowers they like to eat and plant some of those if you can.

Flies

Flies can be important pollinators, and there are lots of different species. I'm not going to tell you to encourage flies to your garden as a starting point, but do be aware of this in how you choose to manage them.

Beetles

Beetles are said to be responsible for up to 88 per cent of pollination worldwide, but they're often not the first pollinators we think of! Consider planting for them, and be aware that many of the beetles perform other important services in your garden also; for example ladybirds (ladybugs) are great for aphid control.

Small birds and bats

In different places around the world, there are all kinds of small birds (such as hummingbirds, honeyeaters and spinebills) that play important roles in pollination. And then there are the microbats, also part of the story. So many important pollinators, in each and every ecosystem.

Good bugs

These are the bugs that prey on the 'bad bugs' (well, they're bad for your vegetable patch, usually, not inherently bad in their personality or anything). Certain types of ladybirds, wasps, beetles and nematodes are fabulous garden helpers when it comes to controlling mites, aphids, caterpillars and more, but they need the right conditions to help you out.

Research before removing 'pests'

Before you squish a bug in your garden, take the time to identify it. Ask a knowledgeable friend, or post in an online forum. You don't want to accidentally kill the larvae of a good pollinator because you mistook it for a pest. Some insects are predatory too, meaning they will eat other insects that can be problematic in the veggie patch. You will find garden friends in the most unlikely of places.

USE AND VALUE DIVERSITY

Don't have a garden?

If you don't currently have access to a patch of soil, you can still help support and steward your local pollinators. We all have to eat, yet often the food we buy has a negative effect on our pollinators.

Your options include:

- buying locally grown fruit, vegetables and nuts wherever possible, preferably organically grown, but if that's not available for you, spray-free is also a step in the right direction. This small gesture has a big effect on our pollinators.
- supporting local beekeepers by purchasing honey from someone near you. If that's not possible, buy honey from your own country. Even if it's not organic, by supporting local beekeepers you are supporting your local economy and your local ecosystem.
- considering the 'wild' spaces near you – your street verge, the edge of your local park, even that vacant block down the road – and perhaps seed bombing these spaces (see page 181) with non-invasive flowering plants to provide habitat and food for pollinators.

Above left: Seed bomb local spaces with flowering plants that provide food and habitat for pollinators. Above: Purchasing local honey supports beekeepers and the ecosystem.

habit 47

MAKE YOUR OWN PROBIOTIC DRINKS

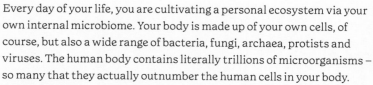

Every day of your life, you are cultivating a personal ecosystem via your own internal microbiome. Your body is made up of your own cells, of course, but also a wide range of bacteria, fungi, archaea, protists and viruses. The human body contains literally trillions of microorganisms – so many that they actually outnumber the human cells in your body.

It's especially important to care for and cultivate the microorganisms in your digestive system. Imbalances in our gut microbiomes have been linked to a wide range of health conditions, both acute and chronic. Even the quality of our sleep has been linked to the health of our guts. At a more basic level, the microbiology in your gut defines which nutrients you can digest and absorb. So enhancing your gut's biodiversity is a great way to increase your overall health and reduce your chances of disease and chronic conditions.

A simple habit that helps you use and value the diversity of microbiology within your gut's local ecosystem is making and drinking naturally fermented drinks. Some of the easiest and cheapest ones to make are kombucha, jun, tibicos and milk kefir. These all have one main thing in common: they're made using different Symbiotic Cultures of Bacteria and Yeast (SCOBY). The SCOBY presents as a jelly-like blob (kombucha) or sometimes like small jelly-like beans or grains (tibicos).

Another thing they all have in common is that they are highly delicious.

All these simple, nourishing drinks are literally living foods: they contain a diverse range of microorganisms that are actively eating and transforming the basic ingredients until they end up inside your tummy as you drink them. So, when you first start drinking kombucha or any other fermented product, a slow and steady approach is best. Limit yourself to one glass a day, to give your tummy time to adjust to the new microbes. Also, be aware that some natural ferments contain caffeine and small quantities of alcohol, so might not be suitable for young children.

By making a habit of brewing one of these simple ferments, you will increase your inner diversity and introduce a tasty new drink option into your kitchen. And once you've got all the bits, these fermented drinks are extremely cheap to make with seasonal or even homegrown ingredients. Try one of our fermented fizzy drink recipes on the following pages. It's a win for the planet, your gut and your tastebuds too.

Facing page, left to right: strawberry tibicos, orange and thyme tibicos, tibicos with SCOBY, lemon verbena kombucha, and kombucha with SCOBY.

Tibicos (water kefir)

Tibicos is a fizzy fruit soda that just happens to be homemade and probiotic. It's usually made with tibicos grains (which are the SCOBY), water, fructose (fruit sugars) and cane sugar. This recipe is a two-day habit, which takes about 5 minutes and results in bottles of delicious fizzy goodness every other day.

You will need

Tibicos grains. These can be bought online if you can't find some locally

2 litre (8 cup) glass jar and two 1 litre (4 cup) glass bottles

Fresh and dried fruit

Half an eggshell

Raw sugar

Rainwater or filtered water

Fresh or frozen fruit, herbs and spices, for flavouring

MAKES 2 LITRES (8 CUPS)

First ferment (2 days)

1. Put 2 tablespoons of tibicos grains in your jar. Add two pieces of dried fruit (for fructose), half an eggshell (for added calcium) and 3 tablespoons of raw sugar. Half-fill the jar with water, stir it around, then fill the jar with more water to 2.5 cm (1 inch) below the top. Cap it lightly to keep out bugs but still allow for gasses to release. This first ferment sits on the benchtop for two days, bubbling away happily.

Second ferment (1–2 days)

2. Strain the liquid into a large bowl or directly into the smaller bottles, returning the SCOBY, eggshell and fruit to the big jar, ready for another first ferment – you can reuse the dried fruit and the eggshell another three times or so, then compost and add fresh ones.

3. Add 1 teaspoon of sugar per bottle (for the microbes to continue to eat; this builds the fizz) plus your flavours of choice. Our favourite combinations include:
   - Strawberry + cardomom
   - Blueberry + orange
   - Lemon + ginger
   - Apple + pear + mint

4. Cap the bottles tightly and stand them on the kitchen shelf for 24 hours, then carefully open the lid (watch out for fizz!) and taste. The tibicos should be fizzy with a hint of sweetness. If you like it dry (like us), leave it another 12 hours, but keep an eye on the bottles because the pressure will continue to build; burp the bottles as needed during this time. Once you're happy with the flavour and the fizz level, transfer to the fridge to cool and slow down further fermentation. And drink it all up!

Kombucha

Kombucha is a fizzy sweet-and-sour drink made from a SCOBY that eats black tea and sugar. It takes a little longer than tibicos, so might be more suitable if you can't spare time each day to tend your ferment.

You will need

4–5 tablespoons loose black tea leaves (or 8 teabags)

3 litres (12 cups) water

4 litre (1 gallon) jar and some glass bottles

1 cup (220 g) organic sugar

1 kombucha SCOBY

Flavours (optional): mashed fruit, fruit juice, grated ginger, cinnamon, blueberries, apple, lemon, pear

MAKES 3 LITRES (12 CUPS)

First ferment (5–10 days)

1. Brew a batch of strong black tea using the tea leaves and water, pour it into the jar, add the sugar and set aside to cool. Add the SCOBY. Lightly cover the jar, then leave it on your kitchen counter for anywhere from 5 days to 2 weeks (it will take longer in cooler weather). Taste it regularly: it's ready when it tastes tangy. You can drink it at this stage, or add more flavours for a second ferment.

Second ferment (1 day)

2. Pour about 80 per cent of the liquid into a bottle or two (reserving the last bit to start your next batch). Add some flavourings to the bottles as desired, leaving at least 4 cm (1¾ inches) of headroom. Add one extra teaspoon of sugar per litre (4 cups) of liquid, then cap the bottle tightly, and leave it on the bench for 12–24 hours to build up some fizz. Don't leave it for more than 24 hours without opening or 'burping' the bottle, otherwise it could build up too much pressure and explode!

3. When the bottle is as fizzy as you like it, put it in the fridge to slow the ferment, drink and enjoy! If anything looks mouldy, or smells cheesy, rotten or unpleasant – discard the tea and start again.

Peach or raspberry fruit soda

No access to SCOBYs to get a tibicos or kombucha started right now? No problem: you can start by making a fruit soda, which is just about the easiest fermented drink there is.

This recipe is super-easy, and also very forgiving for non-exact quantities. You can divide the quantities below in half, if you want to make less. But we recommend you make a big batch – you can thank us later.

The ferment in this recipe comes from the whey. The best way to get this stuff easily is to strain some natural yoghurt through a cheesecloth to make labneh (look that up: it's amazing and simple to make). The watery whey that drips off within an hour or so will work fine. Sometimes whey also forms on top of natural yoghurt; you can use that too.

If you don't want to use whey, you can use a *teeny tiny* pinch of dry yeast instead, or some people use sourdough starter for this. You just need something alive and fermenty to kickstart the soda.

You will need

½ cup (110 g) raw sugar (or ¾ cup raw honey)

2 litre (8 cup) jar

1 litre (4 cups) warm water

2 cups fruit (raspberries, chopped peaches, blueberries)

60 ml (¼ cup) whey (or a tiny pinch of yeast)

MAKES 1.5 LITRES (6 CUPS)

1. Put the sugar into the jar. Add half the water and stir to dissolve the sugar. If you're using yeast, add it at this point: the warmth will help dissolve and activate it.

2. Add the rest of the water, plus the fruit and whey, if using.

3. Stir gently until everything looks well mixed, then cover lightly and leave on the bench for up to 3 days, stirring twice a day to resubmerge all the fruit (it will bob back up, but don't worry, a twice-daily dunking is fine). You should see fizz starting to form in a day or two.

4. After 3 days on the bench, taste your brew and get excited: it should taste great. Strain the liquid into bottles with good lids (swing-tops are great) and put the bottles back on the bench, sealed, for 12 hours or so.

5. Every 12 hours or so from this point on, open the bottles (carefully – there could be a lot of fizz in there) and taste. If they're to your liking, put them in the fridge to halt fermentation, drink and enjoy.

Note

The second ferment, in those sealed bottles, can get seriously fizzy, especially in warmer weather! We've all heard the tales of exploding homemade ginger beer; well, this is not quite that, but still be careful. When in doubt, open bottles with a tea towel (dishtowel) over them to prevent your ceiling (or you) getting covered in fizz.

USE AND VALUE DIVERSITY

INSTALL A GATE IN YOUR SIDE FENCE

How well do you know your neighbours? Is their yard a blank canvas or an overgrown lawn crying out for new life? Or do they have the most excellent of productive food patches and therefore a heap of knowledge you'd love to tap into? It might be that you could have someone well worth getting to know living right beside you. Someone who, with a little bit of effort, could become a friend, a helper, a person or a family to create community with.

This all sounds great, but how do you get that ball rolling? Some folks advocate for the removal of fences completely in urban areas, choosing to share backyards between neighbours. Share the produce, the resources, the land and the work. Using and valuing diversity between neighbours can lead to stronger relationships, more efficient use of resources, more integrated water and waste management, and economies of scale in garden farming.

If all that sounds a bit too radical for you right now, or you think this would be great with the folks on your left, but not on your right, that's completely okay. Here's a smaller and possibly easier first step: agreeing to install a gate between your yard and the yard next door, if it contains neighbours that you get along with. This isn't to say that you have to *use* that gate all the time, but it's a gesture of community that also allows you to interact with your neighbours in the more chilled-out zone that is the backyard, which is quite different from knocking on their front door every time you want to ask or share something.

If you can make it happen, this new shared gate could create a conduit for a deeper relationship. It might allow you to nip between yards (at agreed upon times or frequencies) to grab a bit of fresh parsley when you're cooking; it might be the easy access point for feeding their cat on nights that they'll be out late. Or maybe the gate stays mostly closed, but becomes the low point in the fence that you can pop your head over and chat to each other. A garden gate can be beautiful, too. Jasmine-covered arbour, anyone?

If this isn't cool with your neighbour, perhaps try to find someone else close by who'd like to share; because, ultimately, you'll be helping to create a more skilled and connected community, with people capable of looking after themselves and each other. Who doesn't want to live in a place where people help each other, make things together, fix things for each other and generally know how to do excellent stuff? We do!

This shared gate could create a conduit for a deeper relationship between you and your neighbours.

Ideas for connecting with your neighbours

If you don't want to change your fence situation – or perhaps you don't even have a fence or yard to start with – there are heaps of other ways you can get to know your neighbours and start forging connections.

- Get involved in your local neighbourhood: show up at community meetings, help out at the community garden, attend your local produce swap or lend a hand at working bees with the local environment group, school or whatever.
- Offer to share skills: this can be as simple as opening your kitchen on a Wednesday afternoon to anyone who wants to learn how to make cheese. Or holding a seed-raising workshop outside your local library. Skillshares of any and all descriptions are great, because they build confidence and community in the most unlikely ways and places.
- Place a compost bin in a central spot for two or more homes and collectively contribute food scraps, garden waste and paper. As an added bonus, a larger compost pile is likely to grow more quickly and heat up more, producing better soil as a result.
- Consider sharing a veggie garden bed: map out the spot with the most sun (this might even be on your street verge) and ask your neighbours if they'd like to share watering and other duties.
- See if folks are keen to share essential tools and potentially chip in together for bigger-picture purchases, which reduces duplication and saves households money and space.
- Map out shared children's play spaces that straddle two or more neighbouring properties: more room for small folk to roam, which potentially creates stronger friendships between them too.
- Give what you can, engage where you live and get involved if you are able.

MAKE A LIZARD HOTEL

Dedicated green spaces and wildlife corridors are so important in cities and, well, everywhere, really. Sadly, though, some of the larger species we share our ecosystems with are often seen as pests, especially in urban areas where they have to battle for space, food and water. But they're all essential parts of our ecosystems, and no ecosystem thrives when only one animal (that is, humans) dominates. So, by actively increasing your garden's diversity, you can show up for your wider ecosystem – of which we are residents every day, whether we realise it or not.

Australian permaculture author Rosemary Morrow recommends that at least 10 per cent of any home and garden design should give back to native plants and animals. Doing this is an active way to use and value diversity in your own backyard, helping you cut back on pests and diseases and vastly enrich the ecosystem in which you live.

Here's a super-simple way to get started by making a 'lounge' for lizards in your garden. You could even go a bit further and add a birdbath or frog pond. Preferably all three! If you have small people in your life, this is an activity to get them involved with: grab some hollow sticks or logs, a few nice sunbathing rocks, and get making.

Start by researching the local species. What type of lizards may show up, where you live? This will depend on where you are; in southern Australia, for example, blue-tongue lizards eat slugs and snails in gardens, which is a very handy outcome for any gardener. Find a local reptile guide and figure out what lives near you.

Next, consider what habitat they need. Lizards are cold-blooded – they can't produce their own body warmth and need heat from the sun – so a nice flat rock in a sunny spot is crucial. If they like spiky shrubs, consider growing some of those. All animals need water, so plan for water in your design. Observe your space and see where the best spots would be for each type of garden resident, according to their needs.

Before you know it, your garden will be bursting with diversity, and will be all the more resilient for it, too.

Lizards love rocks that provide spaces for hiding and sunbathing.

A note about pets

For maximum garden diversity, especially for things like lizards, you may want to think about excluding pets from your habitat area. This helps ensure your garden visitors don't get eaten or scared off. Provide plenty of spiky shelter for lizards and other low-lying species to hide from predators if they need to.

Observe your space and see where the best spots would be for each type of garden resident.

Shallow containers filled with pebbles (and other small items!) are best for easy lizard access and drinking.

How to create a lizard-friendly garden

When aiming to bring lizards and other wildlife into your garden, a few key steps will help make the best and most attractive home. Handily, once you've set it all up, you may not even need to 'garden' this spot, as skinks, geckos and other lizards are happiest in semi-wild places.

- Choose a sunny and dry spot, preferably one of the warmest spots in your garden.
- Place a flat rock, a collection of bricks or maybe an old tile in full sun as a spot for lizards to bask in the sun and warm up.
- Nearby, create habitat by stacking things like rocks and branches, and pruning offcuts and logs of different sizes to create places for lizards to hide.
- Plant groundcovers, grasses and small shrubs with twisting branches, providing even more spots to hide. Your local plant nursery might be able to help you choose endemic local native plants for your place.
- Leave several shallow containers on the ground, or design and fill a shallow pond, and regularly refill them with water, providing a place for lizards to drink.
- Keep predators such as cats, dogs and rats out of the area if you can, as they may injure or kill lizards.
- Reduce or completely avoid using chemicals such as herbicides, pesticides and snail pellets in your garden – these are not great for lizards and other wildlife.
- Allow your garden to be a little messy and unruly, which creates even more spots to hide. A dark and wet habitat will also attract more insects and other species for lizards to eat.

SHARE A GARDEN

If you have a bit of garden space at your place – no matter how big or small it might be – you have an opportunity to use and value the diversity of this spot by sharing it with other folks in your local area. This opens you up to a realm of possibilities, including better and stronger relationships with your neighbours and a more resilient community that looks out for and helps one another. What's not to love?

This habit could take many forms. Maybe you have a large garden and you're happy for kids from neighbouring properties to come and play in the treehouse. Or you might be keen to set a designated shared play area across several backyards (see Habit 48). Maybe gardening isn't really your thing, but you have a big back or front yard that would make a great veggie patch: you could advertise for someone to use your land to grow their veggies, in exchange for a share of produce grown fresh at your doorstep.

If you do enjoy growing food, can you increase the diversity of fresh veggies available to your local community by sharing the bounty you grow? While the supermarkets usually fill their shelves week after week with the same tomato variety, for example, your backyard might produce the most exceptional array of delicious heirloom toms, each one perfect for a different reason – this one for eating fresh, that one for cooking, another one just right for making passata.

Get creative about how you pass on your bounty. Sharing homegrown veggies with neighbours via an honesty stall is a great way to get started with building community connection, and it's fun, too. Or share food for free: the 'take what you need, give what you can' philosophy.

The gift economy vs swap economy

Some folks are all about the gift economy: giving, without needing anything in return, for the sake of deepening ongoing connections in all kinds of ways. In some communities, this works beautifully – remember all that we learned about the gift and swap economies in Habit 12 (see page 70)? Experiment and figure out what works best where you live. And as you all get better at it, these economies may well diversify and deepen over time.

This opens you up to stronger relationships with your neighbours and a more resilient community.

Ideas to get you started

Keen to kick off some community connection in your garden, but not sure how to get the ball rolling? Here are some ideas.

Ways to share garden space

- Band together with friends to grow food in your front garden or backyard. You could even create a small urban community-supported agriculture scheme to sell produce.
- Allow a beekeeper to access your rooftop and set up some beehives.
- Find a few city terraces with south-facing side lanes, which are shady and sometimes wet, and start a mushroom growing project (Habit 51: see page 240).
- Chat to your local school about growing food on their grounds, for the kids and the wider community.
- Offer a section of your yard to a landsharer, with the agreement that they will answer questions about how to grow things when they are there, or possibly share a portion of the produce.

Ways to share homegrown produce

- Knock on your neighbour's door or leave a note in their letterbox – would they like some of your excess zucchinis or peaches or whatever?
- Join a local crop swap; groups of gardeners and locals that meet regularly to share produce, seedlings, seeds and more.
- Create a front yard honesty stall from some second-hand shelves or a bookcase, bolt on a cashbox, assign some prices and let passers-by help themselves to your produce.
- Get on board with free food-sharing movements such as Grow Free, Food Not Lawns or Food is Free for ideas on how to connect with your community. Or simply set up a community sharing corner somewhere along your street.

Use edges and value the marginal

✳ Get to know your local fungi

✳ Cook a meal outdoors

✳ Join your local food co-op

✳ Learn to identify and use local seaweeds

✳ Explore your local gift economy

Use edges and value the marginal *reminds us that rather than only focusing on the main game, we need to use our peripheral vision, looking to what is at the edge, because that is often where the most action is happening.*

The fringe is a very interesting space: in permaculture design, we recognise that in nature we can see how the edges between ecosystems are often the most diverse and productive. The edge between water and land, between forest and pasture, is often where the most species are living.

The edge is where it's at. **Charlie Mgee,
Permaculture: A Rhymer's Manual**

In the landscapes of Britain and Western Europe, hedgerows represent the boundaries or edges of old fields. These hedges also contained wild foods that people harvested, and were places that animals such as rabbits – which were also harvested – made their dens. Hedgerows added hugely to the nearby farms' overall production, in addition to what was harvested from the cultivated fields. And not only that, the hedgerows increased the fertility of said fields, by providing habitat for many different species, from which nutrient outputs flowed.

Studies show the same with 'biodiversity belts' of trees planted between cropping fields in Australia: creating edge ecosystems around fields leads to, on the whole, better productivity within those fields and increased biodiversity in the surrounding ecosystem.

You'll also find many species growing at the edges and margins of gardens that are contributing to biodiversity: they're improving soil, they're providing habitat and forage and they may even be harvestable as edibles. These marginal species may not be the main events on our plates, but they can still be valuable additions to your salad, providing minerals and other nutrients. Historically, for many of our ancestors, these same species were often the crucial marginal foods that helped communities survive in times of war or famine.

This word, marginal, is sometimes interpreted to mean 'of little value', but that couldn't be further from the truth when it comes to our ecosystems and our conscious design. These marginal elements – plants, features, other solutions – are supremely valuable in providing backup.

New ideas in society often start to develop in places that are considered 'marginal', whether in terms of their beauty, socioeconomic makeup, or otherwise. But these margins are where the ideas that need to be born most often burst out, from mutual aid systems and art, to fundamentally necessary ideas based on fairness and justice rather than profit or power. Denying the value of these marginal places, clearing them out and redeveloping has been shown again and again to reduce the life, creative energy and possibilities within greater urban systems.

Use edges and value the marginal is one of my favourite principles, because it encourages us to look beyond our points of daily focus and to consider the whole. It counterbalances the power principles that focus on the main game, which, while very important, aren't the whole story of our lives or our ecosystems. And while remaining committed to other principles – such as *Catch and store energy* or *Obtain a yield* – we also need to remember the aspects that exist around the edges of our vision and our homes and our ecosystems, quietly doing essential work. The margins are often where the biggest magic happens.

GET TO KNOW YOUR LOCAL FUNGI

Fungi are literally everywhere. To many of us, they seem a bit mysterious (how do they grow? Can I eat that one?). But with a little knowledge, you can learn to befriend fungi as the important residents of your ecosystem that they are, and once you learn to identify some of them, you might even find edible species growing near where you live. Two great ways to get to know fungi are by learning to identify local wild mushrooms and also by growing some edible mushrooms yourself, at home. These techniques put to use the fringes of your garden space or that forest nearby, and allow you to gain both knowledge and, possibly, a harvest: an excellent way to use edges and value the marginal.

Fungi actually make up a whole kingdom of life, separate from plants and animals, but we still share plenty of genetics with them: we're practically family. It's now thought that more than three million species of fungi exist, outnumbering plants by ten to one, so it's high time you get to know your neighbours.

Fungi don't photosynthesise like plants, they get their energy by consuming the bodies or by-products of other living things, just as animals do. The part that does this – the main body of the fungi – is called mycelium: a distributed, wonderfully fluffy network of tiny filaments that find the fungi's food, while engaging in all sorts of other important ecosystem services and relationships to plants, trees and animals.

Mushrooms are the fruiting body of certain types of fungi, growing out of the mycelium, and they're some of the tastiest, most highly valued foods on the planet. They are packed with important nutrients, including B vitamins, selenium, potassium, copper and vitamin D, and some of them have as many antioxidants as fruits and vegetables.

So, let's look at how can you bring more mushrooms and fungi into your life. Learning to identify your local species is a great place to start.

Mushrooms are some of the tastiest, most highly valued foods on the planet.

Learning to identify wild fungi

The easiest way to learn to identify your local mushrooms, for both reasons of wonderment and also possible foraging, is to find fungi-lovers near you. Ask around in your local community if anyone forages mushrooms or look for a guided mushroom foraging expedition to get you started.

If you can't find anyone, seek out a local mushroom field guide for your area; many of them have identification keys that ask you simple multiple-choice questions to help you quickly work out what species you're looking at. Take the book with you when you go on your fungi foray. There are also a heap of fantastic online resources for identifying mushrooms, from community groups to online forums and websites.

Take lots of photos of the mushrooms you find, and learn to identify from those. There's no need to bring each mushroom home; leave it in its ecosystem to do its important work. Make sure you take a good close-up photo of all parts of the mushroom; the top of the cap, the gills or pores on the underside and the stipe or stem. Also take note of the location, the landscape and any nearby trees.

Many species of wild fungi that are suitable for foraging are mycorrhizal, which means they form symbiotic relationships with particular species of plants. This means that identifying your local tree species can help a lot in identifying the fungi nearby.

Above left: a basket of foraged edible mushrooms. Above: a wood blewit mushroom.

Becoming a beginner forager

The number one foraging rule is: before you put anything in your mouth, you must be 100 per cent certain of its identity. Remember, 'all mushrooms are edible, but some are only edible once'. So learn the identifying characteristics (and the tell-tale signs of any local poisonous lookalikes) so you will be able to confidently identify fungi in the wild. This might sound overwhelming, but it quickly becomes pretty easy, because your mind is a pattern-recognition engine. Remember, your ancestors did this exact thing *a lot* – and successfully, too – which is why you're here today. You can do this.

A few common wild and edible mushrooms

- **Saffron milk cap** (*Lactarius deliciosus*) – one of the easiest to identify and tastiest mushrooms you can forage, found growing in pine forests.
- **Birch bolete** (*Leccinum scabrum*) – grows in association with birch trees and is a versatile edible mushroom, with a complex, nutty flavour.
- **Slippery jack** (*Suillus luteus*) – usually found in pine forests. Several mushrooms in the *Suillus* genus are similar and edible; figure out which one you have before eating.
- **Turkey tail** (*Trametes versicolor*) – a medicinal mushroom indigenous to all continents except Antarctica. Found on fallen trees and stumps.

Make sure you're 100 per cent confident that the mushroom you've got in your hand is actually the one you want it to be, before proceeding to use it for food or medicine. When in doubt, leave that mushroom to do its amazing, interrelated ecosystemic thing – and continue your learning.

Starting your own mushroom garden

Mushroom gardens are a much-loved part of our backyard growing system: they're easy to get going, support our garden ecosystem as they grow and, with very little fuss, pop up regular harvests of tasty, edible mushrooms. It's a great way to increase your household's resilience, enhance your garden's soil, build more relationships within your garden ecosystem and produce delicious mushrooms.

If you have access to a bit of garden space, you can grow delicious edible mushrooms at home. Mix mushroom grain spawn with something the fungi's mycelium will love to eat, such as pasteurised woodchips. Water it occasionally and wait for the mycelium to eat up all the woodchips. When the mycelium is ready, and the seasons create the perfect conditions, this garden will sprout a load of mushrooms for you to eat.

While other methods of mushroom cultivation – such as growing in reusable buckets or jars – are all about tweaking the growing and fruiting environment, you obviously can't control all the climatic conditions when growing outdoors. Your mycelium and the fruiting mushrooms are at the mercy of the local weather. Sound like a disaster? Actually, it's the opposite. It's a beautiful way to get in sync with the seasons at your place.

When we start growing mushrooms in gardens, we begin to observe how extremes of hot and cold temperatures make the mycelium slow down or speed up. We come to cherish the arrival of autumn, and the anticipation as mushroom season approaches, bringing the new daily ritual of checking our patch to see if it's 'time'. And there's something truly magical about walking into your garden to discover a huge harvest of tasty mushrooms to eat and share with your friends and family.

Best species to grow in gardens

Quite a few delicious mushroom species work with this technique, but our favourite is definitely king stropharia (*Stropharia rugosoannulata*), as it's easy to grow, and grows best when exposed to the rich diversity of microbes that exist in your garden.

Other mushroom species suitable for gardens include:
- **Wood blewit** (*Clitocybe nuda*)
- **Shaggy mane** (*Coprinus comatus*)
- **Giant milky** (*Calocybe indica*)
- **Pearl oyster** (*Pleurotus ostreatus*)
- **Parasol** (*Macrolepiota procera*)
- **Morel** (*Morchella spp.*)

Top: Birch bolete; middle: Turkey tail; bottom: Slippery jack

Create your own mushroom garden

We love growing king stropharia mushrooms outside, using a two-stage technique. We start our mycelium in a big tub and then, once the mycelium is nice and strong after the first harvest, we move it to a patch of earth to keep growing.

What you'll need

An outdoor location that is cool, and protected from wind, sun and frost (under a big tree perhaps?)

80 litre (21 gallon) tub with a plug or hose outlet at the base

Hardwood woodchips

Grain spawn (easily bought online)

Stage 1: In the tub

1. Choose your location. It's best to start in spring after those frosty almost-still-winter days are gone, but before the heat of summer creeps up. Gather your supplies.

2. Put the tub in its final, protected position. Fill the tub with the woodchips and then top it up with water. Leave it for a week to start fermenting, then empty out the water while leaving the woodchips in the tub. This process will kill off most of the microbes that will compete with the mycelium you want to grow and is a quick kind of 'pasteurisation'.

3. Mix in your grain spawn to inoculate the tub, making sure to cover it with woodchips on top. Cover everything with some shade cloth or hessian.

4. This is the incubation stage. Within a month, you'll be able to see the mycelium growing through the woodchips. During this time, make sure the tub gets a bit of water each week.

5. You might be lucky enough to have fruit in as little as six weeks, but it's more likely the mushrooms will sprout in six months. As autumn comes around, keep the tub warmer on cool nights by covering it with a plastic tarp, or add a layer of compost and coir on top.

6. While king stropharia can grow comically big (they're also known as garden giants), it's best to harvest them young and small: they taste more delicious and you are less likely to share them with pests.

7. Have your mushrooms for lunch. Make next-level mushroom burgers: slice, pan fry with garlic and load onto a bun with your favourite condiments, garden greens and whatever else warms your burger-loving heart.

Stage 2: In the garden

Now your mycelium is lovely and strong, you can move it to a patch of earth under a shady tree. Simply add another batch of pasteurised substrate into the mix, and the rest of the process will follow steps 4 to 7 (yep, the mushroom burgers are not negotiable!) and your mushroom garden 2.0 is underway.

1 STAGE 1

Gathering

2 Preparing

3 Inoculating

4 Incubating

5 Fruiting

6 Harvesting

7 Burgering

STAGE 2

COOK A MEAL OUTDOORS

habit
52

Cooking outside on a campfire isn't what most of us think of when we think of a weekly eat-together-dinner. Yet developing this simple habit has so many benefits. Gathering firewood, dusting off the outside chairs and watching the sun set as you eat your dinner can be a powerful way to unplug from the week, right in your own backyard. Are you ready to value this marginal activity, break up the routine and get your kids, housemates or neighbours outdoors for a meal this week?

In my experience, what will be enjoyed as a delicious and satisfying campfire meal can be a lot simpler than if I was serving up the same thing inside: a veggie skewer and a few slices of grilled halloumi = dinner, with marshmallows or campfire toast and jam for dessert. Done and dusted.

Keeping things simple means less time spent cooking and washing up, and more time hanging out with your people, outside, with the birds and the trees and the common focus of a good ol' campfire.

Cooking outside also prevents your house from heating up (a winner on a summer's night), and helps you appreciate the seasons a bit more.

Outdoors is a more communal, bigger space, so you can invite friends and enjoy larger groups. Whether it's turning the sausages or eggplant (aubergine) or marshmallows, everyone can get involved. You'll also be saving on electricity and energy bills.

A simple campfire cook up couldn't be simpler, once you have your simple 'camp cooking kit' together (see page 246), and I find it's nearly always fun, delicious and a great way to decompress.

Barbecue starters

Other versions of this habit could be firing up the barbecue on your balcony, or having a regular 'picnic meal' where you take some food in a basket and go somewhere to eat together. We regularly head to our local beach with a little cookstove, a few sausages or the makings of simple veggie fritters, some apples and some bread.

Things to keep in mind

- Make sure fires are allowed where you are; in some places or at some times of the year, they may be restricted.
- Consider where you'll place your firepit, avoiding overhanging branches and dry grass – anything that may ignite and cause the fire to spread.
- Think about how you'll extinguish your fire, both once you're finished for the meal, and in case of emergency. Have water, sand or earth on hand, just in case.
- Choose a location with proximity to a bench or table, comfy places to sit and a bit of a view. And if that's not quite the right spot, try another until you find the ultimate place in your backyard for your campfire cooking times.

Cooking with fire

When constructing a campfire for cooking over, you ideally want to use wood that gives off as little smoke as possible, yet produces a reasonable heat. The upside-down fire technique (see page 249) can help you achieve exactly this, with minimum fuss.

It's best to avoid starting your fire with lighter fluid, paraffin-based firelighters or petrol, as this may leave your food tasting a bit gross. Instead, use natural materials, such as paper, kindling (small twigs) or even straw or wood shavings.

You might need to plan ahead, too, allowing time to light the fire and let it burn down somewhat, as it's no good trying to cook over giant flames when the fire has just started. Much better to cook over hot coals, which need time to develop. You might then choose to rake some coals to the side a little, which gives you a spot with a more gentle and controlled heat to cook over, while keeping the main fire going.

Lastly, get everyone involved: a campfire cook-up is a great way to give everyone a job, while you all wait for the coals to be ready – making jaffles, threading things onto sticks, gathering wood or kindling, chopping up ingredients – and it's a great opportunity to hang out together, while all helping make dinner happen.

A cheap and easy activity everyone can enjoy together: sunshine, moonlight, stars. What's not to love?

Handy fire-cooking equipment

The right cooking utensils can make campfire cooking much easier. You don't necessarily need all of the items listed below – just what works for you. Keep an eye out in thrift stores for second-hand cooking items.

- **Cast-iron frying pan or skillet** without plastic handles and preferably with deep sides to prevent spills into the fire. Great for plonking straight onto coals to fry a few sausages or things on sticks.
- **Cast iron cooking pot or Dutch oven.** Helpful for cooking a big warming stew or any other one-pot-wonder recipe.
- **A metal grid or grill plate.** Lots of options are available from camping stores; some stand on legs or rotate off a vertical pole. We search for old barbecue grill plates and just use those, raised up on bricks either side. Grills are great for cooking chunks of veggies, meat or anything else that will benefit from plenty of direct heat and a bit of smoke.
- **Skewers.** Wooden or metal ones are both great for holding all types of food to grill easily, and can eliminate the need for plates (win!).
- **Metal tongs, egg lifter and wooden spoon.** All long-handled, non-plastic utensils are welcome in campfire cooking! Burnt fingers begone.
- **Jaffle iron** – long-handled, of course. An easy way to keep the cheese toasties coming. Also research dessert jaffle recipes: you're welcome.
- **Oven mitts, old leather gardening or welding gloves, a towel or thick cloth.** Everything is going to get really hot, so don't use your bare hands to handle pots and pans.

Campfire recipe ideas

Cooking over an open fire is an activity limited only by your imagination. Here are a few of our family recipe idea favourites.

Things on sticks

This is about as simple as campfire cooking gets, but it's no less tasty or low-stress for that. Chop your favourite vegetables or meat into 2.5 cm (1 inch) cubes. Thread onto bamboo or metal skewers, then cook on a grill plate over hot coals until done all the way through.

Our fave 'things on sticks' combos:
- Whole pitted olives, capsicum, onion, cubed chicken or halloumi
- Cubed meat marinated in olive oil, salt, pepper and garlic
- Whole small tomatoes and olives
- Chunks of fennel, carrot and beetroot.

Don't forget about dessert things on sticks! You want these in your campfire cooking armoury also. Apart from being delicious, they are excellent for direct bribery of small folk, to get them to eat a bit of dinner first. No apologies – I'm after a low-conflict meal here.
- Chunks of apple, with a drizzle of melted butter on top (and cinnamon)
- Big chunks of pear and little marshmallows
- Whole strawberries (or blueberries) and orange chunks with cinnamon
- Classics: marshmallows, or a simple slice of bread – add butter and jam.

Above left: Build an upside-down fire for less smoky cooking (see page 249). Above: Sausages (meat or vegetarian), sliced zucchini and 'things on sticks' are always campfire winners.

Campfire potatoes

I highly recommend these as a gluten-free, 'no person left unfed' beach fire suggestion: a big basket of precooked potatoes, ready to be reheated, and easy toppings like herbs, butter and sour cream are a low-stress win.

Other easy campfire fare

- **Baked potatoes in their jackets.** Alert! You can cheat and bake these in the oven beforehand – even the day beforehand – then reheat in the campfire and add all the toppings. Or you can bake them in the campfire, if you have a spare few hours. Either way, wrap each potato in foil for the campfire bit, or put naked into a big cast-iron camp oven and plonk on the coals with a good splash of water in the bottom, to reheat them.
- **Sausages, obviously.** Meaty or not meaty, as you like them.
- **Soup and stews.** Premade (or made on the campfire, if you have the time and headspace).
- **Fritters** – oh, how I love the world of fritters! A basic stiff pancake batter with added creamed corn and salt makes corn fritters of dreams. For a sweet version, make a stiff pancake batter with some berries in it. Everyone's happy. Take extra oil for frying.
- **Pakoras (ish).** Also excellent, and gluten free to boot: mix besan (chickpea) flour with grated veggies and a splash of water (sometimes), a bit of salt and spices or herbs to suit your taste: it will magically combine into a fritter-like mix, no other ingredients necessary. Then fry in ghee or oil in a skillet over the coals, and gobble up.
- **Savoury waffles.** If you have a campfire waffle maker, these can be great: use a basic waffle recipe and add grated cheese and onion and some herbs to the mix, for a savoury and entirely acceptable dinner result. If you have an electric waffle maker, these can be made ahead and toasted on sticks once you're in campfire mode. Tasty, simple dinner win.

1. Start with seasoned, dry wood. Take the larger logs – the ones you'd usually put on last – and lay them flat in your firepit. Then cross-hatch successively smaller layers of wood on top, until you're up to the kindling, which sits on the very top of the pile. Try to build your upside-down fire so that it's as stable as possible, so the structure doesn't fall apart while burning. Put some paper on the very top and a scattering of extra kindling on top of that. Trust the laws of physics, and light your fire.
2. The first 10 to 15 minutes will be somewhat unspectacular, as the fire makes its way through the kindling and the combustion gets going. Soon, though, the flames will be roaring and the fire's smokeless (ish) state will be apparent. Now collect whatever bets were placed upon your complete failure and enjoy your upside-down fire.

Learn the art of the upside-down fire

The upside-down technique for building a fire is pretty much failsafe, and it works really well both outdoors and in combustion wood heaters and other indoor fires. This method creates a cleaner burn that produces far less smoke and ash, yet results in better combustion and therefore more heat from a smaller amount of wood – a win for you and the environment. As an added bonus, the first time you make a fire like this in front of a circle of uninitiated folks, you exist in a ring of utter scepticism. Which makes your rockin' upside-down fire all the better when it proves to work beautifully.

Why it works
Heat energy radiates equally in all directions from the point of combustion, not just upwards. So there's no need to build a tentlike structure with small kindling on the bottom and large logs on top. Instead, do the opposite and once the top kindling layer of your upside-down fire combusts, the heat energy will radiate down as much as up.

This means that the larger bits of wood below the combusting material get well heated before catching fire, which in turn facilitates a better burn with less smoke and better coals: great for campfire cooking.

JOIN YOUR LOCAL FOOD CO-OP

When we source our food directly from farmers, growers and small distributors, rather than large supermarkets, we participate in an alternative economy that sits outside the mainstream food system. This in turn creates more resilience for everyone in your community. The money you spend benefits local farmers, not giant corporations with questionable ethics, and it stays in the local economy.

Wherever you live, an alternative to buying everything from supermarkets may well already be operating at the margins of your community, in the form of a food co-operative. A food co-op is a group of individuals who get together to buy food from local farmers, as well as ethical or fair-trade suppliers. Co-ops are run democratically and members are usually responsible for volunteering to run the co-op, too.

With this kind of food-access structure, your weekly grocery spend can become a tool for increasing local resilience on every level possible, while supporting farmers who are stewarding our landscapes, watersheds and catchments. As a co-op member, you'll often save a fair bit of money, too, via the magic of buying in bulk (at the co-op level) and passing those savings on to folks who source their food from there.

And then there's the awesome community aspect of co-ops: belonging, helping, packing, learning. People swap recipes and spare bags and buckets for beans and noodles and broccoli. Stories get told, kids get to be in the thick of a packaging-free food system full of new shapes and smells and sometimes spare strawberries. Community gets cultivated. It's the world we all want to live in, really.

The first step is to investigate if a co-op is already up and running in your area. Do they need volunteers? Do they have events you can join? Go down and say 'hi'. Bring your jars or containers.

Perhaps a co-op doesn't yet exist in your area, but you're interested in getting one going? Give it a go! You can start with just one thing, to get a feel for it – and it doesn't even have to be food. Maybe you could buy toilet paper in bulk with a few folks you know, or buy a huge bucket of laundry powder and split it with a few friends. Once you're comfortable with the process, you can move on to food staples.

All food co-ops start with people just trying to sort out their everyday needs. And as a bonus, this can be done in a way that benefits everyone involved significantly; from the growers of that food to you and your wider ecosystem, too. All you need is a desire for a better food system, a pot of tea and a few friends who like to eat and save money.

Common types of food co-ops

A co-operative approach to food sourcing can take many forms. Each structure can be tweaked and adapted to suit both the needs of the local community and the availability of produce nearby.

Membership-based

One of the most common co-op structures requires 'customers' to also be members. By paying a small membership fee each year, you get access to the co-op shop. Members may be asked to volunteer for a certain number of hours as part of their membership. This leads to remarkably low running costs and overheads so the mark-up on products can be kept to a minimum.

Home-based

Simpler and smaller-scale food share operations can be run from a home garage or front room, and may serve just a few families or a group of friends. Often these kinds of co-ops focus on buying dry goods in bulk – things such as nuts, legumes and grains, noodles, pasta, flour, seaweed, olive oil, apple cider vinegar and potatoes. Volunteers package all this up into smaller volumes, and members come round to collect their share. Everyone shares in the savings from having bought in bulk, and benefits from less packaging and plastic.

Online ordering

Online co-ops are springing up in communities that have little access to organic, local food. Members order online once a month, within a certain time period. The co-op then purchases bulk foods, before splitting and packing to order. Once ready, members collect their order from a central home or shopfront.

Some co-ops start as a bunch of friends and evolve into valued community resources. Alfalfa House, a co-op in Sydney, Australia, has been running for more than 40 years.

Everyone shares in the savings from having bought in bulk, and benefits from less packaging and plastic.

habit
54

LEARN TO IDENTIFY AND USE LOCAL SEAWEEDS

Beachcombing

Seaweeds are a crucial part of marine ecosystems, even when they're washed up on the beach, where they provide important forage and habitat for many birds and insects. So do be mindful in your foraging, and check your local regulations about seaweed gathering. Where we live, it's fine to take beach-cast seaweed, but we only take a bit here and there, and always forage from near the low-tide mark, to ensure we're getting fresh pieces of seaweed, and also not disturbing the habitat further up the beach.

Getting to know your local seaweeds, and how to use them, is an excellent way of using and valuing the marginal. This habit isn't just for coastal dwellers. If you live inland, research good-quality seaweed suppliers and bring these wild nutrients into your garden and kitchen that way. Whether it's for soups, stews and salads, or fertilising your garden, this regenerative resource is very much worth making friends with.

Seaweed is an incredible and nutrient-dense resource which, when harvested responsibly, is one of the best fertility inputs your garden will ever encounter. And it's also delicious, and deserves a place in your home menu – we use it nearly every day.

Learning to identify your local seaweeds is similar to learning about other wild plants near you: take a local guidebook if you can, take lots of pictures and note where in the ecosystem the seaweed is (rockpool? Washed up on the beach? Attached to rocks at the low-tide mark?).

Most seaweeds are edible (in Australia, all of them are), so it mainly comes down to taste and texture if you're looking to forage them for eating. As with any wild food foraging, search out clean locations that aren't affected by sewage outfalls, heavy industry or industrial agriculture upstream; seaweed is incredibly good at absorbing high nutrient loads and heavy metals, but you don't want to bring that home. So if in doubt, just learn to identify your local seaweeds, and fall about in wonderment at their beauty and potential.

In the kitchen

Seaweed is really nutritious – some species are full of iodine, which is helpful for thyroid health – and can be eaten in lots of delicious and imaginative ways: fresh, dried, cooked or powdered. We love adding dried seaweed to soups and stews, powdering it and sprinkling it atop pretty much everything (eggs, salads, soups) and even chopping it up and pickling it. Our favourite seaweeds to forage are wakame, kelp (mostly bull kelp and golden kelp, where we live), nori (the seaweed used in sushi sheets) and *Gracilaria* (a beautiful purple seaweed that can be used as a setting agent in puddings).

In the garden

Seaweed can be used to increase the health of your garden soil, veggies and flowers: it typically contains useful amounts of elements such as iodine, copper, iron, potassium and manganese. Collected from the beach, seaweed can be added to your compost pile to help build a healthy soil food web in your garden. Or use it as mulch around your plants, where it becomes an organic, broad-spectrum, slow-release fertiliser.

You can also create seaweed 'tea' by submerging seaweed in a bucket of water for a few weeks, lid on, then spraying a diluted mix of the resulting infusion over your plants. It's great for starting strong seedlings, as it contains natural hormones that aid plant growth. As a spray for plant leaves, it can also be a helpful anti-fungicide against powdery mildew and some other fungal diseases.

Whether it's for soups, stews and salads, or fertilising your garden, this regenerative resource is very much worth making friends with.

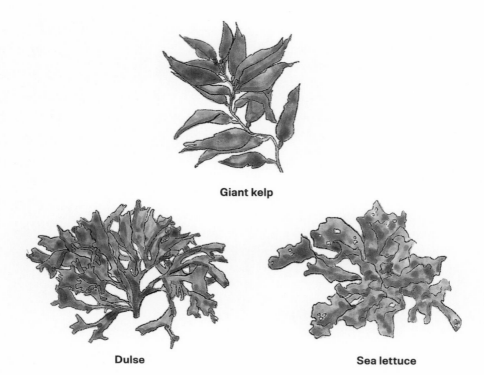

Giant kelp

Dulse

Sea lettuce

Seaweed that washes up around
the low-tide mark is easy pickings
for foragers.

The three main seaweed groups

Seaweed is an algae, so it's not technically a plant even though it
often looks like one. The term 'seaweed' is used to refer to most of the
macroscopic algae that you'll come across in the intertidal region of
beaches and rock shelves between the high-tide and low-tide zones.

Seaweed is generally separated into three main groups:

- The **brown algae** group includes kelps – the long, thick, belt-like
  seaweeds that we know on our plates as kombu, wakame, rimurapa and
  so on. The brown algae group also includes seaweeds called wracks, the
  leafier, smaller-bladed brown seaweeds, often with little round 'floats'
  attached, like knotted wrack and crayweed. You'll find these growing
  at the low-tide mark and below.
- The **red algae** group includes laver or nori, carrageenan and dulse.
  The red seaweeds are generally much smaller than the browns, and
  are sometimes only one cell thick, as in the case of laver, which you
  may know as nori. These generally grow at the mid-tide mark.
- The **green algae** group includes sea lettuce and many of the more
  hair-like, mossy seaweeds you'll find on slippery rocks after high tide.
  They are usually found at the mid- to high-tide mark.

Seaweed press

Another way to get to know your local seaweeds is to press and dry them for crafty projects. They look amazing mounted on card, or in a simple frame (your local thrift store will usually have frames aplenty). If you have a flower press, you can use that.

You will need

Nice bits of seaweed (rinse off sand and pat them dry first)

Baking paper: compostable baking paper is great

Big heavy books

1. Remove any dead or wonky bits and lay the seaweed flat on the baking paper.
2. Open the largest book to about halfway and place the baking paper and seaweed inside. Lay another piece of baking paper on top of the seaweed, so no seaweed bits touch the book and its pages are protected.
3. Gently close the book, trying not to jostle the seaweed too much.
4. Put more books on top to weigh it all down.
5. Wait! A good month is best: the longer you press the seaweed, the drier and more stable it will be. When completely dried, it should feel like paper.

EXPLORE YOUR LOCAL GIFT ECONOMY

The idea of giving, or indeed receiving, something for nothing is a loaded one in our current society. There must be a catch, surely? But what if – stay with me here – you just gave things away? And what if one in five folks you know did that, semi-regularly? What would that mean for the fabric of your community? What would that do for your understanding of reciprocity, on an expanded scale? What would that mean for your sense of belonging, and sense of safety? What would that mean for your attitude towards things you no longer needed, or had too much of?

This habit doesn't need to be a big shift. And it does come with some considerations. But still, what if your community just gave things to each other, as needed, to keep the goodness going around, knowing that it would come back around, in some form, as part of that giving?

How much is enough?

The thing is, this type of gifting with no strings attached functions on a core concept: how much is 'enough' for you? Because once you practise cultivating a strong sense of what is 'enough' – clothes, lemons, time, money, toys, car parts – you can decide what to do with the extra.

You could sell it, and attempt to get a bit more money from it: that's fine. Or you could attempt to barter for other things you need: great! Or you could do both, and keep a few things aside that you know your friend could use, or that the family next door's kids would fit into this winter. No strings attached. Just passing on the goodness.

In doing this, you might discover that paying it forward and sharing your own excess is one of the most powerful ways to build community and reciprocity.

There *are* some considerations here: it's possible that the person you want to give to is not in a position to receive that thing comfortably, without worrying that they can't return the favour, or because they don't want to be beholden to you. Privilege, disparity and all sorts of issues come into this, and it's important to make space for people's reactions, which are all totally valid. So start small, and start with folks you already have a relationship with. But also, be brave!

Not sure where to start? Start softly, with 'pay it forward' thinking: this is a format in which you basically give something to someone, with the loose agreement that they'll give something else to another person, sometime later. It's a great starter technique because it acknowledges the instinct to give in return, but blows that wide open for the receiver to become a giver on their own terms, in whatever way they choose. This can

What if your community just gave things to each other, as needed, to keep the goodness going around?

USE EDGES AND VALUE THE MARGINAL

lead to the sort of behaviour we need more of in our community, and is also at the heart of permaculture ethics: *fair share*.

I can tell you for certain that this habit is small, edgy and powerful ripple-effect stuff. To live in a community where people occasionally just give things to each other when there's a need slowly creates a community-wide network of reciprocity that is the opposite of individualism. This is world-changing behaviour and we all need to cultivate it.

Getting into giving

- Check to see if a Buy Nothing group exists in your community or online, where folks living nearby give and share freely.
- Surprise your neighbour by dropping some homegrown produce or freshly baked goodies around to their place.
- Got a heap of excess lemons or peaches? Put them in a box out the front of your house with a 'free, please take' sign attached.
- Write a note or email of gratitude to someone.
- Show up and donate to your local blood bank.
- Is there a need in the community that you could help out with? Volunteer your time and skills, or offer to trade.
- Identify a local organisation doing amazing work in your community, and ask for donations on your birthday to them, instead of gifts. Or for your wedding, Christmas, your anniversary, whatever.
- Leave a good book for the next person to find. Once you've finished reading, drop the book at a place lots of people pass by: a café, bus stop or train, perhaps. Put a note on the front that it's free to take and is a good read.
- Some cafés have a 'pay it forward' system, where you can buy an additional cup of coffee or a sandwich for a future person who really needs one, but can't afford it.
- Call up your local shelter or refugee support organisation, and ask what they need: it's often specific staple food items or blankets or sanitary items. Tell your friends too – you could gather from a few folks, and do a single drop-off.
- Next time you want to upgrade your smartphone, if your old one still works, reset it and give to your closest domestic violence shelter: they will pass it on to someone who really needs it.

Whether your surplus is lemons, clothes, time or toys, placing a box with a sign at your front gate will make it a gift to someone.

Principle 12

Creatively use and respond to change

*

Raise your voice on the climate crisis

*

Make an emergency plan

*

Do a first-aid course

*

Engage in mutual aid

*

Revisit your personal goal

When we look around us – at our ecosystems, our cities, ourselves – change is literally the most constant thing we can be certain of: it's happening all the time. And it's so important to recognise change, to honour it, to learn from it and to go with the flow to better use that energy, where possible.

Permaculture pioneer Bill Mollison described a process of 'using aikido on the landscape' – rolling with the punches and using those energies to aid us to design what we're seeking, rather than pushing back against them.

There are always forces at work that are larger than us. Whether it's political and social systems, climate change, the weather or the length of the day, these forces are going to create changes that will affect us, whether we like it or not. This is sometimes a difficult thing to come to terms with, because we're so used to the idea that everything is negotiable. But, no, you can't fast-track the seasons, or the length of time it takes to raise a baby into a teenager . . . even if you throw money at it. Some things just take time. And yet, those same things are changing all the time. How can you roll with it and use those changes to create more abundance, rather than pushing back against them and using all your precious energy to try to halt or speed up things that have their own rhythm?

In a time of deep instability, it's easy, and understandable, that you might want to cling to solutions that worked last time, or to a habit that worked for you last year. Might I gently but confidently suggest that, instead, you ***Creatively use and respond to change***, rather than turn your back and ignore it? This calls on you to look forward and embrace the future, no matter how uncertain it seems.

For this principle, I'd actually like you to choose both of the first two new habits, if they're not already something you do regularly – I think they're *that* important. I want you to get political, and rise up in whatever way you can, to help stop catastrophic climate change and demand and participate in creating more just futures – for everyone.

All of the actions and habits that you've considered already in this book are positive, nourishing and excellent things to fold into your life. When done as part of a wider collective, they can help shift power and create the huge changes that we need, right now. But in addition to all that (this is where the 'and also' thing comes in again) we each need to support and demand big change, directly. So dust off your climate-sign-suitable cardboard boxes, lovely. Here we go.

RAISE YOUR VOICE ON THE CLIMATE CRISIS

The climate crisis that we're all facing is very big and scary. And you're just one little person on this Earth. What difference could you possibly make by showing up to a direct action? All the difference in the world, actually; for you, for your family and for our planet. Direct action – standing up and being counted – is the basis of democracy and of fundamental grassroots change, which has a proven track record of redirecting the biggest governments and industries across the entire world to bring about meaningful change. *This matters. And we also know from history that this works.*

Why show up? Because the Intergovernmental Panel on Climate Change (IPCC) and many independent climate scientists say we must limit global warming and we must rapidly and urgently make changes for that to be possible. Today. Tomorrow. And every day after that.

This change is possible, and happily we do have the technology and solutions to make this happen, through agricultural techniques, divestment from fossil fuels, alternative energy generation and so much more. But we cannot hold that line – less than two degrees of warming – without the political will and industry shifts required to take up these carbon-saving and climate-saving tools, technologies and techniques.

It is essential that governments and industries start transitioning now, with every bit of money and privilege and influence that they've got. We must do whatever we can, whatever it takes, to make sure that happens.

Remember, the climate crisis didn't happen because folks like you used too many plastic bags or didn't turn off your lights. These gaslighting narratives are designed to deflect the responsibility for the devastation that unjust power structures and huge companies are knowingly causing in the name of profit, onto you, the end user. And that is not okay. It's disempowering for all of us, and hides the root cause of this crisis, which is that when governments, companies and oppressive systems choose profit and power over healthy communities and ecosystems, there is a reckoning that we all have to bear.

So ensuring a liveable climate for everyone hinges on people like you rising up, holding those companies and politicians to account, demanding change and also imagining and participating in the just and regenerative solutions and structures beyond that change.

But it's big and it's scary, and once you start digging into the converging crises we're facing, there's irreversible damage and more injustice than you can comprehend. It's easy to get dark on this subject – really, really dark. The solutions *are* there, but they need all of us to participate in them, and we need to do it right now.

The solutions are there, but they need all of us to participate in them, and we need to do it right now.

You're never too young (or old!) to protest what matters

In August 2018, a young Swedish student started a school strike for climate, all by herself. In the three weeks leading up to the Swedish election, Greta Thunberg sat on the steps of Parliament every school day, alone, often cold or wet. Yet she remained determined, because she was tired of society's unwillingness to see the climate crisis for what it is: a crisis.

Little by little, Greta's stance gained momentum. Her school strike movement grew to an estimated 1.4 million schoolchildren worldwide, striking in more than 2000 cities in 2019. Governments across the world were forced to reconsider their stance on the climate crisis because of schoolchildren. School strikes continue today, and they continue to apply pressure to governments and industries across the world. Without them, there would be less of the climate action that we need.

Getting active: outside your home

So far, many of the habits, steps and actions we've discussed in this book have focused on the home front, because to change the world for the better *and to have the resilience and stamina to keep going*, it really helps to gather yourself first, and then work it out from there.

But creating a better world, one that is more just and fair, and which supports a liveable climate for everyone, is not just about home-based actions. We must – all of us – work both on the home front and on the streets (the physical streets and the digital ones, too) to make change happen. Direct action can take many forms, and what you do will depend on where you live, and what you yourself are capable of – physically, emotionally, time-wise and otherwise.

Effective places to start

- **Vote like it matters:** elect representatives who will take solid and swift action on climate change rather than denying its existence.
- **Divest your money:** this means taking your savings, superannuation, investments and mortgage out of any bank or financial facility that funds fossil fuels or climate destruction – they are literally funding those companies with your money. Move your money and your debt to an ethical bank or fund that invests in green technologies and ethical ventures *only*: a growing number of choices are popping up. Make sure you let your old bank or fund know exactly why you are going.
- **Stand up at a council meeting:** attend your next local government meeting and ask a public question about what your council is doing to support residents and take action on the climate crisis. Local councils across the world are declaring a climate emergency and calling on their state and national governments to act.
- **Join a climate action group** in your nearest city. These groups are a local solution to a global problem, helping at key moments, such as before elections, or working on local campaigns to protect the environment, reduce plastic and even influence planning laws.
- **Host a Climate Conversation** around your dinner table. Want to really talk about what climate action in your friendship group could look like, but also don't want to be the 'doomer'? A dedicated dinner for the topic allows you to talk about your concerns without embarrassment. You'll be surprised what you can all come up with as a result. You might even be able to invite a trained facilitator to help.
- **Break up with the multinationals:** see if you can go a whole month without financially supporting a multinational company. Or simply choose to break up with the major supermarkets. Choosing to support your small, local shops is another way to divest.
- **Join the next school strike**, whether you have children or not.
- **Set up a tithe system from your income** – even if it's 0.05 per cent – to regularly donate to climate crisis-fighting funds.

Getting active: inside your home

Now that we've looked at the bigger picture, let's zoom back in to remember how home-level ideas spark active hope. When you decide to take on small but significant, meaningful habits and actions at home, these decisions redefine how you live your life.

A household committed to wasting less food, reusing things, connecting with its community and growing even just a few herbs is fundamentally more empowered to talk about what to do next, to live in deeper reciprocity with the ecosystem, to look outward to the community and find one more change to make or to get involved in.

Living with meaning and intention in this age of climate crisis means approaching what you can do with compassion: you're aiming for a soft but strong 'and also' approach, as opposed to an 'either/or' approach.

Simply put, it's about doing whatever you can and *not* beating yourself up for the bits you can't, right now. No-one can do everything! But we can all do something. And it's these simple, humble habits, done by more and more people, that build collective strength, and change.

Your household becomes empowered with each small, home-based step. Now imagine a street full of these kinds of households, each finding their way, moving forward, determined to do what they can. Then imagine two streets full of these households. Then a block, then a suburb, then a town. Imagine what your town would look like if it was full of empowered households, all making small changes which, clustered together, have bigger and bigger impacts.

A community that could support each other, swap skills, car parts and parsley, help each other out occasionally, and (before you know it) decide to do a community solar panel bulk buy. Or start a food co-op. Or a community kitchen. Or clean up the local creek. Or all of these things, *and* elect a town council that will declare a climate emergency and implement climate-positive projects such as street-cooling techniques (planting trees) and suburb-wide compost collection.

Change starts in your kitchen, and on your back step. It really does. Once you begin, self and household empowerment trickles out your front door, and spreads out sideways, like mycelium. It spreads out into your street and onto your neighbours' front porches, then into their kitchens and their backyards. It can influence everything from their health to their superannuation choices and how they respond to others when things get tough.

And this mycelial network of skills, awareness, empowerment, choices and actions grows and grows, to the size of whole towns or cities. It spreads through libraries and waterways, childcare centres and car parks, the corner store, your whole ecosystem and the air you breathe. These changes create far better community resilience in times of crisis, and plenty of goodness on regular days, too – in big and small ways. And each of your actions is a part of this.

Now imagine a street full of these kinds of households, finding their way, moving forward, determined to do what they can.

habit 57

MAKE AN EMERGENCY PLAN

The Intergovernmental Panel on Climate Change (IPCC) has warned us that, as the climate changes, extreme weather events such as fires, floods, cyclones, hurricanes and tornadoes will become more common. So, it's time to stop – really stop – for a moment and consider the impacts of natural disasters in your area. Then put together a plan for how you would deal with each type of event: your flood plan will look different from your fire plan.

Although an emergency may seem unlikely as you go about your day-to-day life, it's an excellent idea to make the time for this, and to prepare a written plan for your home. *Because your plan needs to be done and ready before the point when you need to creatively use and respond to change during an emergency.*

As you start to create your emergency plan, consider what would happen if you were cut off from essential services and travel for a week, at your home:

- Will you have enough food and water?
- How much of these things do you need?
- Do you have enough dry food supplies in your pantry or cellar?
- What would you do regarding electricity (do you have a back-up generator? Do you run on solar)?
- Who will be involved in your plan and who will you tell about it?
- Do you have a safe place to go to and stay if you need to leave home quickly?
- Do you know the route to your safe place? Alternative routes if need be?
- How will you know if roads are cut off and you don't have electricity?
- Have you prepared an emergency kit and is it easily accessible?
- Are your buildings, vehicles and communications systems (including back-up systems if the main ones fail) in good working order?
- Is your plan written down, easy to find and reviewed yearly?
- Are all members of your household aware of the plan, and where all the resources mentioned in it are kept?

Discuss

Prep your home

Emergency info

Bushfire alert levels

Making a bushfire plan

In Australia, as in other parts of the world, one of our most prevalent dangers is fire season. Bushfires have the power to swallow whole communities and leave a swathe of destruction in their path. This particular danger is big and fiery and red – it is immediately tangible, and we can immediately respond. We can do our best to prepare our homes and properties, we can watch and act, and we can support first-responders and evacuees.

Creating a bushfire-resilient household and community takes ongoing thinking, investigation and collaboration with your neighbours. The key points, in very brief detail, are: learn the vulnerabilities of your buildings, review your suburb and the main areas of risk, retrofit your buildings and gardens for safety and help manage adjacent public land.

You also need to consider your psychological and social preparedness for such an event. Consulting with your local experts on the best fire plans for your area is highly advised.

Four-step bushfire plan

- **Discuss** what you will do if a bushfire threatens your home. You have two options here: leave early (often the safest choice) or decide to stay and defend (please remember this can only be done if you are *very well prepared*). Your choice will shape the rest of your plan.
- **Prepare your home.** Each year, as bushfire season approaches, you will need to sort certain things around your home. Don't leave this to the last minute, when a fire front is approaching: that's too late. Preparing your home includes actions such as trimming overhanging trees and shrubs, mowing grass and removing the cuttings, removing material from around your home that could burn, clearing debris from your gutters and organising hoses that can reach all the way around your house, connected to a reliable water source. Consider if installing rooftop sprinklers and fire shutters make sense for where you live, also.
- **Record key emergency information.** Research and save emergency services numbers, local emergency radio frequencies and any apps that let you know if a fire is burning near you.
- **Understand the bushfire alert levels.** Your local fire authority will have ratings to assess the level of fire danger each day, according to the weather conditions, and these should influence your decision-making. For example, under the Australian Fire Danger Rating System (AFDRS), a Catastrophic rating means the fire danger is as bad as it gets – hardly any homes are built to withstand fire in these conditions. If a fire breaks out near you on a Catastrophic fire danger day, leaving early is your only safe option. Similar alerts exist to inform you about levels of danger in situations when an active fire is already burning, but not near to you yet.

Emergency planning: in your home

Preparation is key to being able to respond to an unexpected emergency. Once you have your basic kit set up, staying prepared will involve an annual check to make sure everything is still working and up to date. Here are two main elements to include in your home emergency plan.

Create a RediPlan

The Australian Red Cross has an excellent resource in the form of their RediPlan document, which is a free online template you can fill out with all your most important details. These include:

- emergency contact information
- important phone numbers
- account numbers and names for key services, including electricity, water, internet, phone and insurance
- contact details for alternative places to stay in an emergency
- a basic medical plan, including contact details for your doctor, dentist, pharmacist and local hospital
- a list of any medical conditions you have, as well as current medications and medical aids you need
- a written description of any disabilities you have
- details of where your Will is located
- a list of all your animals and any related details, such as breed and microchip number.

Make a survive and recover kit

A physical kit of items that you can grab and take with you during an emergency is highly useful. You might include:

- a printed copy of your RediPlan
- an amount of cash, in small bills
- a battery-powered (or wind-up) radio
- torches and batteries (remove the batteries from the torch so they will last longer)
- water, in an airtight container (changed every 12 months)
- device chargers (solar-powered and standard)
- food: basic non-perishable staples that don't require heating or cooling
- warm, waterproof clothing and comfortable shoes
- any special medical supplies and equipment that you can't go without
- basic toiletries: a toothbrush, toothpaste, soap and comb
- a first-aid kit (see page 272)
- if you have pets, some extra food, blankets and their registration and microchipping information.

You might also like to make copies of important documents, such as your passport, Will, driver's licence, birth certificate, photographs and receipts for valuable items. Store them in a fireproof box.

Emergency planning: in your street and community

Once your home plan is sorted, look beyond your own front door and play a role in ensuring your neighbourhood and wider community is as prepared for an emergency as possible. Organise a team with your friends and neighbours to share the effort and create a Community Preparedness Toolkit together. This can also be done for organisations, such as community groups, businesses and schools.

Setting goals is crucial here. Organise a meeting with your team and discuss your overall needs and vulnerabilities. Chat with your local emergency management agency, firefighters or other emergency services about what they think might be required; you could even see if they're willing to send someone to speak at your next community group meeting. Then settle on concrete actions, ideally with timelines and one or two people appointed to each action.

Ideas for action

- Conduct a safety drill at work or school, and iron out any kinks in the plan.
- Identify people in your community who might need a hand preparing for emergencies; for example, the elderly, folks with disabilities and others with special needs.
- Work together to ensure someone from every street is trained in first aid.
- Volunteer to help your local firefighters, disaster relief group, community safety organisation or other emergency responders – this doesn't need to be as a frontline worker. There are lots of ways to support and help.

DO A FIRST-AID COURSE

Knowing the basics of first aid is such a great idea – one day you might just save a life. But a first-aid course can also help you learn to deal with more everyday happenings, such as cuts and scrapes, bone breaks and sprains, choking, bleeding and how to help people who are unconscious. Change, in the form of accidents and emergencies, happens every day; you can creatively respond by upskilling to help in these situations.

By studying first aid, you'll be learning self-reliance and joining the ranks of active and capable community members. You'll learn how to stabilise a person until emergency medical services arrive, a result that can be life-saving because many acute illnesses and injuries demand immediate care. Sure, you might be able to consult a first-aid book or manual, but what if there's no time for that? By training in first aid, you will commit the skills you need to your memory, so you can react quickly and do the most good.

Most courses teach you how to use basic household items for times when a first-aid kit might not be available, which helps you build resilience in all sorts of scenarios, wherever you might be. And you'll learn how to remain calm and give clear directions, which can help to ensure that other people involved in the situation cope better.

Having a first-aid certificate can also make you more valuable at work, in your community group, at school or in volunteer work. And learning these skills heightens your awareness of risks in your life and neighbourhood, so you might be inspired to make small changes that reduce the risk of accidents and prevent someone from being seriously injured.

Committing to first-aid training – and regular refresher courses, so the knowledge stays firm in your mind for when it's most needed – is a simple way to help make yourself and your community safer and more prepared.

Ways to study first aid

- Reputable organisations such as the Red Cross and St John Ambulance regularly host short first-aid training courses. In-person classes are best, if you can get to them, as you'll get practical experience with techniques such as cardiopulmonary rescuscitation (CPR).
- Ask your workplace: some employers offer first-aid classes to staff.
- If you live in a rural or remote area, you may be able to access an online class, or request a training course through your local medical centre or ambulance service.
- If a good book is your only option, read it. And watch a bunch of videos on the basics, too; there are some great ones out there.

You'll learn how to stabilise a person until emergency medical services arrive: a result that can be life-saving.

Purchase a ready-made first-aid kit if you prefer, but don't forget to replace anything you use.

Creating a basic first-aid kit

Keeping a well-stocked first-aid kit is a simple way to stay prepared for emergencies and a must for all homes. A small, portable car kit is a good idea, too. Some organisations sell basic kits at reasonable prices, or you can create your own. Don't forget to restock your kit if you use an item, so everything is available for you the next time you need it.

Useful items to keep in your kit

- Gauze, non-stick dressing pads and bandages of various sizes
- Adhesive dressing strips, such as bandaids, of various sizes
- Antiseptic wipes and rubbing alcohol for disinfecting and cleaning superficial wounds
- Stainless steel scissors
- Stainless steel tweezers
- Safety pins and surgical tape
- Disposable gloves
- Emergency thermal blanket
- Notepad and pen
- A basic first-aid how-to manual.

ENGAGE IN MUTUAL AID

Just like the health of our ecosystems, the health of our communities relies and thrives on interdependence and reciprocity.

Mutual aid is the coordinated act of caring for one another – meeting each other's needs – both in times of crisis and also in an ongoing way. Mutual aid systems erupt in situations where it becomes apparent, or people just know from prior experience, that the official systems in place will not meet people's needs for care at that time.

Mutual aid can be a community-coordinated response to disaster recovery, such as providing essential food and medical services to residents after a flood when the government response has not been sufficient. It might be initiating, funding and maintaining ongoing services and support for sectors of a community who are not receiving the care they need because of their status, location, or other challenges.

> *When we talk about community and care we cannot detach it from political, cultural and historical circumstances. Class, race, colonialism and capitalism all affect how care is distributed in society. Social inequalities and disadvantage mean that care often doesn't reach those who need it the most, especially those who are already the most oppressed or marginalised under these systems.* **from 'It Takes a Forest', TransHub.org.au**

Mutual aid is a core part of our personal and collective histories, evidenced again and again in response to disasters and hard times. In every disaster, and in response to need, we see some people rising to meet each other's needs – organising, fundraising, speaking up, showing up – and providing effective relief and care, sometimes for a week until other systems kick in, sometimes in an ongoing way.

Flying in the face of the theory of 'social Darwinism' – that idea that humans have an 'everyone for themselves' approach to all crises as a base response – mutual aid and the act of collectively caring for each other clearly shows up as an innate response to disaster and to need – by ordinary people, for ordinary people.

Mutual aid is a powerful and natural human response that also flies in the face of capitalism and consumerism. The idea that we can provide and care for each other – efficiently, creatively and sometimes *far more effectively* than the official systems in place – says a lot about those systems. And it also says a lot about this part of our 'nature' that we are drawn to care for each other, given a collective framework and the opportunity to help.

Building solidarity

I love the definition of mutual aid outlined by Dean Spade, in his 2021 book *Mutual Aid: Building solidarity during this crisis (and the next)*. Here's a summary:

- Mutual aid is the radical act of caring for each other while working together to change the world.

- Mutual aid projects work to meet survival needs and build shared understanding about why people do not have what they need.

- Mutual aid projects mobilise people, expand solidarity, and build movements.

- Mutual aid projects are participatory, solving problems through collective action rather than waiting for saviours.

Solidarity, not charity

Uruguayan journalist Eduardo Galeano said, 'I don't believe in charity; I believe in solidarity. Charity is vertical: it goes from top to bottom. Solidarity is horizontal. It respects the other and learns from the other. I have a lot to learn from other people. ' This inspired the slogan 'solidarity, not charity' to describe mutual aid ideals. Rather than being disempowered and unable to help ourselves without top-down support from elsewhere, we can gather what we need for a response to crisis from within our communities, and do it ourselves, together.

This is not to say that charity is not a useful and crucial aid in some situations, but it *is* very different from an emergent, community-driven response. Mutual aid systems are 'solidarity systems' that build confidence, networks, skills, decision-making capability and overall capacity within the community, for that community, by that community – to help us care for ourselves.

Getting involved in mutual aid systems is something you do with the skills you already have, as well as adding skills like first aid (see Habit 58), communication and conflict resolution skills (see Habit 19) and, most importantly, cultivating community connections (see the whole book!) so you are well prepared to help out where you can. There's sure to be mutual aid in some form already happening near where you live, and also within communities of care, which may be defined in other ways than by location, such as online or otherwise.

From neighbourhood support services to volunteer-run food banks to knitathons to online abortion support to community kitchens set up during a natural disaster, mutual aid as a response to the need for care, for whatever reason, is a part of our shared history, and is all around us. As activist and organiser Thelma Young-Lutunatabua said in an interview with Rebecca Solnit (whose writing on 'radical hope' I can't recommend highly enough), 'The way we get through this is together.'

So if you're seeking confirmation that individual acts, when done collectively, can change the world and people's lives – immediately and significantly for the better – mutual aid systems provide concrete and ongoing examples of exactly this. Your history and your future are connected to these webs of care. Your small daily habits, acts and choices can combine with others, and build up to far-reaching, transformative futures based on care, connection and purpose.

Getting involved in mutual aid systems is something you can do with the skills you already have.

REVISIT YOUR PERSONAL GOAL

Time to check in. How are you feeling about all these possible projects and futures? Excited? Overwhelmed? Can't wait to get going? Have you scribbled a million notes? Can you more clearly imagine new worlds, with more fun, more possibility and more hope, that you can see yourself being an integral part of? It's possible. It's all possible.

It's time to recentre, by checking in on that personal goal you articulated waaay back at the start of this book.

Revisiting your personal goal on the regular can be a fantastic way to stay firmly grounded with your roots in the earth, while you stretch out, unfurl new buds, flex new skills and send tendrils out every which way towards that wild and precious life you're growing into.

By now I hope you've got a cluster of habits and skills you're keen on trying, marked by dog-eared pages, margin notes, journal lists or whatever works for you.

Before you jump in to any of them, take a minute to test them against that personal goal of yours, and ask yourself:

Will this habit or project take me closer to my goal?

And then listen for the answer.

If it's a firm 'Hell yeah', then go do that thing; I can't wait to hear how you go with it. If the answer is an 'Errrm, I think so?' consider putting that action a bit further down your list, and check back in when you get to it.

Remember: no-one needs to do all the things. But we can each do some of the things. Take on one new habit or one small project at a time, and keep at it until it's part of your new normal. No big deal.

And once it's just something that you do, that you enjoy and that works for you and yours . . . choose the next new habit or project. And build that future of yours, piece by piece.

This is how we build lives that are worth living, and how we change the world. By changing our worlds – each of us, and all of us together – with small endless days that add up to lives that are rooted in meaning, in relationship and reciprocity, and grounded in purposeful action and hope. Living at this time on Earth – with all of the challenges and all of the beauty – with our feet on living soil and our hearts wide open.

Think back to where you started at the beginning of this book and see how far you've already come. You're amazing.

Where to from here?

The resources on the following pages are packed with goodness, and your own hands-on learning will reveal many things. The Milkwood website has free guides we've built up over the past 16 years, as well as the guided Permaculture Living course. I'd love to hear how you go – visit milkwood.net to share your thoughts.

RESOURCES

Agroecology and Regenerative Agriculture: An evidence-based guide to sustainable solutions for hunger, poverty, and climate change by Vandana Shiva (Synergetic Press, 2022)

Climate Change Is Racist: Race, privilege and the struggle for climate justice by Jeremy Williams (Icon, 2021)

Dark Emu: Aboriginal Australia and the birth of agriculture by Bruce Pascoe (Magabala Books, 2018)

Drawdown: The most comprehensive plan ever proposed to reverse global warming by Paul Hawken (Penguin, 2018)

The Earth Restorer's Guide to Permaculture (3rd edition) by Rosemary Morrow (Melliodora, 2022)

Milkwood: Real skills for down-to-earth living by Kirsten Bradley and Nick Ritar (Murdoch Books, 2018)

Permaculture: A designer's manual by Bill Mollison (Tagari, 1988)

Permaculture: A rhymer's manual by Charlie Mgee (formidablevegetable.com.au)

Permaculture One: A perennial agricultural system for human settlements by Bill Mollison and David Holmgren (Corgi Publishing, 1978)

Permaculture: Principles and pathways beyond sustainability by David Holmgren (Melliodora Publishing, 2017)

The Red Deal: Indigenous action to save our Earth by The Red Nation (Common Notions, 2021)

Sand Talk: How Indigenous thinking can save the world by Tyson Yunkaporta (Text, 2019)

This Changes Everything: Capitalism vs the climate by Naomi Klein (Penguin, 2015)

The First Knowledges series by various authors (Thames & Hudson)

Milkwood permaculture resources at *milkwood.net*

A note on the following resources: many of these are so excellent and wide-ranging that they fit into many principles and habits, but in the interests of space, I've included them once each.

Principle 1: Observe and interact
Braiding Sweetgrass: Indigenous wisdom, scientific knowledge and the teachings of plants by Robin Wall Kimmerer (Milkweed, 2015)

Eat Weeds: A field guide to foraging by Diego Bonetto (Thames & Hudson, 2022)

The Sustainable House Handbook: How to plan and build an affordable, energy-efficient and waterwise home for the future by Josh Byrne (Hardie Grant, 2020)

Weed Forager's Handbook: A guide to edible and medicinal weeds in Australia by Adam Grubb and Annie Raser-Rowland (Hyland House, 2012)

An intro to daylighting urban waterways *americanrivers. org/resource/daylighting-streams-breathing-life-urban-streams-communities/*

Nikole Alexis: motivational foraging for everyone *instagram.com/blackforager*

Great UK foraging resources at *gallowaywildfoods.com*

Principle 2: Catch and store energy
Rainwater Harvesting for Drylands and Beyond, Volume 1, 'Guiding Principles to Welcome Rain into Your Life and Landscape' (3rd edition) and Volume 2, 'Water-harvesting Earthworks' (2nd edition) by Brad Lancaster (Rainsource Press, 2020)

Seed to Seed: Seed saving and growing techniques for vegetable gardeners (2nd edition) by Suzanne Ashworth (Seed Savers Exchange, 2002)

Wild Fermentation: The flavor, nutrition, and craft of live-culture foods (2nd edition) by Sandor Katz (Chelsea Green, 2016)

The Winter Harvest Handbook: Year round vegetable production using deep-organic techniques and unheated greenhouses by Eliot Coleman (Chelsea Green, 2009)

Principle 3: Obtain a yield
How to Grow More Vegetables (and fruits, nuts, berries, grains, and other crops) by John Jeavons (Clarkson Potter/Ten Speed, 2017)

RetroSuburbia: The downshifter's guide to a resilient future by David Holmgren (Melliodora, 2018)

Staying Alive: Women, ecology and development by Vandana Shiva (Frog Ltd, 2016)

Principle 4: Apply self-regulation and accept feedback
Emergent Strategies: Shaping change, changing worlds by Adrienne Marie Brown (AK Press, 2017)

Holding Change: The way of emergent strategy facilitation and mediation by Adrienne Maree Brown (AK Press, 2021)

The Intersectional Environmentalist: How to dismantle systems of oppression to protect people + planet by Leah Thomas (Souvenir Press, 2022)

Me and White Supremacy: Combat racism, change the world and become a good ancestor by Layla F Saad (Quercus Books, 2020)

Nonviolent Communication: A language of life by Marshall B Rosenberg (Puddledancer Press, 2015)

On Intersectionality: The essential writings of Kimberlé Crenshaw (The New Press, 2019)

Sister Outsider: Essays and speeches by Audre Lorde (Crossing Press, 1984)

Terra Madre: Forging a new global network of sustainable food communities by Carlo Petrini (Chelsea Green 2010)

The Transition Handbook: From oil dependency to local resilience by Rob Hopkins (Uit Cambridge Ltd, 2014)

Principle 5: Use and value renewable resources and services
The Humanure Handbook: Shit in a nutshell by Joseph C Jenkins (Jenkins Publishing, 1996)

Rocket stove resources at *aprovecho.org*

Principle 6: Produce no waste
A Family Guide to Waste-free Living by Lauren Carter and Oberon Carter (Plum Books, 2019)

The Compost Coach by Kate Flood (Murdoch, 2023)
Consumed: The need for collective change: colonialism, climate change & consumerism by Aja Barber (Balance, 2021)
In Defence of Food:The myth of nutrition and the pleasures of eating by Michael Pollan (Penguin, 2009)
Information about reusing plastics at *ecobricks.org*
Mending Life: A handbook for repairing clothes and hearts by Nina Montenegro and Sonya Montenegro (Sasquatch, 2020)

Principle 7: Design from patterns to details
The Intelligent Gardener: Growing nutrient-dense food by Steve Solomon with Erica Reinheimer (New Society Publishers, 2012)
Permaculture Design: A step by step guide by Aranya (Permanent Publications, 2012)
The Secret World of Weather: How to read signs in every cloud, breeze, hill, street, plant, animal, and dewdrop by Tristan Gooley (Sceptre, 2022)
Soil: The incredible story of what keeps the earth, and us, healthy by Matthew Evans (Murdoch Books, 2021)
Teaming with Microbes: The organic gardener's guide to the soil food web by Wayne Lewis and Jeff Lowenfels (Timber Press, 2010)
Indigenous weather and climate knowledge at *bom.gov.au/iwk/*

Principle 8: Integrate rather than segregate
'A Short History of Enclosure of the Commons in Britain', in *The Land: An occasional magazine about land rights*, Issue 7, summer 2009, *thelandmagazine.org.uk*
The New Create an Oasis with Greywater (6th edition) by Art Ludwig (Oasis Design, 2015)
The One-Straw Revolution by Masanobu Fukuoka (New York Review Books, 2009)
The Small-Scale Poultry Flock (revised edition) by Harvey Ussery (Chelsea Green, 2023)
Water harvesting resources by Brad Lancaster at *harvestingrainwater.com*

Principle 9: Use small and slow solutions
The Art of Frugal Hedonism by Annie Raser-Rowland and Adam Grubb (Melliodora, January 2017)
Bread Baking for Beginners by Bonnie O'Hara (Rockridge Press, 2018)
Edible Forest Gardens, Volumes I & II, by Dave Jacke and Eric Toensmeier (Chelsea Green, 2005)
The Seed Savers' Handbook by Michel and Jude Fanton (Seed Savers Network, 2000)
Tree Crops: A Permanent Agriculture by J. Russell Smith (first published 1928, pdf available online)

Principle 10: Use and value diversity
Wild Drinks: The new old world of small-batch brews, ferments and infusions by Sharon Flynn (Hardie Grant, 2022)

Principle 11: Use edges and value the marginal
Backyard Fire Cookbook: Get outside and master ember roasting by Linda Ly (Harvard Common Press, 2019)
Green Fire: Extraordinary ways to grill fruits and vegetables, from the master of live-fire cooking by Francis Mallmann with Peter Kaminsky and Donna Gelb (Workman, 2022)
Milkwood: Real skills for down-to-earth living by Kirsten Bradley and Nick Ritar (Murdoch, 2018); Mushrooms chapter and Seaweed chapter
Wild Mushrooming: A guide for foragers by Alison Pouliot and Tom May (CSIRO Publishing, 2021)
Food Co-op resources at *fci.coop*
Kids seaweed guide (pdf) at *milkwood.net/2019/01/08/the-milkwood-kids-seaweed-guide/*
Campfire Kids e-book (for recipes and craft) *onwillowsbend.bigcartel.com/product/campfire-kids*
Gift economy resources at *reconomy.org/what-you-can-do/alternative-banking-and-currencies/the-gift-economy-and-community-exchanges/*

Principle 12: Creatively use and respond to change
Essential Bushfire Safety Tips by Joan Webster (CSIRO Publishing, 2012)
Hope in the Dark: Untold histories, wild possibilities by Rebecca Solnit (Canongate, 2016)
It's Not That Radical: Climate action to transform our world by Mikaela Loach (Dorling Kindersley, 2023)
Mutual Aid: Building solidarity during this crisis (and the next one) by Dean Spade (Verso, 2021)

REFERENCES

Pages 5–6 David Holmgren, Permaculture Living courses *milkwood.net/permacultureliving*
Page 8 Sonya and Nina Montenegro, 'A Stumble Toward Something Right', *The Far Woods* blogpost, 28 September, 2022, patreon.com/thefarwoods.
Page 13 *The Australian Wars,* directed by Rachel Perkins (Blackfella Films Pty Ltd, 2022)
Page 177 Bill Mollison, *Permaculture: A designer's manual* (Tagari, 1988)
Page 213 Simon Buxton, *The Shamanic Way of the Bee* (Inner Traditions/Bear & Co, 2006)
Page 234 Charlie Mgee, *Permaculture: A Rhymer's Manual* (Formidable Vegetable Sound System, 2013)
Page 260 Bill Mollison, *Permaculture Two* (Tagari Books, 1979)
Page 273 *transhub.org.au/vitality/mutualaid*; Dean Spade, *Mutual Aid: Building solidarity during this crisis (and the next)*, (Verso Academic, 2021: Part 1, Chapter 1)
Page 274 Eduardo Galeano in *Louder than Bombs: Interviews from The Progressive Magazine*, by David Barsamian (South End Press, 2004); Thelma Young-Lutunatabua in '"The way we get through this is together": the rise of mutual aid under coronavirus' by Rebecca Solnit, *The Guardian*, 14 May, 2020.

THANK YOU

Firstly, thanks to the melukerdee country that we live upon and within, which nourishes and teaches us so much. We are so thankful to be here. Thanks also to the local elders whom we have learned from and continue to learn from, both in this place and beyond.

Thanks to Nick, my partner in life and Milkwood. We made the Permaculture Living course together, and this book came out of that – somewhat slowly, alongside a few very difficult years. Thank you for all the cups of tea, and for being my someone who chooses to show up with all of themselves. Thanks also for chasing and catching that chicken.

To our many students, from whom we have learned so much. It's been an enlightening experience to steward you all through pockets of knowledge and skills – from the on-farm years, to city rooftop garden Permaculture Design courses, to many small halls, farms, schools and community centres across this land – and now that we're teaching online, you're all over the world! Thanks for joining us. We love watching you all grow, and being a small part of your story.

Thanks to David Holmgren and Bill Mollison for your thoughtful and far-reaching work defining permaculture, which inspired us to start Milkwood in the first place. Thanks also to our many, many teachers from whom we've learned and with whom we've created courses: including Rowe Morrow, David Holmgren, Bill Mollison, Dave Jacke, Sandor Katz, Brenna Quinlan, Hannah Moloney and so many more.

Thanks to the team who helped create the Permaculture Living course upon which this book was built – Nick Ritar, David Holmgren, Brenna Quinlan, Dylan Wiehahn, Charlie Mgee, Jess Perini and Lindy Churches.

To the many folks who helped smoosh and rejig that course into an extended book form, including but not limited to Andrea Davison, Koren Helbig and, at Murdoch Books, Jane Morrow, Alexandra Payne, Melody Lord, Kristy Allen, Madeleine Kane and all the team.

Thanks to Brenna Quinlan for her always-awesome illustrations for both course and book, and to Dalee Ella for her delicious linocut contributions.

Thanks so much to photographer Samuel Shelley for chasing (and catching!) the golden light and for being a dog person, and to Michelle Crawford who makes hard things effortless: everything looked so darn great. Thanks to friends Maria, Beth, Miso, Kellie, Mark, Zoe, Daisy, Ashar, Brenna and Michelle for being such gorgeous campfire, picnic and walking buddies.

Thanks to Sadie and Matthew for excellent book chats, general support, and also for letting us roam Fat Pig Farm for detail shots. To Alex Kelly, for her marvellous mind and courageous heart. Thanks to Lizzie, Lucas and Albie May for the backyard retreat that helped reboot my ability to focus and write, with the sea in my ears.

Huzzah to all our Milkwood team both past and present – particularly Isis, Belle, Koren and Lindy – for holding the fort while I went to ground making this book happen.

Thanks to Ashar Fox for getting out of bed while sick to smile happily in our garden, and for being a source of sunlight in shady times. And to our extended family, for their ongoing support.

Lastly – thanks to you, for reading, and for being part of the change that our communities and ecosystems need and deserve. May your every day hold meaning, and your heart stay open.

INDEX

Published in 2023 by Murdoch Books,
an imprint of Allen & Unwin

Murdoch Books Australia
Cammeraygal Country
83 Alexander Street
Crows Nest NSW 2065
Phone: +61 (0)2 8425 0100
murdochbooks.com.au
info@murdochbooks.com.au

Murdoch Books UK
Ormond House
26–27 Boswell Street
London WC1N 3JZ
Phone: +44 (0) 20 8785 5995
murdochbooks.co.uk
info@murdochbooks.co.uk

For corporate orders and custom publishing,
contact our business development team at
salesenquiries@murdochbooks.com.au

Publisher: Alexandra Payne
Design Manager: Kristy Allen
Editorial Manager/Editor: Melody Lord
Designer: Madeleine Kane
Photographer: Sam Shelley
Cover illustration: Dalee Ella
Illustrations: Dalee Ella, Brenna Quinlan
Stylist: Michelle Crawford
Production Director: Lou Playfair

Every reasonable effort has been made to trace the
owners of copyright materials in this book, but in some
instances this has proven impossible. The author(s) and
publisher will be glad to receive information leading to
more complete acknowledgements in subsequent
printings of the book and in the meantime extend their
apologies for any omissions.

*Murdoch Books acknowledges the Traditional Owners
of the Country on which we live and work. We pay our
respects to all Aboriginal and Torres Strait Islander Elders,
past and present.*

ISBN 978 1 92235 192 0

 A catalogue record for this
book is available from the
National Library of Australia

A catalogue record for this book is available from
the British Library

Colour reproduction by Splitting Image Colour Studio
Pty Ltd, Wantirna, Victoria
Printed by 1010 Printing International Limited, China

The information provided within this book is for general
inspiration and informational purposes only. While we
try to keep the information up-to-date and correct, the
author and publisher do not assume and hereby disclaim
any liability to any party for any loss, damage, or
disruption caused by errors or omissions, whether such
errors or omissions result from negligence, accident, or
any other cause. Be sure to check with your local council
and use common sense when handling any potentially
harmful equipment or materials.

OVEN GUIDE: You may find cooking times vary
depending on the oven you are using. For fan-forced
ovens, as a general rule, set the oven temperature to
20°C (35°F) lower than indicated in the recipe.

TABLESPOON MEASURES: We have used 20 ml
(4 teaspoon) tablespoon measures. If you are using
a 15 ml (3 teaspoon) tablespoon add an extra teaspoon
of the ingredient for each tablespoon specified.

10 9 8 7 6 5 4 3 2 1

Kirsten Bradley is the co-founder of Milkwood with Nick Ritar – together they've been teaching permaculture design and skills for living like it matters for more than 15 years. Kirsten and Nick's book *Milkwood: Real Skills for Down-to-Earth Living* was published by Murdoch Books in 2018. When she's not helping folks to create meaningful change through their everyday actions, Kirsten can be found tending her backyard ecosystem of veggies, bees, berries and family, on melukerdee country in lutruwita/Tasmania.

Discover more at milkwood.net.